Creating Interdisciplinarity

VANDERBILT ISSUES IN HIGHER EDUCATION is a timely series that focuses on the three core functions of higher education: teaching, research, and service. Interdisciplinary in nature, it concentrates not only on how these core functions are carried out in colleges and universities but also on the contributions they make to larger issues of social and economic development, as well as the various organizational, political, psychological, and social forces that influence their fulfillment and evolution.

SERIES EDITOR
John M. Braxton
Peabody College, Vanderbilt University

EDITORIAL ADVISORY BOARD
Ann E. Austin (Michigan State University)
Marcia B. Baxter Magolda (Miami University)
Alan E. Bayer (Virginia Polytechnic Institute
    and State University)
Ellen M. Brier (Vanderbilt University)
Clifton F. Conrad (University of Wisconsin)
Mary Frank Fox (Georgia Institute of Technology)
Roger L. Geiger (The Pennsylvania State University)
Hugh D. Graham (Vanderbilt University)
Lowell Hargens (Ohio State University)
James C. Hearn (University of Minnesota)
George D. Kuh (Indiana University)
Michael T. Nettles (University of Michigan)
Joan S. Stark (University of Michigan)
John C. Smart (University of Memphis)
William G. Tierney (University of Southern California)
Caroline S. Turner (Arizona State University)

I Creating Interdisciplinarity

*Interdisciplinary
Research and Teaching
among College and
University Faculty*

LISA R. LATTUCA

VANDERBILT UNIVERSITY PRESS
Nashville

This book is printed on acid-free paper.
Manufactured in the United States of America

Library of Congress Cataloging-in-Publication Data

Lattuca, Lisa R.
    Creating interdisciplinarity : interdisciplinary research and
teaching among college and university faculty / Lisa R. Lattuca.— 1st
ed.
        p.   cm.   — (Vanderbilt issues in higher education)
Includes bibliographical references and index.
    ISBN 0-8265-1367-0 (cloth : alk. paper)
    ISBN 0-8265-1383-2 (pbk. : alk. paper)
        1. Universities and colleges—Curricula.   2. Interdisciplinary
approach in education.   I. Title.   II. Series.
LB2361 .L33   2001
378.1'99—dc21   2001003443

CONTENTS

ACKNOWLEDGMENTS

Confidentiality prevents me from naming most of the people whose participation was essential to this study. Although the faculty who took part in this research must remain anonymous, they should not go unrecognized. Their words and experiences are the lifeblood of this book, and I thank them for the gift of their time, which is always in short supply. Confidentiality also prevents me from thanking the administrators at each research site who allowed me access to their campuses and provided assistance in developing a pool of potential participants. Their knowledge of their respective faculties was critical to accomplishing this work.

I would also like to thank a number of individuals who were instrumental (in the most meaningful sense of the word) in bringing this study and this book to fruition. Bill Newell, professor of interdisciplinary studies at Miami University of Ohio and a foundational figure in the study of interdisciplinarity, encouraged me, invited me to one of his workshops, and provided a forum in which to conduct the exploratory focus group. Julie Thompson Klein, professor of humanities at Wayne State University and author of numerous works on interdisciplinarity, met with me and generously shared drafts of works in progress. Both of these experiences were central to the development of this study. Lois Voigt, who in her latest incarnation is a doctoral student at Loyola University Chicago, read this manuscript too many times. Maintaining, to my surprise, her good humor, she edited my writing, checked my organization, and questioned my excesses. I am very grateful for her diligence and her comforting presence. I am also thankful to Loyola University and the School of Education for funding the assistantships that provided me with so intelligent and generous a colleague. Joan Stark, professor emerita of the University of

Michigan, was present when this book was but a thought. I have been graced with Joan's guidance and unending support for many years and doubt that I can point to a professional accomplishment in the last ten years for which she is not in some way responsible. May she never retire from mentoring and may she never tire of me.

A few other individuals deserve thanks for absorbing the shrapnel of my anxiety as I worked on this volume: my mother, Josephine Lattuca, who has no idea how soothing her voice can be; Ed Blucher, whose patience and intelligence always astound me; Gail Elden, who keeps me focused; and my *most excellent* colleagues at Loyola: Jennifer Grant Haworth, Terry E. Williams, and Terri Pigott.

I thank everyone for their support and beg their indulgence on the next project.

Considering
Interdisciplinarity

To the untrained eye the world is interdisciplinary—or, more accurately, nondisciplinary. In Western society our attempts to understand it, however, are often discipline-based. In Cartesian fashion we use our analytic skills to divide the world into smaller and smaller units, hoping that in understanding the parts we will eventually understand the whole. Our colleges and universities, and to a lesser extent our elementary and secondary schools, teach us by word and deed that knowledge is divided into academic disciplines. The more schooling we have, the more entrenched our sense of disciplinarity can become; we are introduced to disciplines in elementary school and learn to live by them in high school and college.

Disciplines provide the rationale for the departmental structure of U.S. colleges and universities and strongly influence faculty appointments; hiring, promotion, and tenure practices; teaching assignments; student recruitment and enrollment; and even accounting practices. Those structural and operational realities link the fortunes of interdisciplinary research and teaching to the disciplines. Moreover, despite increases in interdisciplinary activity in postsecondary education, disciplinary frameworks still organize most faculty members' understandings and interpretations of information and experience. The extent to which this assumption will hold true in the future, of course, is open to debate as more and more faculty question the foundations of the disciplines and seek alternative ways of knowing.

Until the last quarter of the twentieth century, scholars could take for granted the role of academic disciplines in college and university life. Most did not think much about how disciplines influenced the daily work life of college and university faculty and shaped their views of how knowledge is created and advanced. Academic departments that followed disciplinary lines provided a seemingly logical arrangement of scholarly activity. Disciplinary associations served to connect scholars to one another and to advance their given disciplines. Over time, however, it became clear that departments and disciplines had some drawbacks. The exponential growth of knowledge in the twentieth century revealed how disciplinary cultures and perspectives could discourage inquiries and explanations that spanned disciplinary boundaries. Disciplines, it now seems clear, are powerful but constraining ways of knowing. As conceptual frames, they delimit the range of research questions that are asked, the kinds of methods that are used to investigate phenomena, and the types of answers that are considered legitimate (see, for example, Becher 1989, and Kuhn 1970, 1977). Research generally supports this conceptualization, demonstrating close ties among the attitudes, cognitive styles, and behaviors of groups of faculty within disciplines and the character of the knowledge domains in which they work (see Becher 1989; Biglan 1973a, 1973b; Donald 1983, 1990; Jacobson 1981; Lodahl and Gordon 1972; Price 1970; and Shinn, 1982).

As disciplines grow, they also become more complex. Today most disciplines are comprised of smaller communities of scholars who coalesce around shared interests and/or methods of inquiry. In some cases these specializations substantially resemble their parent fields, but as the number and variety of specializations grow, academic specialties can estrange faculty from their colleagues (Becher 1987a). Our nostalgic view of the disciplines is that they are tightly knit communities in which everyone knows what everyone else is doing. Like local parents keeping the neighborhood kids in line, members of the community observe and cement disciplinary norms through conversations across the backyard fence. As the disciplines have grown larger and more diverse, the neighborhood community, however, has been replaced by more distal connections. Scholars in a specialization may have a disciplinary home, but they often travel elsewhere to work. Where once everyone knew all the folks on the block, perhaps even in the town, they now wave from their driveways but rarely invite the neighbors in. The growth of specializations parallels the decline of the front porch from which everyone could survey their territory. Now the more private world of the backyard deck excludes all but a select few.

It is no longer safe to assume that faculty within particular disciplines share areas of interest, methods, or even epistemological perspectives. The field of economics is unusual among disciplines because it enjoys considerable consensus on subject matter and methods. However, in the disciplines of anthropology, art, literature, and sociology, to name a few, there is extraordinary variation in content, methods, and epistemologies. Furthermore the gaps between those who adhere to traditional approaches to knowledge and those who argue that these approaches are misguided and misleading is widening. The qualitative-quantitative cross currents in the social sciences and the increased use of poststructuralist theories in the humanities and social sciences are two obvious examples of how differences in perspectives can disrupt disciplinary relations.

It is difficult to separate the willingness to question conventional disciplinary perspectives from the growth of knowledge in the past century; each drives and is driven, at least in part, by the other. Both developments, however, have moved interdisciplinarity from the academic periphery to a more central scholarly location. The border crossing of early interdisciplinarians was largely instrumental, that is, it was motivated by the need to solve a given problem using borrowed theories, concepts, or methods. Early interdisciplinarians were also fewer in number and generally acted as trespassers, not warring parties; they crossed disciplinary boundaries, but they rarely tried to demolish them. Many of today's interdisciplinary scholars are more revolutionary in their ideas and ideals and are eager to interrupt disciplinary discourse and to challenge traditional notions of knowledge and scholarship. In the sciences and related professional fields, such as engineering and medicine, interdisciplinarity is still largely instrumental. There is also a good deal of instrumental interdisciplinary work in the social sciences and humanities and in professional fields such as education, business, and social work. However, an increasing number of faculty in the humanities and social sciences pursue interdisciplinary work with the intent of deconstructing disciplinary knowledge and boundaries.

In the past when interdisciplinarity was criticized for not being "disciplined," the charge was a presumed lack of rigorous thinking and methodology. Scholars attempting interdisciplinary work were suspected dilettantes who knew too little and claimed too much. This is still the most common, and probably the least demonstrated, criticism of interdisciplinary scholarship. More recently, as interdisciplinarity has become more prevalent in a host of emergent areas, such as cultural studies and women's and ethnic studies, it suffers not only from a reputation for superficiality, but from the unfamiliar and unsettling effects of its ideas. Poststructural and postmodern ideas are often unacceptable to those who support "modern" forms of academic work in the disciplines; traditional disciplinary scholars resist these forms of interdisciplinarity because they find the premises that guide them untenable.

This book began as an attempt to understand interdisciplinary scholarship in all its variety.* It grew from my interests in disciplinary influences on faculty work and the desire to understand how individuals negotiate them. I also wanted to understand how and why faculty pursued interdisciplinary projects, how their institutional, departmental, and disciplinary locations affected them and their work, and what kinds of rewards they reaped from interdisciplinary work.† I wanted to compare interdisciplinary scholarship and motivations across disciplines and in so doing to learn how they might be similar and different. In the course of studying thirty-eight faculty doing interdisciplinary work across sixteen fields of study and four institutions, it became clear to me that as interdisciplinarity has evolved, it has outgrown its own definitions. The traditional conceptualization of interdisciplinarity as the integration of disciplinary perspectives conceals the disciplinary critique that drives much interdisciplinary scholarship today. This book therefore is as much about the need to revise our definitions of interdisciplinarity as it is about the processes, contexts, and outcomes of interdisciplinary scholarship. It is an attempt to construct a deeper and broader understanding of interdisciplinary work and of the many scholarships that are collected under that rubric.

Interdisciplinary Moves

Some scholars claim interdisciplinarity can be traced to the ancient Greeks, while others dispute these claims. Newell (1998) wondered whether it is meaningful to talk about interdisciplinarity prior to the advent of the disciplines themselves and argued convincingly that "the interdisciplinary motiva-

---

*I use the terms *interdisciplinarity* and *interdisciplinary work* interchangeably. I use the term *interdisciplinary scholarship* to refer specifically to teaching and research activities.
†See the appendix for a description of the study design and methodology.

tion to seek a more comprehensive perspective would have little urgency prior to the development of the distinctive worldviews of reductionist disciplines" (p. 533). He suggests that we distinguish between interdisciplinarity and predisciplinarity.

Before the modern disciplines assumed primacy in colleges and universities in the late 1800s, knowledge was categorical: the medieval university divided the seven liberal arts into the quadrivium (arithmetic, geometry, astronomy, and music) and the trivium (logic, grammar, and rhetoric). These studies provided the medieval university student with the basis for the study of Aristotle's three philosophies: natural philosophy (what we know as physics), moral philosophy (ethics), and mental philosophy (metaphysics). Changes in the curriculum were slow to materialize. During the first hundred years of higher education in the United States, the college curriculum greatly resembled the classical curriculum of the English college, with its emphasis on rhetoric, ancient languages, and moral philosophy. In the early 1800s critics of this classical curriculum, including many students, pressed educators to include more mathematics and philosophy, as well as the study of literature, history, the natural sciences, and practical fields such as engineering in the college course of study. As student demand grew, advances from science and industry were reflected in the curriculum. Similarly interest in literature, once relegated to the extracurriculum, fueled the growth of the humanities.

As the first academic departments were created at Harvard and the University of Virginia in the 1820s, early reformers such as George Ticknor advocated further expanding the course of study in U.S. colleges and universities by adding elective courses to the curriculum. Expansion, however, was not easily accomplished, and traditions in the classical college held fast. In 1825, when a small group of instructors at Yale suggested that Greek and Latin should be eliminated from the required curriculum so that other subjects could be added, the Connecticut legislature supported them by issuing a report claiming that Yale's curriculum was impractical and regressive. The response from the Yale Corporation, led by President Jeremiah Day, successfully defended the classical course of study and deflected extensive reform until mid-century. Institutions that wished to provide instruction in areas of study that could not be incorporated into the standard curriculum established parallel courses of study and separate schools.* Student demand for education in the emerging "scientific" disciplines, the impact of Jacksonian democracy, and concerns about the U.S. economy eventually convinced educators and legislators that the country needed instruction in more practical subjects. The Morrill Act of 1862 promoted the development of a utilitarian mission that emphasized postsecondary education that would enable citizens to participate in the economic and commercial life of the country. Colleges and universities could now serve the needs of their regional populations, providing access to specialized training in professions such as nursing, education, and engineering.

The history of U.S. higher education since the nineteenth century has been one of increasing disciplinary specialization and organization. Interdisciplinarity as we know it today was not on the minds of higher education administrators, faculty, and students who were engaged in the heady process of building disciplines and forging new professional fields. In time concerns about the proliferation of academic specialties prompted some educators to think about the problems associated with the disciplinary structure of colleges and universities and about developing coherent and integrated courses of study for students. The seeds of interdisciplinarity then began a long and slow process of germination.

By the end of the nineteenth century, the social, political, and economic upheaval of the Civil War years and the increasing belief in the practical benefits of science had helped transform a number of classical colleges into research universities. Aspiring to be a comprehensive source of knowledge, the emerging research university sought to provide instruction in a range of subjects and left selection issues to individual students and faculty. Although academic departments were established in the 1820s, it was not until the turn of the twentieth century that faculty and administrators began to worry in earnest about the fragmentation that might accompany disciplinary divisions. Eventually, great increases in the number of courses and new concentrations raised concerns about haphazard course selection and overspecialization by students. University reformers of this era argued that the university had failed in its mission to shape college graduates into models of humanity and intelligence. Curricular reform was needed to restore unity and moral character in undergraduates. Despite such pressures to return to their religious character and

---

*Faculty at Harvard and Yale established the first scientific schools in the mid nineteenth century. Harvard awarded its first bachelor of science degrees in 1851, protecting the bachelor of arts from contamination by students graduating from a school with lower admissions standards and presumably less academic integrity. See Rudolph (1977) for a discussion.

mission, most universities skirted the issue of moral development in favor of simply adding more structure to the undergraduate curriculum (Reuben 1996). Calls for intellectual unity were met by restricting the number of electives a student could take. Knowledge, many conceded, had become too far-reaching for the individual to master. Although the distribution and concentration requirements appeased reformers by encouraging more directed study among students, these structures did not reinstitute a unified view of knowledge.

Rudolph (1977) contends that for U.S. higher education in the decades between the Civil War and World War I, "the elective system was something of a safety valve. No comparable device could have contained the energies that were seeking expression in the undergraduate curriculum" (p. 191). The elective system allowed universities to respond to the advances in occupational training and in technology, to the professionalization of the disciplines, of scholarship, and of scientific research, and even to a population of older and more serious students who now entered college after attending high schools with standardized curricula.

By the 1900s rumblings of discontent with the disarray of the undergraduate curriculum were heard in colleges and universities and colleges and universities moved again toward general education requirements.* Although colleges and universities tried for some time to add structure to the elective system, it was the general education movement that shaped higher education in the first three decades of the twentieth century. Efforts to define a common curriculum hastened during and after World War I as many felt the need to preserve and strengthen a sense of cultural and national identity and responsible citizenship. After the war comprehensive survey courses emphasized the content and values of Western civilization. The need for instructors who could effectively synthesize knowledge and make it accessible to undergraduates contrasted with the kind of scholarship promoted by specialization and scientific methods. Despite concerns about disciplinary fragmentation and despite the focus on the dangers of academic specialization, few innovators considered interdisciplinary curricula, a term virtually no one used. The Experimental College at the University of Wisconsin, which lasted only from 1928 to 1932, is

---

*Rudolph (1977) reports the results of a 1901 survey of ninety colleges: thirty-four allowed students to elect at least 70 percent of their courses; twelve allowed 50 to 70 percent election; and fifty-one allowed less than 50 percent of courses to be elected by students.

perhaps the most famous exception. The concept of "interdisciplinarity" is more likely attributable to research rather than teaching activities.*

In the 1920s the Social Science Research Council was established to promote integration across the social science disciplines. In the post war period of the 1930s and 1940s, issues of war, social welfare, crime, labor, housing, and population shifts appeared to require attention from several disciplines.† Klein (1990) notes that a "spirit of reform encouraged integrative thinking in both governmental and private agencies, and, though the concept of an applied social science initially emerged from outside the university, academic social scientists began to see its importance and inherent interdisciplinary nature" (p. 24). The development of area studies in the 1930s signaled an attempt to focus multiple disciplinary perspectives on a single geographic area, such as the Pacific or Asia. With extensive financial support from the Ford Foundation and funding provided through the National Defense Education Act, area studies programs proliferated in U.S. universities from the 1950s to the 1970s (Pye 1975).

World War II encouraged interdisciplinary research applications in service of military and political ends. The development of radar systems, for example, required the cooperation of teams of scientists from different disciplines. Some of these cooperative projects led to the development of new fields of study, such as solid-state physics, operations research, and radio astronomy. The problem-based research missions of the World War II era continued in the 1960 and 1970s. The need to address problems in the areas of defense, aerospace, and industry contributed to the expansion of federal funding and the creation of the National Science Foundation (NSF) and National Institutes of Health (NIH) to support both basic and applied science. By the 1970s most of the impetus for interdisciplinary projects had shifted, and interdisciplinary engineering centers took up concerns for product safety, environmental

---

*According to Klein (1996) the first citations of "interdisciplinarity" can be found in *Webster's Ninth New Collegiate Dictionary* and *A Supplement to the Oxford English Dictionary*. These reference a 1937 issue of the *Journal of Educational Sociology* and an announcement for postdoctoral fellowships at the Social Science Research Council. Frank (1988) claimed that the term as used by the SSRC connoted research involving two or more of the professional societies of the council.

†In *Interdisciplinarity: History, Theory, and Practice*, Julie Thompson Klein offers a detailed history of federally funded interdisciplinary projects and an extensive and useful history of interdisciplinary activities in the university. These provide the basis for much of this discussion.

quality, technology assessment, and information systems. In Europe interdisciplinary projects were sponsored by the United Nations Educational, Social, and Cultural Organization (UNESCO), by the Society for Research into Higher Education, and by the Centre for Educational Research and Innovation, which organized the first international investigation of the concept of interdisciplinarity. The 1980s witnessed the further development of interdisciplinary science and technology centers. In the United States the Carnegie Foundation, the National Endowment for the Humanities, and the Fund for the Improvement of Postsecondary Education joined the NSF in supporting interdisciplinarity.

Interdisciplinary curricula also gained prominence during the social transformations of the 1960s. In 1965 the Wisconsin legislature chartered the University of Wisconsin—Green Bay to devise a future-oriented innovative curriculum. Influenced by the ecology movements of the time, Green Bay offered an interdisciplinary curriculum focused on the relationships between humans and their environment. The university organized its colleges around environmental themes rather than academic disciplines and divided its curriculum into nine problem-centered concentrations. Students elected one of these interdisciplinary majors and could develop disciplinary expertise through a minor concentration. Over time, however, Green Bay added disciplinary majors and interdisciplinary minors to its original structure. In 1967 Evergreen State College in Olympia, Washington, opened as a nontraditional liberal arts college. Its coordinated studies program allowed its students to participate in full-time interdisciplinary study. Outside the United States, the University of Sussex (Britain), Griffith University (Australia), University Center Roskilde (Denmark), the University of Tromso (Norway), and the University of Tsukuba (Japan), institutions similarly concerned with avoiding the dichotomy of general and specialized work, opened between 1961 and 1972.

Interdisciplinary problem-based research and curricular projects continued through the 1980s and 1990s, but during these decades a new kind of interdisciplinarity appeared. In 1972, when the Centre for Educational Research and Innovation published *Interdisciplinarity: Problems of Teaching and Research in Universities*, general systems theory and structuralist thinking provided the theoretical foundation for the contributors' claims. In the social sciences and humanities of the 1960s and 1970s, structuralism and semiotics defied disciplinary boundaries in their search for underlying systems or forms that would unify theory in disparate areas. In the 1970s and 1980s, poststructuralist approaches that rejected the search for unity, systems, and underlying forms as illusory and futile became influential. Feminist theory trained attention on how difference, reflected in the form of gender, ethnicity, class, and power, influences the social world. Postmodernists, reacting to what they interpreted as a failed Enlightenment project, taught, wrote, and researched in ways that repudiated scholarly attempts at objectivity, neutrality, universality, and generalizability. Interdisciplinarity was, and is, evolving, and definitions of the adjective *interdisciplinary* reveal its various guises.

Defining Interdisciplinarity

Attempts to define interdisciplinary work began in the 1930s but reached a peak during the 1970s and 1980s. During this fifty-year period theorists specializing in or influenced by the philosophy and sociology of science offered numerous definitions of interdisciplinarity, most modeled after scientific inquiry in the natural and physical sciences (see the edited volumes *Interdisciplinarity and Higher Education* and *Interdisciplinarity: Problems of Teaching and Research in Universities* for examples). These definitions focused on disciplinary integration achieved (for example, Heckhausen 1972; Cotterell 1979; Hausman 1979; Kockelmans 1979; Epton, Payne, and Pearson 1983; Hermeren 1985).

Proponents of integration argued that interdisciplinary projects achieved a higher level of disciplinary integration than multidisciplinary projects that merely concatenated disciplines or their components. Faculty involved in multidisciplinary projects, they argued, behaved as disciplinarians with differing perspectives. Their disciplinary contributions might have been mutual and cumulative, but they were not integrated, and communication among the disciplines was presumed to be minimal (for example, Hanisch and Vollman 1983). Since no real cooperation among the disciplinary practitioners was assumed, multidisciplinary projects did not result in changes or enrichment of the participating disciplines. Such disciplinary relations were thought to be transitory and limited (Klein 1990).

In contrast interdisciplinary projects were defined as projects that emphasized integration over discrete disciplinary studies (Klein 1990). Consequently more cross communication and cross coordination among the disciplines would occur in interdisciplinary than in multidisciplinary efforts. Rossini and Porter (1984) likened interdisciplinary work to a seamless woven garment that stands in contrast to the patchwork quilt of multidisciplinary work—in true interdisciplinary projects, a concatenation of disciplinary perspectives is replaced by integration of those perspectives.

Other forms of multi- and interdisciplinary work have also been postulated and examined, including pluridisciplinarity, crossdisciplinarity, and even auxiliary, linear, and method interdisciplinarity. For some proponents of interdisciplinarity, transdisciplinary approaches—which strive for an overarching synthesis that transcends disciplinary worldviews (Miller 1982)—are the ultimate goal of disciplinary cooperation.* A more recent definition differentiates between two forms of interdisciplinarity: instrumental interdisciplinarity and conceptual interdisciplinarity. Salter and Hearn (1996) define instrumental interdisciplinarity as a pragmatic approach that focuses on interdisciplinarity as a problem-solving activity and does not seek synthesis or fusion of different perspectives. Conceptual interdisciplinarity emphasizes the *synthesis* of knowledge, a "theoretical, primarily epistemological enterprise involving internal coherence, the development of new conceptual categories, methodological unification, and long-term research and exploration" (Salter and Hearn 1996, p. 9).

Theoretical and philosophical treatments of interdisciplinarity often included speculation about different forms of disciplinary cooperation (see, for example, Kocklemans 1972, Piaget 1972, Jantsch 1972). These definitions occasionally made their way into discussions of teaching and learning (e.g., Mayville 1978). The difficulty of moving from theory to practice is evident in the empirical studies of the 1970s and 1980s. Limited by definitions that were not based in real-world observations, operational definitions of interdisciplinarity focused on its separate characteristics and rarely produced a holistic picture of interdisciplinary work. In addition, most were developed for use in studies of the management of interdisciplinary research projects in industry and higher education and therefore focused on team-based interdisciplinary research projects in the sciences, social sciences, and applied fields such as

---

*See Kockelmans (1979) and Klein (1990) for further discussion of other forms of interdisciplinarity.

engineering. These definitions are not therefore easily applied to research in the humanities, to collaborative research that is not team based, or to projects that involve interdisciplinary teaching rather than research.

An overview of typical operational definitions of interdisciplinary research also reveals the limitations of an emphasis on disciplinary integration. Birnbaum, for example, argued that interdisciplinary research "refers to research teams in which the effort is integrated into a unified whole" (quoted in Epton, Payne, and Pearson 1983, p. 3). Similarly Lindas suggested that interdisciplinary research implies continuously integrated research "in which the specific contributions of each researcher tend to be obscured by the joint product" (quoted in Epton, Payne, and Pearson 1983, p. 4). Other definitions emphasized process over product. Russell (1983), for example, stressed the collaborative nature of interdisciplinary research: "In general the term interdisciplinary refers to a specific plan, approach or set of efforts which blends the components of two or more administrative units within a university or among a set of colleagues drawn from a variety of institutional settings" (p. 246). Porter and Rossini (1985) tried to operationalize the degree to which a research project was interdisciplinary through survey responses. Their final decision as to whether a project was interdisciplinary was based on these five factors: the principal investigator's (PI's) judgment of how interdisciplinary a project was, the number of disciplines on the team, the range of skills represented, the percentage of the team from outside the PI's disciplinary category, and the researchers' own judgment of how interdisciplinary the project was. Since many of the projects were still underway at the time of the research, the PIs and researchers could judge only some of these products.

In their anthology on interdisciplinary research management, Epton, Payne, and Pearson (1983) formulated some formal propositions based on common themes in scholarly discussions of interdisciplinary research. In their estimation form was the key to defining interdisciplinarity. Research tasks requiring contributions from more than one discipline could be carried out using either of two different organizational forms:

> The "pure" multidisciplinary form in which the portions of the task are carried out by organizationally separate units each of which includes practitioners of only one discipline. The products of their activities are com-

bined into a coherent whole by a task co-ordinator who bears ultimate responsibility for so doing.

or

The "pure" interdisciplinary form in which the elements of the task are carried out within a single organizational unit consisting of the practitioners of the disciplines necessary for the completion of the task. The members of the unit share the responsibility for integration of individual contributions into a coherent whole. (Epton, Payne, and Pearson 1984, p. 70)

Roy (1979) proposed a similar breakdown between multidisciplinary and interdisciplinary research but added a further requirement: "interdisciplinary research (or activity) requires day-to-day interaction between persons from different disciplines. It requires, therefore, some learning of the other discipline's basic language and the interchange in interactive mode of samples, ideas, and results" (p. 170).

Birnbaum (1977) developed a set of indicators to determine the extent to which a project meets the criteria for interdisciplinary research. These indicators are (1) different bodies of knowledge are represented in the research group, (2) group members use different problem-solving approaches, (3) members of the group perform different roles in solving problems, (4) members of the group work on a common problem, (5) the group is responsible for the final product, (6) the group shares common facilities, (7) the nature of the problem determines the selection of group members, and (8) members are influenced by how others perform their tasks.

The focus on integration also created challenges for scholars exploring interdisciplinary teaching. In *Interdisciplinary Courses and Team Teaching: New Arrangements for Learning*, James Davis (1995) limited his discussion to team-taught interdisciplinary courses. Although he recognized that professors teaching alone could make interdisciplinary connections, he defined interdisciplinary courses as those that "involve two or more professors collaborating in significant ways" (p. 5). Davis adopted the emphasis on integration, noting that the goal of a team-taught interdisciplinary course is to provide "integrative disciplinary perspectives" (p. 8). While acknowledging differences of opinion about what constitutes genuine interdisciplinarity, he stressed the importance of "at least some efforts at integration" (p. 5). His criteria for interdisciplinary teaching centered on four collaborative tasks: planning, content integration, teaching, and evaluation. Each of these criteria can fall on a point in a continuum from low collaboration to high collaboration. According to these criteria, any team-taught course involving faculty from different disciplines is interdisciplinary since it will require some degree of collaboration, however minimal, in planning, teaching, and evaluation. The kind of content integration required of interdisciplinary research is not necessary.

The focus on team research and team teaching portrays interdisciplinarity as an interaction among individuals from different disciplines. Only one series of linked studies focused on individuals engaged in interdisciplinary research (see summary by Robertson 1983). Other scholars broached the question of individual interdisciplinary work but did little more. Taylor (1986), for example, briefly contested the idea that "the ideal polymath" existed; an individual, he argued, cannot be truly interdisciplinary. Petrie (1986) considered the possibility of individual interdisciplinarity, but recalling the research on team interdisciplinarity, merely suggested that the problems faced by the individual interdisciplinary researcher would parallel those faced by an interdisciplinary team. In a later article he wrote, "almost all interdisciplinary problem solving occurs in groups" (Petrie 1992, p. 314). Yet in programs such as women's studies, black studies, and environmental studies, which have existed for more than a generation, individual faculty members provide students with interdisciplinary understandings of social and natural phenomena and produce scholarship that purports to be interdisciplinary.

Newer scholarly approaches such as feminism, poststructuralism, and postmodernism challenge conceptualizations of interdisciplinarity based on collaboration by individuals from different disciplines. Some also challenge definitions that require disciplinary integration, claiming, rather, that interdisciplinarity is a critique of disciplinary knowledge.

Critiquing Disciplinarity

In *Interdisciplinarity: History, Theory, and Practice*, Klein (1990) noted that "The bulk of the literature [on interdisciplinarity] consists of case studies and anecdotal wisdom, but very little empirical analysis and even less epistemological reflection" (p. 109). In part the lack of epistemological reflection Klein identified resulted from a sample of writing and research that was heavily weighted toward scientific forms of interdisciplinarity. By 1996 in *Crossing Boundaries: Knowledge, Disciplinarities, and Interdisciplinarities,* Klein could highlight epistemological reflection on interdisciplinarity by analyzing scholarship from women's studies, ethnic studies, cultural studies, and literary studies. Although work in these areas is considered to be inherently interdisciplinary, calls for interdisciplinarity are also frequently part of a larger project to redefine knowledge, and reflection on epistemological assumptions is paramount. For some scholars working in these areas, the redefinition of knowledge might logically conclude in integrated disciplinary perspectives. However, for many feminists, poststructuralists, and postmodernists, the redefinition project is about dismantling disciplinary perspectives, not maintaining and integrating them.

There is no single definition of poststructuralism and even less agreement on what constitutes postmodernism (for example, see Rosenau 1992; Hollinger 1994; Bloland 1995). The concepts have been invoked to describe developments in a number of disciplines and fields. Although variations are important, the majority of poststructuralists, postmodernists, and feminists share some assumptions.* Structuralism as a general orientation assumes that interior structures, forces, or processes are responsible for what we observe; poststructuralism is a reaction against this premise. Most inquiry in the human sciences is compatible with structuralism. Gergen (1994) noted that Marxism is structuralist because of its focus on material modes of production and underlying capitalist theories of the economy, the individual, and value. Chomsky's attempts to locate a deep grammatical structure and Freud's attempt to use spoken words to explore the structure of unconscious desire are also structuralist in nature. In literary theory poststructuralism disavows the presumption that language provides truthful descriptions or explanations; in linguistics it repudiates the supposition that interior dispositions rather than the exterior world structure communication.

Positivist approaches to knowledge rely on the correspondence between observations and what is represented in language because this correspondence

---

*Throughout this book the term poststructuralism indicates an overarching category that includes postmodernism and feminism.

renders knowledge objective and verifiable. In denying correspondence, poststructuralists challenge the positivist paradigm. Postmodernists take the critique of positivism a step further, contending that objectivity, value neutrality, and rationality—doctrines that grew out of the Enlightenment—are deeply flawed and responsible for a multitude of evils, including the erosion of community and moral values and the destruction and disenchantment of the natural world (Rosenau 1992; Gergen 1994; Hollinger 1994). Postmodernists also defy the disciplinary bases of knowledge, rejecting the idea that knowledge has an absolute foundation that is permanent, universal, and objective (for example, Foucault 1980; Rorty 1991), as well as the premise of a disciplinary basis for interdisciplinarity (Lyotard 1984). Opposed to any kind of foundationalism, even in the service of interdisciplinarity, postmodernist critics propose conceptualizations of scholarship that stress the hermeneutic and poetic (Rorty 1979), the local and the plural (Lyotard 1984), and the contextual (Fish 1989) aspects of knowledge.

Like postmodernists feminists reject notions of neutrality, rationality, and objectivity, as well as other disciplinary assumptions about knowledge and the world (Sherif 1987; Nielsen 1990; Gumport 1991; Rosser 1997). In addition, they argue for methods of inquiry that place women at the center rather than the margins, and they espouse an interdisciplinary perspective that redresses fragmented and dichotomous viewpoints by recognizing the interconnectedness of reality (Perreault 1984; Collins 1986). A defining characteristic of both feminist and postmodernist critiques of knowledge is the epistemological warrant for interdisciplinarity. Because the disciplines themselves are viewed as power structures, the epistemological and the political are inseparable. Disciplinary approaches to research and teaching result only in partial and thus distorted knowledge that serves to keep those who have power in power and those without power subordinate. Interdisciplinary approaches result in less distorted forms of knowledge and thereby redistribute power to individuals who would otherwise be powerless. As such, interdisciplinary approaches are the only routes to genuine understanding and equality. In this view interdisciplinarity is therefore both a means to an end and an end in itself. In comparison much of the literature on interdisciplinarity views interdisciplinarity as a useful approach to answering social or technological questions and not as an end in itself. Klein (1990) argues that this view of interdisciplinarity as means rather than end was the prevalent view among those who studied interdisciplinarity.

The poststructuralist view of interdisciplinarity as both means and end can also be contrasted with structuralist and general systems theory approaches to interdisciplinarity (see Miller 1982 and Vosskamp 1986 for discussions). Like poststructuralists, feminists, and postmodernists, structuralists and general systems theorists view interdisciplinarity as both method and goal. However, systems theorists and structuralists search for structural parallels between disciplines and seek to create a unified science that integrates all the disciplines (Miller 1982; Vosskamp 1986). In contrast poststructuralists, including feminists and postmodernists, reject the very notion that there are universals to be discovered and argue that a belief in universals disguises the inherent contradictions, ambiguities, and oppositions that exist in the world (Bloland 1995; Salter and Hearn 1996). Superficial agreements about interdisciplinarity as a method and end obscure deep epistemological and ontological rifts between these perspectives. Furthermore the view that all knowledge is political and subjective separates feminists and postmodernists from those working within a scientific paradigm in which knowledge is objective and value neutral. As a result feminist and postmodernist critiques of disciplinarity have imbued interdisciplinarity with new meaning.

Although many of the definitions of interdisciplinarity are flawed, feminist and postmodern theories of interdisciplinarity create another set of issues. If the standard for interdisciplinarity is rejection of disciplinarity, great numbers of individuals working in a modern, or positivistic, mode—although doing what has typically been considered interdisciplinary work—are excluded. Most individuals working in the physical sciences would fall into this abyss. The question is whether to impose a standard that is epistemologically untenable to great numbers of individuals. Should we propose a definition of interdisciplinarity that discriminates against faculty on the basis of epistemology or is it possible to develop a definition that would allow disparate epistemologies to coexist?

The definition offered by Centre for Educational Research and Innovation (OECD 1972) seems to accommodate different, and even competing, types of interdisciplinarity. CERI's definition specifies a range of interdisciplinary interactions:

> Interdisciplinary—An adjective describing the interaction among two or more different disciplines. This interaction may range from simple com-

munication of ideas to the mutual integration of organising concepts, methodology, procedures, epistemology, terminology, data, and organisation of research and education in a fairly large field. An interdisciplinary group consists of persons trained in different fields of knowledge (disciplines) with different concepts, methods, and data and terms organised into a common effort on a common problem with continuous intercommunication among the participants from the different disciplines. (OECD 1972, pp. 25–26)

This definition focuses on interactions, a broader notion than team research or collaboration. Although the definition clearly assumes a disciplinary basis for interdisciplinarity, it does not exclude postmodern interdisciplinarity in which the disciplines are not central to modes of inquiry since a critique of disciplinary knowledge implies an interaction with the knowledge of the disciplines. This definition also recognizes a wide range of interdisciplinary work; rather than establishing a fixed point at which interdisciplinary integration occurs, the CERI definition suggests that interdisciplinarity exists on a continuum. On one end of this continuum is the informal communication of ideas, such as might happen in a conversation between colleagues from different disciplines; on the other end is formal collaboration, such as research or teaching teams comprising one or more faculty from different disciplines. Research supports both the conceptualization of a continuum of interaction as well as the suggestion that conversation itself can promote conceptual change (Roschelle 1992). We might conceivably map more recent critical interdisciplinary work on a continuum from modern, or discipline-based, interdisciplinarity to postmodern, or adisciplinary, interdisciplinarity.

Creating Interdisciplinarity

The wave of interest in interdisciplinarity that began in the 1970s has not diminished significantly since then. Early observers of interdisciplinarity struggled to understand the underlying foundations of interdisciplinarity. Descriptive literature appeared in a number of disciplines, and a small body of empirical studies accumulated, driven by researchers' interests in problem-based research and research management. These early discussions and studies of interdisciplinarity almost exclusively featured scholarly activity in the form of research in the natural and physical sciences and assumed that research in the natural sciences exemplified academic inquiry. Interdisciplinarity, then, would look basically the same regardless of the disciplines involved—and it would be characterized by the integration of disciplinary perspectives. Klein (1996) and Salter and Hearn (1996) were among the first to explore interdisciplinarity in disciplines and fields outside the natural and physical sciences in depth and to demonstrate the considerable variety of interdisciplinary approaches to scholarship.* Although writing on interdisciplinarity has increased dramatically and now covers a variety of academic areas, there is still a striking absence of empirical work that examines interdisciplinarity *across* academic contexts.

In *Outside the Lines*, a volume of essays describing interdisciplinary research in the social sciences, Salter and Hearn (1996) noted that there is little conceptual clarity in current scholarly debates about interdisciplinarity because the debates involve professional, social, political, cultural, and epistemological issues. While the early literature on interdisciplinarity hinted at these issues, largely by noting resistance to interdisciplinary research and the ethnocentrism of the disciplines (Kockelmans 1979, pp. 133–134), it rarely examined the epistemological issues at the heart of the matter. Today scholars writing about interdisciplinarity rarely ignore the influence of epistemological, political, and cultural factors on scholarship. While the contemporary picture of interdisciplinarity is now more balanced in terms of disciplinary representation and more cognizant of epistemological issues, it is largely analytical rather than empirical. There are also few works that combine discussion of interdisciplinary teaching and research. The Centre for Educational Research and Innovation's edited volume, *Interdisciplinarity: Problems of Teaching and Research in Universities* (1972), Mayville's (1978) monograph, *Interdisciplinarity: The Mutable Paradigm*, Klein's *Crossing Boundaries: Knowledge, Disciplinarities, and Interdisciplinarites* (1996), and Newell's anthology, *Interdisciplinarity: Essays from the Literature* (1998) are still among the only works

---

*A few other treatments of interdisciplinarity in the social sciences preceded these works. For example, in 1995 the journal *Social Forces* examined the issue of interdisciplinarity in the social sciences in a series of articles exploring aspects of the major social sciences disciplines. Disciplinarity and, to a lesser extent, interdisciplinarity are also the focus of chapters in the edited volume *Knowledges: Historical and Critical Studies in Disciplinarity*, Messer-Davidow, Shumway, and Sylvan, eds. (1993).

that treat interdisciplinary teaching, curricula, and research as equally important dimensions of interdisciplinary scholarship. While it could be argued that
treating teaching and research individually will result in greater clarity, doing
so lessens our ability to see meaningful connections between teaching and
research and precludes a comprehensive understanding.

The limited body of empirical work on interdisciplinarity focuses on processes such as integration, the effects of disciplinary and institutional contexts
on interdisciplinarity, and the outcomes that result from interdisciplinary work.
These aspects of interdisciplinarity, however, have been studied in isolation;
researchers have only rarely examined the relationships among processes, contexts, and outcomes. Moreover, these dimensions of interdisciplinarity are in-
terdependent: processes may differ by context, and contexts may influence processes; different processes may produce different outcomes, as may different
contexts; and conversely outcomes may influence contexts and later processes.
To understand interdisciplinarity fully, processes, contexts, and outcomes must
be examined together and in relation to one another.

Scholars concerned with the processes by which interdisciplinarity is accomplished typically focused on concepts such as the borrowing of methods
and theories from other disciplines or examined the structures, such as research
teams, that permit individuals to work across disciplines. Their intent was to
determine whether particular practices promoted the success of interdisciplinary projects. They were not interested in studying the processes by which
interdisciplinarity was achieved for the sake of understanding interdisciplinarity itself. In contrast, I believe it is important to examine processes because
they increase our understanding. Questions such as, "What does interdisciplinary practice look like?", "How does it differ from disciplinary practice?", "How
does it respect or challenge the disciplinary conventions of academic culture?"
should reveal the limitations of present definitions and portrayals. As ethno-
methodologists have demonstrated, it is in breaches of the taken for granted
that we come to understand our values, norms, and taboos (Feldman 1995;
Holstein and Gubrium 1998).

It is fruitless to talk about the process of doing interdisciplinary work without discussing the influence of the contexts in which it is done. Since the
1970s, when interdisciplinary research and programs began their ascent on
college and university campuses, scholars and researchers have dissected the
influences of various contexts on interdisciplinarity, focusing primarily on the

institutional context for interdisciplinary scholarship. Consequently the literature on interdisciplinarity is replete with discussions about the influence of
different institutional, divisional, and departmental environments on interdisciplinarity.* The departmental structure of the university and its influence on
institutional reward systems are considered major barriers to interdisciplinarity since these are based on disciplinary models of research and teaching. Many
of these studies, however, were completed in the 1970s and early 1980s, and
the question of whether institutional environments have changed is well worth
asking.

Although some institutions support interdisciplinary scholarship through
a variety of institutional policies, the impact of the presence or absence of
such facilitators has not been examined. And what of faculty who pursue interdisciplinary projects without institutional support and without regard to disciplinary barriers? What, if any, rewards do they reap? Does interdisciplinary
scholarship result in institutional rewards, such as promotions or research support? Are the rewards tied to products such as course syllabi or reports on interdisciplinary projects? While these more tangible outcomes of interdisciplinarity are important, it is equally important to explore more intangible outcomes,
such as changes in practice, in ideas, and in perspectives on knowledge. Over
time such changes may expand disciplinary perspectives and/or introduce new
models of inquiry.

We can look also at the broader disciplinary context for interdisciplinary
work that exists outside the institution. Disciplinary associations have often
influenced, or attempted to influence, the lives of their members. Although
we sometimes overlook the gatekeeping role that such organizations play, they
can send strong messages to members through the editorial practices of the
journals they sponsor, the content of the conferences they hold, and committee membership. What role, if any, do disciplinary associations play in the lives
of interdisciplinary faculty? Do these associations lead or lag behind interdisciplinary trends in scholarship? Does it make a difference for faculty if their
disciplinary association welcomes their work or rejects it?

Questions like these prompted this study, which is admittedly a first step
toward understanding interdisciplinary scholarship. Although this research

*See Newell (1975); Newell, Saxberg, and Birnbaum (1975); Birnbaum (1979); Rossini and Por-
ter (1981); Porter (1983); Russell and Sauer (1983); Teich (1986); and Klein (1990).

began as a straightforward attempt to understand why and how college and university faculty pursued interdisciplinary research and teaching projects, in time it developed into an examination of the concept of interdisciplinarity itself. The words and experiences of the faculty who participated furnished the basis for a grounded definition of interdisciplinarity that challenges existing conceptualizations of the term and that brings into relief the significant characteristics of interdisciplinarity.

Disciplining
Knowledge

The realities of today's academic organizations oblige observers of higher education to study interdisciplinarity and disciplinarity in point and counterpoint. Most scholars define the locus of interdisciplinarity as the integration of disciplinary perspectives. Moreover, understanding how interdisciplinarity is received, and how it is conceived, depends on an understanding of the nature of academic disciplines and their influence on faculty life in colleges and universities. Despite their relative youth — the academic disciplines we know today are largely the products of the late nineteenth and early twentieth centuries — the disciplines are institutionally entrenched and cannot be ignored. But the study of interdisciplinarity directs our attention to aspects of disciplines and disciplinary knowledge that often remain hidden. The very thought of disciplinary integration forces us to consider the assumptions and conventions that define particular disciplines and that make them similar to or different from others.

Disciplines are complex phenomena. They can be defined as sets of problems, methods, and research practices or as bodies of knowledge that are unified by any of these. They can also be defined as social networks of individuals interested in related problems or ideas. The first definition stresses the infrastructure of the disciplines, the second their social, cultural, and historical dimensions. While most studies of academic work stress one or the other of these foci, neither is complete in isolation. Those who believe the key to understanding the disciplines is to identify and examine their basic structures share the premise that, regardless of differences in particulars, all disciplines share different classes of components, such as *content* or *method*. These analyses provide a number of important insights into the nature of the disciplines and can also illuminate interdisciplinarity. They tend, however, to downplay or even ignore the historical and cultural dimensions of disciplinarity. Poststructuralist analysis shifts our attention from the structural to the cultural and sociohistorical and reminds us that structures such as content and methods are socially constructed; they exist as expressions of human ideas and are subject to change. In the study of the disciplines, these two approaches, despite their theoretical antagonism, tend to align on an uneasy continuum. Structural analyses of the disciplines do not completely discount the cultural: they focus on the disciplinary community and on its norms and practices, as well as on disciplinary components such as methods. Similarly poststructural accounts of the disciplines implicitly acknowledge structures when they highlight power differentials associated with various epistemologies and methodologies. Each framework has its limitations.

Structuralist accounts of disciplinarity define the discipline as a framework for understanding and interpreting information and experience, for judging the validity and adequacy of solutions to problems by defining what is acceptable, appropriate, and/or useful. Implicit in this model is a role for the individual, who interprets, judges, etc., and a role for the disciplinary community, which maintains disciplinary boundaries. But structural views tend to focus on how human agency is constrained by influences external to the individual. In abstracting and decontextualizing disciplinary components, structural depictions downplay or ignore the interaction of structures and cultures and give a false impression that the disciplines are characterized primarily by structures that promote conformity and stability. In the structuralist scenario disciplinary change is resisted unless it is in approved directions and influence appears unidirectional: the community is shaped by the discipline.

In contrast a poststructuralist perspective directs our attention to the community, portraying the discipline as a heterogeneous social system composed of individuals with varying commitments to ideas, beliefs, and methodolo-

gies—and to one another. By focusing on the communal construction of meaning, the existence of multiple perspectives, and the linkage of individual perspectives to social processes, poststructuralism replaces the idea of a structure
with the more fluid concept of a space in which persons and ideas exist in
relation to one another. Because meanings are seen as socially constructed,
disciplines are sites of ontological, epistemological, methodological tensions,
and these tensions animate structures such as subject matter and methods.
The structural perspective abstracts underlying frameworks that are believed
to define a phenomenon, while the poststructural approach eschews abstrac-
tion and attends to the local and the particular, which are time and context
bound.

All ways of seeing are, of course, selective. They emphasize a particular
perspective over others and in doing so limit our field of vision. If the danger
inherent in structural analyses is that the discipline becomes monolithic, with
tightly controlled boundaries and conventions, the siren call of poststructuralist analysis is cultural chaos. Taken to an extreme, the poststructuralist view
portrays the individual as personally defining and redefining the discipline
from moment to moment. The discourse community is present as a power
structure and little else: the discipline hardly seems to exist in the material
world. Although my own disposition is more poststructuralist than structuralist, structural analyses of the disciplines help me understand how interdisciplinarity transgresses, as well as how it respects, scholarly conventions. Poststructural analyses help me understand *why* transgressions are or are not
consequential; the poststructural focus on social and power relationships is
essential to understanding the pas de deux of disciplinarity and interdisciplinarity because the disciplinary structures that are important to understanding
interdisciplinarity are not spontaneously generated or magically maintained.
Individuals in social relationships create disciplines and determine which ideas
and which individuals are accepted within a disciplinary community at a given
point in time.

The paradigm shift from a Newtonian-Galilean model to a quantum
model in the physics community provides a useful illustration of how combining insights from structural and poststructural perspectives can lead to a multi-
faceted view of disciplinary phenomena. In the first decades of the twentieth
century, quantum mechanics gradually replaced Newtonian-Galilean physics

as the dominant view of the physics community. By 1930 the argument was largely over, and the quantum view became synonymous with modern physics. Still, despite great consensus, members of the physics community, including notables such as the Nobel laureate P. W. Bridgman, continued to dissent as their colleagues adopted the new paradigm (Kline 1995).

Should we interpret this move to a new organizing principle as a structural change, that is, a change in the conceptual or cognitive system underlying the discipline of physics, or should we view this as a moment of cultural change? Should we foreground the intellectual event, the synthesis of theory and technology, or the development of a dominant group whose agenda pushed the quantum view to nearly hegemonic status? It seems that neither view is completely adequate, and a stereoscopic approach increases our understanding of this episode in the history of physics. The cultural perspective emphasizes the role of the members of the physics community in considering and accepting significant change in the fundamental principles guiding their discipline. The adoption of the quantum view signaled, to use Kuhn's (1970) term, a revolutionary paradigm shift in physics; it was the result of individuals coming to consensus on an idea. In the same moment that the social and dynamic character of the discipline was most visible, ontological and epistemological beliefs underlying the discipline drove a search for stability and order: "the important point is that the dominant workers in the physics community thought of this new view not as one view among many . . . but as an improved basis from which everything else can be derived, at least in principle" (Kline 1995, p. 216). Once physicists adopted the quantum view, it became *the* view that would allow for a unified conception of the physical world. Following the shift to a new paradigm, the positivistic teleology embedded in the discipline consciously or unconsciously motivated urges for unity and control consistent with its epistemological foundations.

If we were to follow the history of particular disciplines, we would identify many instances of movement and change as well as moments of resistance and protectionism. The development of molecular biology also constitutes a moment of great change as biology accepted not only the technology and instrumentation of physics, but also the cognitive reframing of the fundamental problem to be solved by the discipline, that is, understanding the structure and mechanisms of the gene (Fox Keller 1993). In the social sciences the willingness to consider alternatives to the positivist paradigm was part of a movement toward interpretive modes of inquiry. Attempts to understand disciplinarity, then, profit from a consideration of how the components of a discipline—its subject matter, its modes of discovery and validation, its language and its value system—influence disciplinary and interdisciplinary work.

Parsing Academic Disciplines: Subject Matter, Cognitive Frameworks, and Paradigms

In the field of education the first analyses of the disciplines took a structural perspective. Dressel and Marcus (1982) described a discipline as a systematic way of organizing and studying phenomena. Building on the earlier work of Phenix (1964), Dressel and Marcus conceptualized disciplinary structures as composed of five components: the substantive component (which includes assumptions, variables, concepts, principles and relationships); the linguistic component (the symbolism whereby elements can be identified and relationships defined and explored); the syntactical component (the search for organizing processes around which the discipline develops); the value component (commitments about what is worth studying and how it should be studied); and the conjunctive component (the discipline's relation to other disciplines). According to Dressel and Marcus, the interaction of these components gives each discipline its distinctive character. Other scholars developed more encompassing definitions. Toulmin (1972) focused on epistemological aspects such as concepts, methods, and fundamental aims, but he also acknowledged the role of the academic in conceiving those epistemological dimensions. Carrying Toulmin's definition a bit further, Whitley (1976) defined disciplines as organized social groupings. King and Brownell (1976) also provided an inclusive description. In addition to its conceptual and syntactical structure, domain of knowledge, and specialized language, King and Brownell defined a discipline as being an expression of human imagination, a tradition built on the discourse of forebears, a heritage of literature and a communications network, and an instructional community.

As analysts moved beyond a purely structural approach, they focused attention on the disciplinary community as a group of actors with varying perspectives, beliefs, and motivations, highlighting the social construction of the enterprise. Individuals within the community were endowed with agency; that is, they were viewed as acting upon the discipline and upon one another. Foucault (1970) complicated our understanding of discipline by positioning the word *discipline* in relation to the concept of power. For Foucault discipline implies the regulation of human conduct and social relations as well as the development of roles and norms that are tightly tied to systems of power. Agents, then, are capable of recruiting members, rejecting them, or bending the rules to advance their own political agendas. The role of power becomes particularly salient when one considers the possibility that individuals and collectives, such as departments or institutions, can reward or penalize interdisciplinary scholarship. Salter and Hearn (1996) argue that "Academic disciplines are evidence of the political deployment of knowledge products" (p. 17).

There are some obvious overlaps in the disciplinary components identified by theorists. The syntactical component identified by Dressel and Marcus is equivalent to King and Brownell's conceptual structure. Whitley's organized social groupings can be equated with King and Brownell's community and communication network components. Toulmin's concepts, methods, and fundamental aims are subsumed under Dressel and Marcus's substantive and syntactical categories. Foucault's discussion of power extends Whitley's notion of disciplines as social groupings and complicates King and Brownell's notions of community; his notion of the discipline as keeper of norms is a compatible, if a less benign, portrayal of disciplinary communities.

Kuhn (1970) conceptualized the cognitive framework of a discipline as consisting of three elements: its underlying theory (generalizations); idealized models and analogies (fabricated examples that are abstracted from real cases to ideally describe phenomena); and exemplars (specific instances of generalizations and models). The disciplines, he argued, differ not only in the way they make generalizations, but also in the set of exemplars used to illustrate these generalizations and the way the two are related. According to Kuhn, models and exemplars serve an important purpose:

> One of the fundamental techniques by which the members of a group, whether an entire culture or a specialist sub-community within it, learn to see the same things when confronted with the same stimuli is by being shown examples of situations that their predecessors in the group have

already learned to see as like each other and as different from other sorts of situations. (Kuhn 1970, pp. 193–194)

These models are designed to further understanding of disciplinary principles and to test and thereby modify and/or extend theory. Gold (1977) contended that the construction of shared models bridges disciplines. But the character of the disciplines involved may determine whether such bridges can be erected:

> Impermeable boundaries are in general a concomitant of tightly knit, convergent disciplinary communities and an indicator of the stability and coherence of the intellectual fields that they inhabit. Permeable boundaries are associated with loosely knit, divergent academic groups and signal a more fragmented, less stable and comparatively open-ended epistemological structure. (Becher 1989, pp. 37–38)

Petrie (1986) argued that academics studying essentially the same phenomena could disagree in important ways, but that a convergence of interests is also possible. Becher suggested that "open-ended epistemological structures" permit sharing across disciplinary boundaries. Epistemological change also permitted what Geertz (1980) identified as a cultural shift that aligned the humanities and social sciences, exemplified by the move from physical analogies of the sciences to symbolic analogies of literary scholarship. While convergence does not signal the unification of disciplines, it does suggest that shared perspectives can facilitate interdisciplinary research — or at least may eliminate one possible source of conflict. Crane (1969), for example, suggested that the acceptability of a new idea is affected by the amount of cognitive reorganization that is required to integrate new information with previous knowledge. Similarly Gold and Gold (1983) suggested that collaboration between members of different disciplines might be enhanced by similarities in cognitive structures.

Communication can be a difficult aspect of interdisciplinary collaboration. One of the most distinctive and binding aspects of a disciplinary community is the language it employs. The jargon and technical terms of a discipline or field are a form of intellectual shorthand that simplifies communication between colleagues (King and Brownell 1976; Becher 1989). Disciplines such as mathematics and physics sciences have developed entire systems of symbols that differ from ordinary language. Other disciplines use general language but imbue common words with particular meanings. Cameron (1985) used the concept of "register" to refer to the manner in which individuals in different disciplines understand information, make arguments, and discuss issues. Disciplinary discourse therefore reveals the disciplines' cultural features, including differences in the way arguments are typically generated, developed, expressed, and reported and how the work of peers is evaluated (Becher 1987b).

Those working in disciplines other than the ones in which they are trained need to understand what they read and hear. The need for interlingual speaking, as Bauer (1990) called it, may be most evident in interdisciplinary research teams. Studies demonstrate that poor communication among team members from different disciplines inhibits the success of research teams (Luszki 1958; Hagstrom 1971; Nilles 1975; Bauer 1990). Kuhn (1977) observed that the task of translating from one discipline to another is more than a mechanical process:

> To translate a theory or worldview into one's own language is not to make it one's own. For that one must go native, discover that one is thinking and working in, not simply translating out of, a language that was previously foreign. That transition is not, however, one that an individual may make or refrain from making by deliberation and choice, however good his reasons for wishing to do so. Instead, at some point in the process of learning to translate, he finds that the transition has occurred, that he has slipped into the new language without a decision having been made. Or else, like many of those who first encountered, say, quantum mechanics in their middle years, he finds himself fully persuaded of the new view but nevertheless unable to internalize it and be at home in the world it helps to shape. (pp. 203–204)

Kuhn (1977) suggested that translation does not indicate conversion from one discipline to another, but the decision to try to translate may create a climate in which it is more likely to occur. Whether conversion is necessary or even desirable is a matter of individual choice. It is clear, however, that faculty can create a climate more conducive to interdisciplinarity by sharing ideas and information. Appreciating different disciplines requires learning how their methods, theories, or perspectives compare and perhaps even how they complement one another. In a two-year study of the process of integrating the disciplinary components of technology assessment projects, Rossini, Porter, Kelly, and Chubin (1984) hypothesized that the greater the diversity in disciplinary background among team members, the greater the difficulty they would have in integrating their work.* The researchers created a simple index of intellectual distance among disciplines to explore the issue. To their surprise the greater the intellectual distance among the core team members, the more substantively integrated the study output. Attempting to explain these findings, they argued that the presence of diversity on an interdisciplinary team might increase awareness of the need to work consciously toward integration. Conversation, then, may help overcome an impediment to interdisciplinary research—lack of understanding of others' disciplinary perspectives. It may also reveal insurmountable incompatibility. Anticipation of the challenge of interdisciplinary communication may prevent faculty from taking the very steps needed to form an interdisciplinary team: "Without . . . successful communication, the research simply does not happen" (Nilles 1975, p.12).

Kuhn's (1977) observation that disciplines are characterized by the existence, in varying degrees, of paradigms that specify appropriate problems for study and appropriate methods for studying those problems is well known, but it has not been the subject of much research. Kuhn claimed that in some fields, such as the physical sciences, paradigms are highly developed; in others, such as the humanities and social sciences, they are less so.† Among the most no-

---

*Rossini and his colleagues were not alone in their thinking. Earlier Pearson, Payne, and Gunz (1979) used a classification of disciplines as a means of structuring interactions among disciplines. They characterized disciplines as restricted (R) or configurational (C). R-sciences, or the hard sciences, deal with highly specific objects with a restricted set of relevant properties whereas C-sciences, or the soft sciences, deal with more complex objects exhibiting a broad range of features. They postulated that it was likely, a priori, that R-sciences would combine better with R-sciences and C-sciences with other C-sciences. Attempts to combine R and C sciences were expected to face considerable communication and value barriers. Vosskamp (1986) similarly argued that disciplines such as mathematics and physics that shared a common code would find interdisciplinary collaboration relatively simple to achieve.

†For the moment, I will ignore the value judgment inherent in this conceptualization of the disciplines to focus on what we may learn from Kuhn's theory and the discussion that it generated. I disagree with Kuhn's contention that the social sciences are less developed paradigmatically than the sciences because it assumes the existence of a single paradigm of inquiry to which disciplines must eventually aspire.

table attempts to study Kuhn's claims are the series of studies by Anthony Biglan in the 1970s and Becher's work in the 1980s. To identify the nature of the differences that distinguished paradigmatic and nonparadigmatic fields, Biglan (1973a) asked faculty members at two institutions to judge similarities among areas of study. This research on the characteristics of subject matter in different academic areas led him to conclude that the three most important dimensions of the "cognitive style" of an area were (a) the extent to which a paradigm exists; (b) the degree of concern with application; and (c) a concern with life systems, as opposed to non-life systems.* Comparing and combining the contributions of various scholars, Becher (1989) summarized the major subject matter distinctions among general categories of knowledge found in the literature. He concluded that hard, pure knowledge, the domain of the natural sciences, is marked by relatively steady cumulative growth. In these areas knowledge is typically generated in a linear fashion. Becher contrasted this growth by accretion to the predominantly recursive or reiterative pattern of development, which characterizes the soft knowledge domains. Steady growth of knowledge is associated with the predictability of problems that are directly relevant to advances in knowledge: "Scientists in hard pure fields seem able at any given time to identify what questions they should attempt to answer next" (Becher 1989, p. 14). Becher suggested that this readiness might be attributable to the well-defined boundaries that demarcate knowledge in the hard, pure disciplines. In the soft domains, "academic work often traverses ground already explored by others. Basic issues maintain their currency from one generation to the next" (Becher 1989, p. 13). In the softer domains, where boundaries are less circumscribed and more penetrable, consensus is less likely.

Becher also identified other clusters of properties that distinguish the disciplines. He observed that whereas the natural sciences and mathematics break down complex ideas into simpler components such as reduction and atomization, the humanities, and to some extent the social sciences, repudiate this

---

*In a follow-up study Biglan (1973b) observed that, depending on the characteristics of their academic area, scholars differed in (a) the degree to which they were socially connected to other faculty; (b) their commitment to teaching, research, and service; (c) the number of journal articles, monographs, and technical reports they published; and (d) the number of dissertations they sponsored.

process. In the soft pure domains, complexity is a legitimate and necessary feature of a holistic appreciation of phenomena. He also argued that a quantitative/qualitative dichotomy exists: scientific knowledge is concerned predominantly with universals; nonscientific knowledge tends to be concerned with particulars. Furthermore the natural world of the hard sciences makes causal connections easier to establish; in contrast, "human data demand complex forms of reasoning in which judgment and persuasion play a more prominent role" (Becher 1989, p. 14). Finally Becher contrasted the impersonal, value-free nature of scientific knowledge with the personal, value-laden knowledge of the social sciences and humanities. Becher noted that while these constituent properties may not be exhaustive, they are useful and familiar enough to provide acceptable characterizations and comparisons. Such general categories, however, mask opposing viewpoints that exist among faculty in the same discipline. For example, not all biologists believe that research in the natural sciences is objective and value-free; they acknowledge that personal biases and desires influence choices of topics, interpretations of findings, and decisions about what to publish.

Comparing the hard applied and soft applied fields of knowledge is not as easy; authors have had little to say about the social- or science-based professions. While understanding in this area is still under construction, Becher made some generalizations. The hard applied fields, he noted, are amenable to heuristic, trial-and-error approaches. Knowledge does not necessarily grow cumulatively, although it may in some areas, and it is not entirely quantitative since application always involves qualitative judgments. Hard applied fields generally work toward some practical end and are judged by how effectively they work to this end. Their primary outcomes are products and techniques. Soft applied knowledge draws upon soft pure knowledge as a means of understanding the complexity of human situations and enhancing the quality of social and personal life. Soft applied knowledge generally does not grow cumulatively. The primary outcomes of most fields are protocols and procedures, which are judged mainly using pragmatic and utilitarian criteria. Becher (1989) also argued that when knowledge is both cumulative and amenable to fragmentation, research labor can be divided among researchers. Fragmentation, ironically, promotes greater social connectedness among scholars in the hard disciplines, particularly in terms of research activities as researchers in these fields tend to work with significantly more people (Biglan 1973b). Similarly Biglan found that faculty in applied fields and life sciences fields prefer to work with more people and report more sources of influence on research goals than faculty in pure and nonlife fields.

Examining disciplinary structures provides clues to the role that they play in the processes of interdisciplinary research and teaching. This exploration of subject matter and method suggests some disciplinary intersections. For example, we might look at the interactions between two sets of subject matter or at the junction at which the subject matter of one discipline intersect with the method(s) of another. Do these junctions suggest different types of interdisciplinarity? Do faculty describe doing interdisciplinary research and/or teaching in terms of intersections or do they perceive it as something different? Is interdisciplinary research and teaching more than the integration of disciplinary components? When method and subject matter are combined with community norms, the picture of interdisciplinarity may become even more complex, given the opportunities for faculty in different disciplines to disagree on goals, appropriate frameworks for pursuing those goals, and appropriate evaluation of the results of their research multiplies (Gold and Gold 1983).

Disciplinary Subjects: Communities and Norms

Disciplines are more than canisters of subject matter and inquiry methods. They are social groupings of people who, to varying extents, share assumptions, behavior patterns, and beliefs about scholarship. The value judgments made by individuals within a discipline concerning the appropriate topics for investigation, the kinds of questions that are valid to ask, and judgments regarding what constitutes a valid answer are social conventions, and these conventions lead to different views of scholarship. Bauer (1990) observed that scientists discover truths about nature and their task is to "lay out those facts" (p. 108). In contrast originality of thought and subtle sophistication of expression are more highly regarded by humanities faculty than the disclosure of facts. Strong normative influences are also apparent in the willingness of faculty from different disciplines to allow personal values to influence their academic work. Becher (1989) claimed that the values and philosophies that individual academics espouse are generally imported from outside the university, and he demonstrated how practitioners' values were likely to appear in the fields of

sociology and economics.* Although some fields of inquiry appear less open
to the influence of external ideologies and values, Becher noted it is too sim-
plistic to attribute this difference to the subject matter of the discipline, that is,
whether the field deals with people or things. For example, engineering is a
field concerned with both people and things, but most academic engineers
would describe their work as objective and apolitical.

Disciplines have been described as cultures, which have in turn been defined as sets of shared meanings or understandings about a group or organization and its problems, goals, and practices (Cameron and Ettington 1988;
Reichers and Schneider 1990; Peterson and White 1992). Thinking about disciplines as cultures can enrich our understanding by suggesting how the community aspects of faculty life influence perceptions and behaviors related to
interdisciplinary research.

> For each discipline, there is a natural set of corollaries embracing matters
> clearly tied to the subject, for instance, epistemic or methodological
> stance, but also such apparently unrelated matters as political affiliation
> and style of behavior. In other words, each discipline can be aptly viewed
> as a culture. . . . By seeing disciplines as cultures, one recognizes that a
> field or subject—its knowledge, methods, theoretical approaches—can-
> not be separated from its practitioners. Outsiders cannot properly practice
> an intellectual discipline just as foreigners find it difficult to assimilate
> into a national culture. (Bauer 1990, p. 110)

Within disciplines there are often subgroups of faculty who share particular
interests or perspectives. Van Mannen and Barley (1984) defined subcultures
as subgroups of an institution. The members of these subgroups interact regularly with one another, perceive themselves as a distinct group within the institution, share a commonly defined set of problems, and act on the basis of collective understandings unique to their group. A group of faculty working in a
specialization within a discipline could also be an example of a subculture.
Faculty can also be divided along epistemological lines, and further subdivided

---

*Becher (1989) was careful to point out the difference between being committed to a set of val-
ues–and perhaps allowing these to influence the choice of a specialism–and permitting them to
distort the evidence to fit one's preconceptions.

along other lines, perhaps ad infinitum. Focusing for the moment on faculty as members of disciplines will help illuminate some of the issues faced by individuals pursuing interdisciplinary scholarship in U.S. colleges and universities.

Schein (1986) observed that the functioning of groups depends on a clear consensus on who belongs to the group and who does not. One of the results of setting boundaries is that group members are provided with a sense of identity. The manifestation of group identity is clearly observed in the university; individual faculty identify themselves with their departmental colleagues and cultures. It has been suggested that faculty in highly prestigious, research-oriented institutions often have a greater sense of professional identity than institutional identity. These faculty identify strongly with their discipline as a result of interactions with a national network of disciplinary colleagues: "The discipline rather than the institution tends to become a dominant force in the working lives of academics" (Clark 1983, p. 30).

According to Becher (1987a), the discipline is the central source of faculty identity. Socialization into a discipline, beginning with graduate training, instills in the faculty member a strong sense of belonging. To be accepted into the disciplinary community the individual must not only demonstrate technical competence but must also show that she or he is loyal to the collegial group and will adhere to its norms. In defining its own disciplinary identity, a disciplinary culture also defines its territories and boundaries:

> The tribes of academe, one might argue, define their own identities and defend their own patches of intellectual ground by employing a variety of devices geared to the exclusion of illegal immigrants. Some . . . are manifest in physical forms ("the building occupied by the English department . . ."); others emerge in the particularities of membership and constitution. . . . Alongside the structural features of disciplinary communities, exercising an even more powerful integrating force, are their more explicitly cultural elements: their traditions, customs and practices, transmitted knowledge, beliefs, morals and rules of conduct, as well as their linguistic and symbolic forms of communication and the meanings they share. (Becher 1989, p. 24)

While members of disciplinary cultures may be similar in terms of espoused values and behavior patterns, all members of a given discipline do not share the same career and work experiences; the culture of the institution affects the strength of the disciplinary culture (Austin 1990). Faculty therefore tend to define their values in ways that make them consistent with local settings. In some cases local definition of professional concerns may weaken the normative core of the disciplines (Ruscio 1987). Although cultures are maintained by teaching newcomers accepted views, newcomers may also shape, to some degree, the culture of the subgroup (Van Mannen and Schein 1979). As interdisciplinarity gains ground, norms concerning academic work may be adjusted to meet the needs of a growing mass of interdisciplinary researchers.

One of the perceived barriers to interdisciplinarity is that it requires faculty members to temporarily (or perhaps permanently) leave their disciplinary communities and thus risk a loss of professional identity. Similarly advocates of interdisciplinarity ask members of disciplinary cultures to accept the presence of nondisciplinary colleagues into their previously homogeneous groupings, again muddying professional identity. As individuals they are likely to have varying amounts of tolerance for either of these situations. Reif and Strauss (1965) explained that faculty members have a large investment in themselves as researchers pursuing certain lines of work; it is not easy to change self-concepts, role models, and values. They are likely to be reluctant to give up the position of influence and status they have attained as a result of their disciplinary achievements. The quest for disciplinary status is in some ways analogous to the individual's concern with academic reputation (Becher 1989). It is stimulated not only by pride, but also by an extrinsic need to justify the existence of the discipline and to secure the necessary resources for the advancement of the discipline. In this way, Becher argued, status can promote competition among disciplines and among individuals.

Departmental objectives generally revolve around raising the scholarly prestige of the department, but it has been suggested that the sources of prestige resulting from interdisciplinary work are limited. For example, one source of prestige is the number of doctorates generated by a department. Birnbaum (1983) noted that interdisciplinary research generates fewer Ph.D. degrees than departmental research. Another source of prestige is the amount of publications in refereed disciplinary journals, but interdisciplinary researchers may find it difficult to produce publications, especially single-authored journal articles, for two reasons: (1) the complexity of the problems investigated makes single authorship sometimes impractical, and (2) journal editors may be reluctant to publish the results of interdisciplinary research that lie outside the narrow interests of their primary readership. Other forms of publication, such as technical reports, papers, and books that are more common products of some forms of applied interdisciplinary research may be accorded less weight in hiring, promotion, and tenure decisions than more recognizable journal articles and monographs. Interdisciplinary research, it has been argued, then can be hazardous for untenured faculty since it often results in fewer publications in respected journals than does disciplinary research. Without this traditional yardstick of quality, colleagues socialized into disciplinary cultures may be unwilling to accept the legitimacy of interdisciplinary approaches or may be uncertain of how to evaluate them or their colleagues who use such approaches.

Tenure policies and faculty perceptions of disciplinary prejudice may also inhibit participation in interdisciplinary research. Sixty percent of the faculty respondents in Hurst's (1992) study of an environmental studies program considered pressure on untenured faculty to work within their disciplines a major obstacle to interdepartmental collaboration. Such fears of disciplinary biases in evaluation and review may be justified. In a comparative study of forty predominantly interdisciplinary research projects sponsored by the National Science Foundation, Porter and Rossini (1985) found a moderate correlation between the peer rating given to a proposal and how interdisciplinary the proposed project was: the more interdisciplinary the project, the poorer the rating. Porter and Rossini also observed a marked tendency for reviewers to rate proposals from principal investigators from their own discipline more favorably. Porter and Rossini further noted that certain comments made by proposal reviewers suggested discomfort with interdisciplinary work.*Thirty percent of the faculty whom Hurst surveyed believed the difficulty of evaluating the work of colleagues from other disciplines was a major obstacle to interdepartmental collaboration.

Studies conducted in the 1970s and 1980s offered indirect evidence of a widespread belief among faculty that interdisciplinary work was not well re-

---

*For example, one economist faulted a proposal for including noneconomic aspects. Other forms of discomfort were observed in comments such as that of a reviewer who indicated reluctance to grade a proposal outside his domain of expertise.

ceived by colleagues. Birnbaum (1981a) noted that interdisciplinary research-ers tended to be scholars without tenure concerns: either they had already at-tained it, or they were not in tenure-track positions.* Those researchers who were in tenure-track positions but who had not yet been awarded tenure ap-peared to be concerned that interdisciplinary work would not help their ca-reers. Nilles (1976) reported that participation in interdisciplinary research by untenured faculty in the U.S. tended to drop steadily as the tenure decision date approached.

Faculty are familiar with the notion of an academic pecking order in which disciplines are ranked according to status and prestige (Becher 1987a; Birnbaum 1982). Although Becher argued that this pecking order is not con-stant across institutions or countries, it is fairly stable in some aspects. Schol-arly prestige is accorded on the basis of the strength of scholarly traditions; high paradigm fields such as the physical sciences are generally considered to be of higher status than low paradigm fields such as the social sciences and education. Anecdotal evidence of this pecking order abounds in maxims such as "mathematicians talk to God, physicists talk to mathematicians, chemists talk to physicists, biologists talk to chemists . . ." (Birnbaum 1982, pp. 14–15).

In a study of collaboration among faculty in schools of public health, Stewart (1980) hypothesized that prestige and status, as well as power and in-fluence, would influence collaboration in research. She believed that faculty from high prestige groups would participate more in interdisciplinary research than faculty from low prestige groups and that faculty from groups with power and influence would be less likely to collaborate than members of groups with-out power and influence. Stewart found, however, that neither prestige and status nor power and influence predicted participation in collaborative inter-disciplinary research. Similarly she found no significant differences by rank or tenure status in the collaborative research patterns preferred by respondents. Rather she noted that discipline was the most consistent predictor of the kinds of collaboration in which individuals engaged. Stewart's findings are consis-tent with those of Gillespie and Birnbaum (1980), who studied eighty-four in-

*Teich (1986) referred to those professional researchers who do not hold faculty appointments as the "unfaculty" in recognition of their second-class status within the university. While many hold Ph.D.s and have qualifications comparable to regular faculty, they generally are not eligible for tenure, seldom participate in decision-making bodies of universities, and are frequently de-nied perquisites of academic life.

terdisciplinary research teams from fifteen leading universities. Defining status concordance as a match between team members' academic ranks and their position on an interdisciplinary team—a team is concordant when senior faculty of higher prestige disciplines head teams composed of junior faculty and faculty from lower prestige disciplines—the researchers found that status concordance was not a critical factor in ongoing interdisciplinary research efforts. Moreover status concordance could depress, as well as elevate, a team's overall success.* Gillespie and Birnbaum concluded that while concordance might strongly impact initial attempts to achieve a unity of effort and to convince funding agencies of a project's merit, once firmly established, factors more directly related to the nature of the team's operation became more salient bases for its status system.

The work patterns that characterize the disciplines may either facilitate or hinder interdisciplinary research. Kleinman (1983), for example, contended that there is a bias against collaboration and in favor of the "lonely scholar" image in the field of sociology. Doctoral students learn that research and writing are ways of standing out among peers; professional development is viewed as increasing individualization. In history and languages norms are similar: research and writing are personal and inseparable from the individual. In contrast many of the hard and applied sciences favor collaborative research activities (Becher 1989).

The literature cited thus far focuses on differences *among* disciplines. Academic specialties, however, create differences *within* disciplines as well. While a disciplinary reference group might include hundreds of individuals, affiliation with an academic specialty generally reduces that number to a much smaller cadre.† Becher (1987a) noted that a specialty is more than an affiliation representing sectional interests within a discipline; it is an area of inquiry

---

*Stewart alluded to this in her discussion of how specialization can create tension among interdisciplinary collaborators engaged in a research project since the degree to which an area of specialization is critical to an endeavor will determine the amount of power individuals having that expertise are accorded in the group. This unequal distribution of power can be detrimental to the extent that it undermines the belief that collaborators are partners of equal status. Lindas (1979) arrived at a similar conclusion after examining evaluations of four interdisciplinary projects. She argued that leaders of interdisciplinary research groups should not be individuals who are too highly regarded since the status accorded them may create an undue emphasis on their disciplines.

†Becher noted that, to his surprise and with the exception of the more populous areas in physics

that requires substantial investments of time and effort. Some specialties are readily accessible, while others require longer periods of induction:

> It is easy to predict—and the prediction is borne out by testimony—that those who become involved in a high investment area are reluctant to leave it until they feel they have adequately realized the dividends of that investment. Conversely, those who might wish to move into such an area are often dissuaded from doing so, particularly in mid- or late career, by the prospect of having to commit substantial intellectual capital of the entry process. Considerations of this kind help to maintain the boundaries of specialist fields and to promote a relatively stable pattern of activity within any given discipline. (Becher 1987a, pp. 292–293)

This is not to say that movement among specialties and disciplines is typically thwarted; shifts in the internal structures and external boundaries of disciplines are a significant source of change in the academic world.‡ Movement across boundaries and into specialties where interaction patterns are different than in the parent discipline may be difficult because of the need to master both new knowledge and a new language. Becher noted that specialties from different disciplines are often more similar to each other, on the other hand, than the specialty is to the parent discipline. Such similarities, when based on subject matter or cognitive frameworks, may promote interdisciplinarity.

So much of the literature focuses on the barriers to interdisciplinarity created by disciplinary cultures and institutional environments that it is sometimes hard to imagine that these same social structures might encourage interdisciplinary work as well as impede it. But the assumption that institutional and departmental contexts have a largely negative influence on interdisciplinary work is challenged by the frequency with which interdisciplinary teaching and research take place. There are several possible explanations for this.

---

and chemistry, that the figure of six to twelve members of a specialty was commonly quoted in almost every field in each discipline he studied.

‡Becher (1987a, 1989) examined the migration of academics among specialties within fields (broadly defined, for example, as the biological sciences) and among neighboring disciplines. Internal mobility, he suggested, is easier in the biological and physical sciences, particularly in the more theoretical areas, while movement across disciplinary boundaries is much more limited.

First, some departmental and institutional environments may actually support interdisciplinary scholarship. Alternatively faculty may be able to circumvent or ignore the less supportive aspects of their environments.

Anecdotal evidence suggests that tenure concerns, for example, have a chilling effect on interdisciplinary research. But while observers have implicated the academic reward system in this way, only a few studies directly examine this influence. A reexamination of the role of reward systems, as well as other institutional policies on sabbatical leaves, release time, and grant giving, for example, could provide some valuable insights into the influence of context on interdisciplinary research and teaching. What are the characteristics of departments and institutions that discourage and encourage faculty to pursue interdisciplinary activities?

Similarly, the empirical literature on interdisciplinarity has not examined in detail the influence of extra-institutional factors on interdisciplinary teaching and research. How might the larger disciplinary community influence faculty members' dispositions toward interdisciplinary scholarship? How do faculty assess their disciplinary community's attitude toward interdisciplinary work? Although disciplinary communities are generally perceived as discouraging interdisciplinary scholarship, little has been written about the differences that may distinguish local disciplinary contexts, typically departments, from national or international community contexts. Local contexts, it has been argued, act to modify disciplinary contexts, and we know that different types of institutions, such as research universities, liberal arts colleges, and community colleges, place differing emphases on research and teaching. How do faculty perceive their home departments in relation to their larger disciplinary communities? How do these perceptions influence the calculus they use to assess these environments and their decisions to do or not to do interdisciplinary work?

Finally, research on faculty behaviors suggests that while the attitudes and opinions of colleagues both inside and outside the institution are important to faculty, they may have a limited impact on decisions about what and how to study and teach—perhaps even before tenure. Faculty tend to make decisions about what to study by assessing their own strengths and interests. Confidence and determination, therefore, may play an important role in decisions related to interdisciplinary research and teaching. Understanding faculty assessments of departmental, institutional and professional environments can help unravel the complicated linkages between interdisciplinary research and teaching and the contexts in which it is pursued.

Interdisciplinary Work in Disciplinary Spaces: The Quest for Support, Resources, and Rewards

Since the 1970s, when interdisciplinary research and programs began their current ascent on college and university campuses, scholars and researchers have focused intently on the institutional context for interdisciplinary scholarship (for example, Newell 1975; Newell, Saxberg, and Birnbaum 1975; Birnbaum 1979; Rossini and Porter 1981; Porter 1983; Russell and Sauer 1983; Teich 1986; Klein 1990). Typically the departmental structure of the university and institutional reward systems are considered major barriers to interdisciplinarity since they presumably are based on disciplinary models of research and teaching. Rossini and Porter (1981) observed some general agreement in the literature about influences on interdisciplinary research. Most studies identified internal factors, such as project management and team communication, as well as external factors, such as university structures and funding constraints (see Newell, Saxberg, and Birnbaum 1975; Birnbaum 1979; and Hattery's 1986 review of the literature).

For some the university promises "a ready and ideal setting for interdisciplinary research efforts" (Baldwin and Faubion 1975, p. 4). Among its advantages are the availability of "hard money" and the resultant flexibility and opportunity to initiate projects that might not be funded by outside sources; the opportunity to create interdisciplinary project teams on an ad hoc basis; the availability of a pool of disciplinary experts to work on interdisciplinary research projects; and an environment in which academic experts have the freedom to choose their research projects and collaborators without administrative or other approval. However, while some perceive the university setting as a catalyst to interdisciplinary research, others see faculty members' freedom to pursue their own research interests as tempered by structures, policies, and practices that value disciplinary contributions to knowledge over interdisciplinary ones (Kast, Rosenzweig, and Stockman 1970; Birnbaum, Newell, and Saxberg 1979). Many focus on the potential barriers to interdisciplinarity (see, for example, Kast, Rosenzweig, and Stockman 1970; Nilles 1976; Birnbaum 1981b; Gold and Gold 1983; Porter and Rossini 1985; Petrie 1986; Hurst 1992). When Newell (1975) generated a ranking of issues from the literature on interdisciplinary research management, university structure was one of the ten most frequently mentioned problems facing interdisciplinary research. Even today the departmental structure is consistently identified as one of the most significant constraints on interdisciplinary research. The basic concept of interdisciplinary research, it is argued, conflicts with the single disciplinary orientation of academic departments. During the heyday of discussion about interdisciplinary research, as opposed to interdisciplinarity in general, a typical view appeared to be that "High quality interdisciplinary research is performed in spite of the traditional university environment, not because of it . . ." (Nilles 1976, p. 160).

Has this picture changed in the twenty or more years that have elapsed since the early studies of interdisciplinary research were conducted? Perhaps. Federal agencies such as the National Science Foundation have encouraged the development of interdisciplinary research programs and centers. Despite some setbacks interdisciplinary programs such as women's studies, area studies, and cultural studies have increased in number on college and university campuses. Have the attitudes of faculty and administrators changed as well? In 1970 Kast, Rosenzweig, and Stockman contended that the university structure of schools, colleges, departments, and divisions made interdisciplinary efforts difficult and often led to competition among disciplines. In 1992, in a study of faculty involved in environmental studies teaching and research, Hurst still found this to be a common belief. In a national survey of faculty, conducted in 1989 for the Carnegie Foundation for the Advancement of Teaching, 75 percent of respondents disagreed or strongly disagreed with the statement that multidisciplinary work is soft and should not be considered scholarship. Twenty-five percent either agreed or were neutral on the issue (Boyer 1990). The question of whether Ph.D.s from interdisciplinary programs will be hired in the same numbers as their discipline-trained counterparts, however, still appears to be open (Wilson 1998).

In addition to institutional policies and departmental structures, disciplinary contexts also influence interdisciplinary scholarship. These can be local, that is, a department of economics can have its own particular ways of seeing and being, or national, as in the case of the professional associations of the individual disciplines. A poststructuralist approach encourages examination of disciplinary cultures and directs our attention to primary patterns of behavior that reflect deeply embedded values, beliefs, and assumptions. Some researchers differentiate culture from climate, a more specific construct that is defined as common perceptions regarding various organizational phenomena (Allaire and Firsirotu 1984) and that has a particular referent, for example, the climate for interdisciplinary research (Schneider and Rentsch 1988). The difference is important, researchers argue, because while culture represents closely held values that continue over time, climate is more transient—as changes occur in an organization, participants' perceptions of the climate of that organization may change as well (Peterson and White 1992). In view of these distinctions, disciplines are cultures that exert relatively strong and embedded influences on faculty. Institutional phenomena such as policies or administrative support are elements of institutional climate because they are more malleable and transient.

Climate is generally conceptualized as a product of individual perceptions of an institutional context "that are learned through processes involving actual interactions with environments, social influences, vicarious learning experiences, self-reflection, and insight" (James, James, and Ashe 1990, pp. 41–42). These perceptions tend to be shared by individuals who have internalized an institutional norm such as research productivity or an emphasis on teaching, but because they are personally constructed, individuals within the same work environment may differ in how they experience a particular phenomenon. Individual perceptions of the institutional climate for interdisciplinarity, then, can vary considerably within the same environment, and individual faculty will make different assessments of whether their work environment is personally beneficial to them.

Climate has both behavioral and normative aspects (Peterson and Spencer 1990). The institutional climate for interdisciplinary research therefore consists of patterns of faculty behavior related to interdisciplinary research and faculty perceptions of the climate for such research, particularly their perceptions of the attitudes of their departmental and disciplinary peers toward interdisciplinary research. Probing individuals' perceptions of the institutional climate for interdisciplinary scholarship may provide insights into the influence of this context on faculty who do interdisciplinary work. Researchers interested in interdisciplinarity have explored three sources of perceptions related to climate: administrative support, institutional resources, and reward systems.

Studies of administrative support for interdisciplinary research are limited both in quantity and focus. The few studies assessing administrative support concentrate exclusively on research universities and the interdisciplinary centers and institutes that they sponsor. Although they are dated, they offer guidance to researchers and observers of interdisciplinarity today. In a study of research administrators at top research universities, Saxberg, Newell, and Mar (1981) concluded that central research administration officials did not actively encourage interdisciplinary research. Postsecondary faculty, most of these administrators believed, should be free to pursue their own lines of research without administrative interference: "Entrepreneurial, creative, and good faculty researchers were seen as automatically defining their academic life around research and therefore successful in obtaining funding for their research. Those who are already thus involved do not need further support beyond that of grants and contract administration . . ." (Saxberg, Newell, and Mar 1981, p. 34). Offices of grants and contracts tended to reflect the same orientation toward research support as their central administrations, confirming earlier findings by Ikenberry and Friedman (1972) that administrative superiors, other potentially influential university figures, and even advisory committees did not typically shape the activities or program objectives of interdisciplinary research centers or institutes.

Saxberg and his colleagues, however, found a minority view among the interviewed representatives of university central research administration. Some representatives believed in providing strong direction to research activities, including deliberate encouragement of interdisciplinary research through the use of seed money and other funding in support of preproposal and proposal activities. The offices run by these administrators tended to distribute information from funding agencies to faculty and to attempt to match faculty profiles to requests for proposals. Only in a few instances did university officials attempt to determine what type of research activities were in the best interests of the university. The university environment "was generally characterized by a lack of university policies to guide or direct interdisciplinary research" (Saxberg, Newell, and Mar 1981, p.40). Perceptions of support for interdisciplinary research and teaching, however, may be an important element of institutional context. For example, in a survey of University of Southern California faculty who participated in interdisciplinary research, Nilles (1976) found a major impetus to further participation was faculty members' perception that the university administration was favorable toward such research.

Although political and market influences may be eroding it, the norm of faculty autonomy is still strong in U.S. colleges and universities, and it is likely that administrative oversight of research is much the same today as twenty years ago. Still, institutional leadership may also be an important force in enabling interdisciplinary research. Russell and Sauer (1983) claim that effective leadership for interdisciplinarity may consist of explicitly allowing time for nondepartmental research, facilitating linkages among departments, encouraging communication concerning interdisciplinary research and teaching opportunities among department heads, and generously recognizing effective interdepartmental efforts. Similarly university incentives can have a positive influence on interdisciplinary activities. Endorsing interdisciplinarity and instituting policies that permit interdepartmental flexibility in grant accountability are additional ways that university incentives can augment initiatives for interdisciplinary research. Institutional leadership can also encourage interdisciplinary teaching through incentives. Course development funds or release time ease the burden of creating interdisciplinary courses and programs. Funds for travel to interdisciplinary workshops and conferences allow faculty to meet with individuals who are knowledgeable about their subject matter and share pedagogical strategies for presenting interdisciplinary material. Sponsorship for interdisciplinary teaching forums where faculty can discuss concerns, strategies, and problems associated with interdisciplinary teaching can also be a sign of administrative support.

Most major universities have the breadth of talent within their faculties to provide expertise for many kinds of interdisciplinary research activities. Laboratory, library, and computing facilities are not typically problematic either, although restriction of financial resources and uncertainty about their continuation are major constraints on staffing of interdisciplinary research projects (Epton, Payne, and Pearson 1985). Financial constraints may limit travel to conferences and other institutions and other information-gathering activities. Such restrictions may inhibit successful research. Blau (1973), Pelz and Andrews (1976), and Reskin (1977) observed that the amount of collegial exchange and interaction among colleagues appeared to be related to individual research performance. These constraints can also hinder the activities of interdisciplinary research teams.

Conflicts over physical resources may be detrimental as well. Some interdisciplinary research projects require an easily accessible location in which to conduct interactive, interdisciplinary work (Nilles 1976). This minor but sometimes important factor can inhibit intragroup processes in universities where different disciplines are located on different parts of the campus (Epton, Payne, and Pearson 1983). Solving the problem is not inherently difficult, but it is less often achieved than may be desirable. Researchers are often responsible for this difficulty as they are reluctant to give up their location, and their identity with the parent discipline, but provision of duplicate space to those involved in interdisciplinary research is often an administrative problem, especially for small and untried programs (Nilles 1976).

Epton, Payne, and Pearson (1983) noted that friction over administrative and financial control can develop between the university and affiliated organized research units (ORUs). Moreover the university environment is itself a constraint on ORUs, which have, over time, developed their own power and influence bases. These institutes can offer financial and other inducements to top graduate students and thereby directly compete with the host institution. In addition very large and well-established ORUs can offer careers and working conditions that are better than those offered by smaller ORUs.

Interdisciplinary teams can also flourish in institutions where policies facilitate departmental sharing of generated resources and conveniently permit cross-departmental purchase and sharing of equipment, faculty, and graduate student time (Russell 1990). Policies on departmental sharing in overhead returns from externally sponsored research may additionally encourage interdisciplinary research.

Interdisciplinary educational programs suffer when resources are constrained. In many institutions interdisciplinary programs borrow their faculty from discipline-based departments; a half- or full-time director is responsible for finding suitable individuals to teach program courses. Departments can supply or not supply faculty, based on their own teaching needs. This situation is alleviated if faculty from particular departments are contractually affiliated with interdisciplinary programs. Interdisciplinary team teaching also creates a resource-related accounting problem: how to determine the teaching load for a team-taught course (Davis 1995). Institutions have established various procedures for counting faculty effort in these courses, but these may create other problems. For example, some institutions calculate course loads on the basis of course enrollment. If a course taught by two individuals enrolls twenty students, each faculty member is assumed to be responsible for half of the students. However, the increased preparation and implementation time required by interdisciplinary courses in order to integrate and coordinate materials, teaching activities, and evaluation suggest that this may not be a fair assessment of the effort put forth by the faculty.

While rewards are often considered the purview of the department, it is typically the higher administration, rather than the department, that structures reward policies, oversees their implementation, and gives final approval to departmental decisions on hiring, promotion, and tenure. Departmental colleagues, of course, have considerable input, but rarely are departmental decisions that conflict with institutional policies and practices upheld. In a review of the literature on interdisciplinary research, Birnbaum, Newell, and Saxberg (1979) documented the common perception that the traditional university reward structure inhibits interdisciplinary research. Although the probability of reward or loss of it is surely influential, studies of faculty motivation indicate that rewards are not the sole predictor of engagement in interdisciplinary research. In a review of more than three dozen studies, Finklestein (1984) concluded that personal standards of performance, rather than reward systems or perceptions of payoffs, were the primary determinants of what faculty did with their time. Similarly Blackburn and Lawrence (1995) found considerable support for their motivation-based framework for understanding faculty behavior. They contended that (1) faculty do what they think they are good at doing; (2) devote energy to what interests them; and (3) engage in activities in which they believe they can influence outcomes. Individual predilections, preferences, and perceptions appear to be more powerful than reward systems in influencing faculty behavior.

Although faculty may subscribe to internalized standards, the influence of institutional context on faculty work should not be ignored. Blackburn and Lawrence argued that social support influences the behavior of faculty members; the intellectual climate — that is, the atmosphere in which faculty work — can reinforce an individual's decision to pursue a theory, pedagogical notion, or line of inquiry. For example, several studies across disciplines support the relationship between intellectual climate and publication e.g., Braxton 1983; Over 1982; Reskin 1978; and Parsons and Plat 1968).

In considering the role of discipline in interdisciplinary scholarship, it is easy to focus on the potential snags in the process. Researchers also have a tendency to direct their attention to that part of the process that requires the most visible and/or intensive efforts. As a result researchers and theorists alike often suggest that overcoming the differences in language and methods among the disciplines is critical to the success of interdisciplinary work. And although the notion that faculty need to recognize and perhaps even reorganize their cognitive frameworks to do interdisciplinary work is often emphasized, there has been little exploration of the ways that faculty learn about the other disciplines in order to do interdisciplinary work. Focusing on disciplinary difference, and on the sciences, also leads to a focus on collaboration as the normative form of interdisciplinarity. While some interdisciplinary teaching and research is collaborative, individuals can also pursue interdisciplinary research or teaching projects. Although there is no division of labor, fundamental epistemic differences, if they exist between or among disciplines that contribute to the project, must still be negotiated. Few beyond those interested in interdisciplinary team projects have asked how we should portray interdisciplinary processes of research and teaching. Although we assume that faculty negotiate spaces in which to accomplish interdisciplinary work, we have not examined the art or science of negotiation. And while Kuhn's theory of paradigms appeals to some, there is a need for more conscious attention to the reality of multiple paradigms and how these can help us better understand why and how faculty engage in scholarship. For example, what, if any influence, does paradigm have on how faculty select topics for interdisciplinary teaching or research projects, on their choice of collaborators, and on the level of success and satisfaction they experience?

Faculty Learning and Faculty Rewards

Discussions of institutional and disciplinary barriers to interdisciplinarity tend to focus on their impact on tangible scholarly outcomes, for example, on publications or project reports (for example, Heathington, Cunningham, and Mundy 1978; Birnbaum 1983; Russell 1983; Russell and Sauer 1983). In studies of interdisciplinary research projects outcomes were typically conceptualized as dependent variables, a by-product of researchers' desire to identify factors that predicted the success of interdisciplinary team projects (see, for example, Birnbaum 1977; Birnbaum, Newell, and Saxberg 1979; Stewart 1980). Until recently, intellectual outcomes of interdisciplinary scholarship were left virtually unexamined. The few empirical studies examining cognitive factors have included them as independent variables that influence, rather than are influenced by, interdisciplinary activity (for example, Robertson 1981). An exception, Thorburn's (1985) study of faculty in an interdisciplinary general education program, revealed that faculty who taught interdisciplinary general education courses reported increased vitality, new collegial relationships, intellectual stimulation, increased tolerance or respect for other disciplines, and the use of new teaching strategies. Newell (1998) noted that studies of interdisciplinary courses claim that students experience a range of cognitive outcomes, such as critical and creative thinking, contextual understanding, coping with complexity, receptivity to new ideas, tolerance of ambiguity, willingness to challenge assumptions, and the ability to shift perspectives, to synthesize, and to integrate. It seems likely that faculty will also experience outcomes related to ways of thinking and, perhaps, to their disciplines. For example, the adoption of a new methodology or theory might call into question epistemological commitments and changes in disciplinary perspectives might follow.

Petrie (1986) argued that to do collaborative interdisciplinary research or to participate in an interdisciplinary teaching team, collaborating faculty must learn something about the discipline(s) of the other member(s) of their research or teaching team. Strike and Posner's (1982, 1985, 1992) model of conceptual change defines learning as an interaction between an individual's experiences and his or her current conceptions and ideas. These conceptions serve as frameworks for understanding and interpreting information that is gathered through experience and for judging the validity and adequacy of solutions to problems. They can also, however, result in difficulties when individuals perceive discrepancies between experience and current beliefs. As Pintrich, Marx, and Boyle (1993) noted, a paradox exists for the learner: "On the one hand, current conceptions potentially constitute momentum that resists conceptual change, but they also provide frameworks that the learner can use to interpret and understand new, potentially conflicting information" (p. 170).

Strike and Posner postulated that an individual's conceptual ecology—the constellation of conceptions that organize his or her thinking about particular topics and the world—influences selection of a new conception. Following Toulmin's (1972) metaphor, conceptual ecology is based on the belief that people's ideas or concepts are the result of a process of natural selection. Hewson and Hewson (1984) explained:

The intellectual environment in which a person lives (including cultural beliefs, language, accepted theories, as well as observed facts and events) favours the development of some concepts and inhibits the development of others. Thus the intellectual environment acts as an ecological niche. Conceptual ecology involves a dynamic interaction between a person's knowledge structures and the intellectual environment in which he or she lives. (p. 5)

When a new conception is introduced into an existing conceptual ecology, it can be incorporated either by assimilation or by accommodation. Assimilation, according to cognitive-structuralist theorists, occurs when an individual's existing conceptions about a topic are not fully developed and new information can be readily incorporated with existing ideas. For faculty a new theory still in its early stages might be an example of an idea that is not fully developed. Accommodation, in contrast, occurs when new conceptions come into conflict with well-developed conceptions.* Accommodation is a more radical kind of incorporation in which central commitments are modified or reorganized.†

Although conceptual change theory seems to explain how individuals' ways of thinking about particular phenomena might change, it does so by focusing primarily on an internal process—cognition—and backgrounds the social context in which learning takes place. Yet the schemata that individuals test new conceptions against are themselves social constructions (Resnick 1991). They are influenced by the kinds of beliefs and reasoning schema that are available to the individual in his or her surrounding culture—what Hewson and Hewson called the intellectual environment and what some researchers and theorists interested in the sociocultural aspects of cognition refer to as discourse communities. Within cultures discourse communities share preferred ways of thinking, speaking, and writing. Disciplinary communities are one kind

---

*Although Strike and Posner borrowed the term accommodation from Piaget, they disavow any commitment to his theories. See Posner, Strike, Hewson, and Gertzog 1982, p. 212.

†The difference between assimilation and accommodation is largely one of degree; the extent of change in the learner's framework that occurs in a given situation is less important than the fact that new conceptions are understood, judged, and acquired or rejected within the context of an existing conceptual framework. Generally individuals will not replace an old conception with a new one unless the old conception is considered inadequate.

of discourse community and as such are repositories of beliefs and reasoning schemata. They also provide the community standards that are typically used to judge the quality of new ideas. Collaboration among individuals from different disciplines occurs within the context of different discourse communities—and disciplinary communities may only be one of these. The collaboration itself is also a social setting influencing the conduct and cognition that occur between or among the individuals engaged in the collaboration. If learning occurs in the intersection of the social and the cognitive, then we must consider how social contexts are integral to interdisciplinary (and disciplinary) learning.

Ethnographic and sociological analyses of the construction of scientific theories (Knorr-Cetina 1981; Latour 1986; Mulkay, Potter, and Yearly 1983) indicate that scientific collaboration shares most of the features of everyday, informal interaction, including the act of negotiating meanings through conversation. Research also demonstrates that interactions of many kinds can promote conceptual change. Investigations of classroom teaching have shown that over time students' cognitive structures become more similar to the content structures of the courses that they take (Shavelson 1972; Geeslin and Shavelson 1975; Fenker 1975; Stasz, Shavelson, Cox, and Moore 1976). These cognitive structures also become more like those of the instructor who teaches the course (Gorodetsky and Hoz 1985; Naveh-Benjamin et al. 1986; Thro 1978). The increasing similarity over time suggests that as a student learns more about a topic, she adjusts her cognitive structure or conceptual framework to reflect her expanded knowledge of the topic or phenomena. Faculty who teach an interdisciplinary course or do interdisciplinary research, either individually or in collaboration, may experience similar kinds of conceptual change. How are the operative social contexts implicated in this change?

Interdisciplinary scholarship may expand an individual's intellectual repertoire or disciplinary framework when theories, methods, analogies, and concepts are borrowed from other disciplines. But borrowing might also result in modifications of disciplinary perspectives. Research on the intellectual outcomes of interdisciplinary research and teaching might establish whether such changes in disciplinary perspectives are common or rare. It may also shed light on whether different levels of engagement with interdisciplinary work are associated with different kinds of outcomes for faculty, that is, are some faculty "more interdisciplinary" than others as a result of significant engagement in interdisciplinary research and/or teaching? Research could also help answer a number of questions about epistemology, social contexts, and intellectual outcomes: How does epistemology influence engagement in interdisciplinary scholarship? How do faculty reconcile disciplinary and interdisciplinary ways of thinking? What kinds of social interactions are most influential in producing interdisciplinarity? How does interdisciplinary scholarship influence faculty beliefs about the academic enterprise in general, about research, instruction, and about what faculty teach?

It is commonly assumed that interdisciplinary scholarship does not garner institutional or disciplinary rewards. Yet there appears to be increased interest in interdisciplinary research and teaching. Expectation and motivation theories suggest that faculty who pursue interdisciplinary approaches to research and/or teaching do so because they see some advantage or benefit in this choice. Research on what faculty *think* they gain from interdisciplinary work would be helpful in sorting this out. Does interdisciplinarity help faculty achieve personal research, teaching, or other goals? Questions about rewards again raise questions about contexts. How do institutional actors who govern hiring, promotion, and tenure view interdisciplinary scholarship? How is interdisciplinarity viewed at different kinds of institutions, for example, research universities or liberal arts colleges, and how might this influence faculty work?

Profiling
Interdisciplinarity

To gather information on the processes, contexts, and outcomes of interdisciplinarity, I interviewed thirty-eight college and university faculty who had engaged in interdisciplinary scholarship in the two years prior to the study.* Following the definition of interdisciplinarity developed by the Center for Educational Research and Innovation, discussed in chapter 1, I included individuals with a wide array of interdisciplinary experiences, both formal and informal. Formal activities were defined as participation in interdisciplinary teaching or research projects on an individual or collaborative basis. Informal activities included participation in interdisciplinary colloquia, symposia, workshops, or conferences or participation in such activities in a discipline other than the home discipline, self-defined by the faculty member but typically the doctoral degree discipline.

A good example of an informal interaction is participation in a faculty workshop in which individuals share syllabi for prospective interdisciplinary courses. Depending on the intensity of the discussion or the openness of the faculty member to change, discussions with colleagues who look at a given topic through different disciplinary, or interdisciplinary, lenses might motivate a search for new sources of information, experimentation with different pedagogical tech-

---

*A more detailed description of the study design and procedures can be found in the appendix.

niques, or reading in related disciplines. Participation in informal interdisciplinary activities therefore can reflect substantial engagement with an interdisciplinary topic. For most faculty, even attending a conference that only lasts a few days is preceded by a longer period of engagement prior to the decision to attend since in most institutions limited travel funds make casual conference-going rare. Similarly even regular attendance at a campus seminar requires a commitment of time and mental energy that faculty with heavy research and/or teaching responsibilities cannot make lightly. Furthermore it is impossible to know a priori from the type of interaction how intense the engagement with interdisciplinarity is. Formal activities such as joint teaching assignments may not require faculty members to adjust disciplinary perspectives, while sustained engagement in an interdisciplinary seminar may have a profound effect on ways of thinking.

Participation in an informal activity such as an interdisciplinary faculty seminar, conference, or institute was the minimum requirement for inclusion in the study, but the majority of informants participated in both kinds of interdisciplinary interaction. Thirteen reported that they participated in informal activities; nine reported that they participated on a regular basis over an extended period of time. Several served as directors of such seminar programs, which included topics in the sciences, social sciences, and humanities. The majority of informants who participated in interdisciplinary seminars, conferences, or institutes also had interdisciplinary teaching or research experience. All but six of the thirty-eight informants taught at least one interdisciplinary course in the two years prior to the study.* Of these informants twenty taught at least one course through an interdisciplinary academic program; others described their interdisciplinary teaching as occurring within their home department. Of the twenty who taught in interdisciplinary programs, most taught in undergraduate programs that grant baccalaureate degrees such as women's studies, black studies, and urban studies. A few taught in interdisciplinary programs such as international studies that do not grant degrees but offer minor concentrations to undergraduates. Three informants taught in an interdisci-

---

*A 1998–1999 survey of 33,785 faculty at 378 American colleges and universities found that 36.6 percent of faculty reported teaching an interdisciplinary course in the past two years. A summary of the survey results were published in the report "The American College Teacher," available from the Higher Education Research Institute at the University of California, Los Angeles (Sax, Astin, Korn, and Gilmartin 1999).

plinary graduate program. These programs did not grant advanced degrees; rather students were enrolled in other degree-granting programs but took courses and participated in research through the program. Nearly half of the informants who said they taught at least one interdisciplinary course also team taught such a course with a colleague from another discipline.*

Several informants who taught in degree-granting programs described their role in moving those programs from their original status as minors to degree-granting programs with undergraduate majors. A number served as directors of these programs: two of the individuals who taught in interdisciplinary graduate programs at one time directed those programs while four of the individuals teaching in undergraduate programs served as directors. Three individuals were directors of special programs that they defined as interdisciplinary; these included general education, critical thinking, writing across the curriculum, and institutional honors programs. Although I had not anticipated that service activities would constitute a category of interdisciplinary interaction, several participants noted that they served on interdisciplinary program committees. About one-third of the informants served at varying times as members of committees that conceptualized or monitored programs such as black studies, urban studies, and environmental studies.

Twenty-two of the thirty-eight informants were full-time university faculty: twelve were affiliated with a research I university, and ten were affiliated with a doctoral I university. Sixteen informants held full-time faculty positions at two selective liberal arts colleges: nine were affiliated with one institution, seven with the other. These informants were not the only individuals on their campuses who were identified as having engaged in interdisciplinary interactions; they are those who were selected and contacted and who agreed to participate. See Table 3.1 for a profile of faculty informants.

In developing the sample I also considered informant characteristics such as tenure status, gender, race/ethnicity, and disciplinary affiliation that may influence participation in interdisciplinary scholarship. Several studies (for example, Nilles 1976; Birnbaum 1981; Hurst 1992) suggest that untenured faculty are wary of involvement in interdisciplinary research because it is not well regarded by departmental and institutional hiring, promotion, and tenure committees. The difficulty that I encountered in identifying untenured faculty who

---

*In a few cases team-taught courses involved three or more individuals from different disciplines.

Table 3.1
CHARACTERISTICS OF STUDY INFORMANTS

	Number	Percent of Sample
Men	20	52.6%
Women*	18	47.4%
Total	**38**	100%
White	34	89.5%
Ethnic Minority**	4	10.5%
Total	**38**	100%
Rank		
Assistant Professor	5	13.2%
Associate Professor	15	39.5%
Full Professor	18	47.4%
Employing Institution		
Research University	12	31.6%
Doctoral University	10	26.3%
Liberal Arts College	16	42.1%
Doctoral Institution		
Research I University	35	92.1%
Research II University	2	5.3%
Doctoral I University	1	2.6%
Doctoral Discipline***		
Natural/physical Science	10	26.3%
Social Science	20	52.6%
Humanities	8	21.1%

*   In 1998–1999 women accounted for 36 percent of full-time faculty in U.S. colleges and universities (Magner 1999).

**   In 1998–1999 members of ethnic minority groups accounted for less than 10 percent of the full-time faculty in U.S. colleges and universities (Magner 1999).

***   In 1998–1999 approximately 20 percent of all faculty were affiliated with natural and physical sciences departments, 18 percent with social sciences departments, and 26 percent with humanities departments. Faculty in other areas, such as agriculture or forestry, engineering, and health-related fields, accounted for the remainder (Magner 1999).

were doing interdisciplinary work may attest to this fact although it is also possible that assistant professors were less well known to administrators and faculty members who were asked for nominations. Six informants were assistant professors without tenure. Eighteen informants were full professors, and all fourteen associate professors were also tenured. In the general faculty population, 55 percent of faculty were tenured; 86 percent of the faculty informants in this study were tenured.

One study of interdisciplinarity (Robertson 1981), as well as studies of collaboration among women faculty (for example, Cameron and Blackburn 1981; Hood 1985, Wong and Sanders 1985), suggests that gender may influence participation in interdisciplinary research. Identifying female faculty was easier than I imagined, given their underrepresentation in faculty ranks in selective colleges and universities in the U.S.* Women faculty accounted for eighteen out of thirty-eight informants, nearly half, and the ease with which they were identified may be the result of the growth of interdisciplinary women's studies programs on college and university campuses. Thirteen of the eighteen women informants taught at least one interdisciplinary course through a women's studies program. In addition to research or teaching focused on women, however, many women informants also conducted interdisciplinary scholarship in their home discipline or were associated with interdisciplinary programs such as environmental studies or black studies. Some of the thirteen had ended their association with women's studies programs, others continued their involvement. Many of the twenty male informants in the study were also involved in interdisciplinary programs, although they tended to affiliate with a greater variety of programs than the women faculty. Male informants taught in a variety of undergraduate degree programs, such as environmental studies, black studies, and urban studies, in interdisciplinary graduate programs, and in special academic programs, such as critical thinking or honors programs.

Academic disciplines can have a profound effect on faculty thinking and attitudes toward scholarship. Different perspectives are encouraged, or required, for participation in particular disciplinary communities. I purposefully limited this study to faculty who had been trained in a liberal arts or science field rather than a professional field such as business, education, or social work.

---

*According to "The American College Teacher," women accounted for 36 percent of all full-time faculty in U.S. institutions of higher education (Sax et al. 1999).

There were two reasons for this choice. My interests in the influence of discipline on interdisciplinary work suggested the need to limit the study to informants trained in a discipline. In addition graduate study in professional fields
is often geared to solving real-world problems and is typically multidisciplinary,
requiring individuals to complete courses taught from a variety of disciplinary
perspectives. Boyer (1990) coined the term *the scholarship of application* to
describe this form of academic work that focuses on applying knowledge to
"consequential problems" (p. 21). For example, in doctoral programs in education, graduate students may take courses in educational psychology, as well as
in the sociology, history, and philosophy of education so they may better understand student learning and what influences it. This exposure to multiple
disciplinary perspectives may significantly affect attitudes toward scholarship
and toward particular theoretical and methodological approaches. Interviewing faculty trained in a single discipline should therefore more clearly reveal
the influence of discipline on interdisciplinarity than interviewing individuals
trained in multidisciplinary fields. In fact multidisciplinary fields such as education have often been criticized for their presumed lack of disciplinary rigor
and their inattention to method and theory (for example, Heath 1999, Lagemann 1999).

The thirty-eight informants received their doctoral degrees in sixteen different academic disciplines. Ten individuals earned doctorates in natural or
physical sciences disciplines, including biology, botany, chemistry, geology,
physics, and zoology. Twenty earned doctorates in social science fields, including anthropology, economics, political science, psychology, and political science. Eight individuals held doctorates in humanities areas such as English
literature, history, Romance languages, and philosophy. Compared to the general population of faculty, social science faculty are overrepresented in this
sample, and humanities and science faculty are underrepresented.

Within these sixteen disciplines informants specialized in diverse areas.
The political scientists concentrated on constitutional law, organizational
theory, and area studies. Of the philosophers interviewed, one was schooled in
the U.S. analytical philosophy tradition and focused on applied ethics, while
another studied Continental European philosophy—an orientation that is
often situated in opposition to the U.S. analytic tradition—and focused on
postmodernist and critical theory. The psychologists' training included cognitive psychology, which is largely concerned with the brain, and human devel-

opment, which is more broadly based. These types of variations can constitute important differences; as Becher (1989) explained, specializations within
fields often have different epistemologies, languages, methods, and foci. Doctoral field of study and departmental location, however, were not necessarily
synonymous. A few informants had earned their degree in one field, but were
hired as faculty members in a department with a different disciplinary base.
For example, a political scientist was hired by a sociology department; a zoologist by a psychology department; a philosopher by a history of art department.
Two individuals were teaching in merged sociology/anthropology departments,
and this required that they teach and advise undergraduates in both disciplines.

A simple, and not entirely inaccurate, model of interdisciplinarity begins
with the assumption that faculty are first trained in a discipline and discover
interdisciplinarity later in their academic careers as they encounter problems
that they cannot solve using disciplinary methods and theories. This linear
progression from disciplinarity to interdisciplinarity is consistent with theories
of conceptual change (for example, Strike and Posner 1985, 1992) that hold
that individuals modify their conceptions when they confront information that
calls previously held beliefs into question. While some faculty described such
encounters with concrete intellectual obstacles, others suggested different
kinds of experiences. For example, some ventured outside their graduate field
of study during their graduate programs, although many noted that their graduate programs severely restricted taking courses outside the discipline. A few
informants held teaching or postdoctoral research positions in disciplines outside their graduate field of study either during or immediately following graduate school. A number of individuals were first introduced to interdisciplinarity
as an academic option when they were recruited to teach an interdisciplinary
course for an interdisciplinary program such as women's studies or black studies. Others, however, claimed to have *always* thought in an interdisciplinary
way.

Although it now strikes me as naive, I was surprised during the pilot interviews for this study when four of the five faculty members whom I interviewed
claimed to always have been interdisciplinary. Their stories had a strong impact on my thinking about where interdisciplinary scholarship fit into faculty
careers and the effects it might have on individual faculty. I wondered whether
this pattern would be maintained in the interviews followed. It was not. The
thirty-eight faculty whom I interviewed reported a variety of interdisciplinary

experiences and routes to interdisciplinarity, and I offer a sampling of their early interdisciplinary experiences here. For readers who wish to make connections among quotations, I have assigned a code, located in brackets after each quotation, that identifies the informant who made the statement. I use this coding system whenever I directly quote faculty informants.*

Becoming Interdisciplinary

A few informants described themselves as being naturally or always interdisciplinary and described intellectual and personal influences that they believed influenced their commitments to interdisciplinary thinking. These influences ranged from life on the farm to life in an extended family and from precollege to graduate school experiences. For example, a historian believed that interdisciplinarity came naturally to him: "I have never formally ever identified a place where I made those [interdisciplinary] connections. I think I have always thought that way" [V]. He described a childhood in which farm life and religion encouraged him to see the connections between things in the world rather than their separateness.

> I was born on a farm in Virginia; at that level all life is related. Feeding the chickens and going to school was a continuum of activity. . . . A rural environment—at some level, it's so essentialist: if you don't plant the corn you will not have crops. I don't divide the world into separate and distinct spheres. That certainly speaks, too, at some level, of my religious training. I was a black fundamentalist—in the church God is not separate and distinct. As I perceived at that time, it was not something indistinct from the human being. . . . So, everything is related, everything is there and everything is tangible. . . . So I didn't sort of come to this. I didn't have a cathartic experience that happened one day and I figured it out. I think it has always been there for me. [V]

---

*To ensure confidentiality, throughout this book I describe informants broadly. It is counterproductive to mask discipline in a study in which it is central, so I have masked other kinds of identifying information, such as references to graduate institutions, employing institutions, and type of institutions, that could be used to identify informants.

Similarly an assistant professor of psychology attributed her commitment to interdisciplinary ways of thinking to early experiences, particularly to her family life:

There's a way in which I think being in my family—my relationships with my grandparents, my parents, and other members of my extended family—helped me develop a kind of social theory that was interdisciplinary. . . . [T]

Because the explanations of black family life that she encountered in graduate work conflicted with her personal theories, she not only questioned what she read, but developed and tested new ways of thinking about the black family.

I really began to position myself and the kinds of questions I was likely to ask in opposition to a lot of what I was receiving in my graduate training. It was always clear to me that there was really a huge gap between whatever kind of social process or phenomena they were talking about and how I came to understand the world. I knew there was this big theoretical gap and so mostly everything I did in all of my papers was try to find a way to understand this particular gap and how would I approach this question differently given the kinds of issues I was interested in. [T]

Although her experience was not altogether positive, some of her graduate training did open her eyes to the various perspectives that might help her understand her chosen area of study: "I did have a couple of powerful courses that really helped me to recognize that I had interests in history and that even though my training was in psychology, there was a strong sociological focus to my work—and that I was also interested in what psychologists were interested in as well" [T].

Educational experiences in particular seemed to bring the difference between disciplinary and interdisciplinary thinking into the foreground. For some, college was a good place to try out interdisciplinary thinking and explore different disciplines. A psychologist compared the specialized training he received in graduate school to the learning he did as an undergraduate:

I do have the feeling—I started having this feeling shortly after I finished graduate school—that I learned far less in graduate school than I did in college. In college I learned to write and to think and to read; in graduate school I learned a lot of specific things, a lot of methodology. I became a statistics whiz. I learned to use computers. I learned how to do experimental research, how to do literature searches, that sort of thing. But I didn't have the feeling that I'd learned that much compared to what college was about. College was a real intellectual adventure for me. [J2]

A political scientist also appreciated the opportunity to explore and experiment in college: "I went to [ ] College in the early 70s and it wasn't explicitly interdisciplinary because that sort of discourse hadn't arrived yet, but basically that's what people were encouraging us to do—to be very eclectic." He described his senior thesis as "very interdisciplinary" and used it as an example that "even then . . . I was not really thinking in disciplines" [P].

A botanist described his experiences in a small botany program in a small New England college, where he believed his interdisciplinary interests were nurtured.

We all knew each other. There were probably a dozen faculty members. It was an unusual time in the life of that program, in my own life. . . . Maybe three or four of us were undergraduates; the rest graduate students—all of whom became close personal friends. . . . As a group, going through it together, there was this sense of discovery and excitement. I also got very interested in geology and took a glacial geology course from a man who is a wonderful teacher—the chalk glaciers [that he drew on the blackboard] sort of moved. Each of those experiences in different areas—although, I could see the connections of those areas—became interesting to me. At that time I became interested in (a) how plants work; (b) how plants interact with their environment; and (c) the history of the earth. [I1]

Undergraduate experiences, however strong, could be difficult to maintain once the students became faculty members. A foreign language scholar active in area studies also attributed her interest in interdisciplinary studies to her undergraduate training: "I was interested in foreign cultures so that by the time I came . . . to studying French literature, I came to it through being interested

in history and politics and current events and geography and Europe, etc."
[N]. She felt "very alienated" when literary scholars challenged the way faculty and students had been studying literature and advocated teaching literature as text, feeling that her interdisciplinary interests had been called into
question.

The botanist quoted earlier suggested that it was a combination of early
childhood experiences and academic interests that created his interdisciplinary approach to scholarship. He talked about growing up in "an academic
family" and about his father, who was also a professor of biology. As a boy he
was "an outdoors sort of kid" who also "read a great deal."

> Among the things that I read were the original Tom Swift novels. And
> Tom Swift often traveled around the world to interesting places and the
> excuse to go there was often a crazy professor who wanted to collect the
> rare frog which was only in the bottom of the Grand Canyon. I have al-
> ways been interested in geography. So I think early on, those interests were
> important to shaping the sort of career I developed. Although, it wasn't a
> conscious effort on my part—it may well have been subconscious. [I1]

The interdisciplinary questions he tended to ask stimulated an interest in a
variety of subjects during college and graduate school. Some of those subjects
were eventually put to use in interdisciplinary research projects involving cli-
matology.

> When I got into college, about the middle of my undergraduate career,
> my interests became quite broad. I learned a lot about the ice age and
> became quite interested in how people understood the ice age and later
> what the ice meant. I became interested in climatology very early. In
> graduate school I got a degree in plant ecology with an emphasis on physi-
> ology and genetics but I did all the course work for a Ph.D. in meteorol-
> ogy which twenty years later is a useful combination for which I can claim
> no foresight. I have always been an interdisciplinary sort of person. [I1]

Several informants described undergraduate experiences that allowed
them to challenge disciplinary boundaries and traditional modes of academic
inquiry. An anthropologist talked about being allowed to "move around the

edge" of anthropology during college. An unusual undergraduate experience in which she took all the required graduate courses in anthropology and completed fieldwork led to an equally unconventional graduate experience in which the question of "what is anthropology" became central: "when I did my comps, I redesigned them. Instead of doing them in anthropology, I said 'This is bullshit to do this in anthropology; it's political economy . . ." [H1]. These interests in political economy led her to study the history of labor relations in multinational businesses. She described her research trajectory as moving through "social history, but as an anthropologist." The interdisciplinary nature of her interests was apparent even as an undergraduate.

> In anthropology doing history was almost subversive because it was asking questions about the construction of reality, the construction of exploitation, the construction of domination — not as something that was natural, but as something that you can see those in power need. And I think that kind of perspective has been sort of crucial to doing anthropology of political economy. So it started as an undergraduate. [H1]

A philosopher/art historian explained the connections — and distinctions — between his undergraduate and graduate studies: "My graduate work was a very logical extension of the studies that I had been initiated at my undergraduate school in that there was the training in traditional art historical methodology, formal analysis, intentionalist criticism, doing archival work, etcetera." Once in graduate school, he soon realized that "we can interpret art in lots of different ways and what you say a work of art means depends on the perspective from which you are coming to this work of art." He began to explore topics from a variety of disciplinary vantage points, and ultimately this process led to the study of the philosophical bases of critical theory.

> I became interested in the various perspectives by which I can understand works of art. And that led very naturally to some courses in sociology having to do with Marxism and Marxist interpretative methods and also to Continental philosophy — people like Kant, Hegel, Nietzsche, Heidegger, Derrida — that informed a lot of critical theory I was reading. So I went from art history informed by these various European philosophical methodologies to studying the European philosophical methodologies.

Then when I went back to graduate school—there was a hiatus of three years until I decided what I really wanted to do—I decided I wanted to keep studying the European tradition that informs these critical methodologies. [E]

Several informants were interested in or influenced by critical and interpretative methodologies, whether those of the early critical theorists or more recent advocates of deconstruction or social contructivism. A political scientist suggested that her work could be pursued from a number of disciplinary perspectives, none more important than any other: "When I applied to graduate schools I was looking for people who were open to the social construction of reality and interpretative methods of looking at the world. . . . If I had to do it over again I might very well have gone to an anthropology department instead" [L].

Role models, typically teachers, were often influential in informants' decisions to pursue interdisciplinary scholarship. A botanist credited a mentor with realizing that she needed a graduate program that would nurture her interdisciplinary approach to the study of plants. He strongly urged her to apply to one specific program because, he argued, she "wouldn't be happy anywhere else." She admitted,

I didn't know what he was saying then, but that's what he was saying—that there would be a responsiveness to this breadth and encouragement of it, which was true. . . . I think had it been more narrow, I think I would have said, "Forget this." I mean, I wouldn't have continued. I never had a very focused, narrow interest in botany. [A1]

An anthropologist who classified most of her work as interdisciplinary talked about the influence of graduate school mentors on her thinking. She argued that she didn't learn to do interdisciplinary work; rather interdisciplinarity has always been her approach to learning, teaching, and research.

My major mentor [in graduate school] was a symbolic anthropologist. [He and his wife] would hold seminars where at least half the folks there were religious studies people or cultural area studies from different parts of the world. . . . I think I only took that course once for credit but I must have sat in six or seven of them, just because it was a learning experience and you always got something out of it. So I guess my understanding that being the part of a discipline didn't mean that you couldn't do other disciplinary things, or other things period. It was always there. It's just been part of what I do. [M]

Not every informant who was an early interdisciplinary explorer, however, could point to positive schooling experiences. Many suggested that graduate programs expressly discouraged interdisciplinarity. A political scientist recalled:

One reason that I chose that as a discipline was that I was under the impression that it was a lot more conducive to interdisciplinarity than it turned out to be. It seemed to me that everything came into play when you were thinking about politics and political process. But I got to graduate school and it turned out that they were a lot more hidebound than I had expected. . . . I was really surprised that there wasn't more collaboration. . . . And we weren't encouraged to kind of take classes in other disciplines at all. It was just very territorial, but nonetheless, my thesis topic was pretty interdisciplinary; it was also really an outlier for them. . . . I [was] sort of moving into history—they [political scientists] like things that are contemporary with an eye toward predicting what's going to happen in the future—so they were horrified and they called me an anthropologist because I was doing this long fieldwork. [P]

An anthropologist commented:

The anthropology department tended to give us a lot of encouragement and support, told us that we were the smartest kids on the block, patted us on our backs, and sent us on our way. And were fairly good about finding material support. . . . I should also point out—ironically, given what I just said—the university was extremely unsupportive of any interdisciplinary effort. You were strongly discouraged from taking classes outside of anthropology and having any real involvement with anyone outside of the field, so in that respect, my thesis was very peculiar. I had two of the four people from outside anthropology—one philosopher, one psychologist—

and it probably would have been more problematic had the thesis been more empirical because there I think the anthropologists might have felt a little surer of how to evaluate it. But because it was entirely speculative, they didn't know what to think. [S]

Another informant was left with a similar impression. An area studies scholar, she earned her degree in sociology. Her interests in other disciplines, however, were often hampered during her doctoral program.

[The university] was totally noninterdisciplinary. Rumor had it that one of the people in my cohort took a course in anthropology and got an "F." As hard as it was to believe, it was just that they didn't want those sociology students here. . . . So you really had to push and push to get to even take a course outside your field. They didn't even want you to even think about other disciplines. [K1]

According to several informants, graduate school often required that interdisciplinary interests be temporarily suspended. Graduate training has traditionally been conceptualized as the development of a specialization—and numerous informants appeared to dislike this aspect of their training. A biologist wistfully recalled his college experiences.

I don't feel like my graduate training expanded my interests; it rather narrowed them down. . . . In fact, that's one of the things I liked about my college, that I had this distribution to fill. I can remember just basically lying to my ecology professor, who wanted me to take more biology, "Oh, no, I have to take this for distribution." I had filled my distributions long ago. But I remember being very sort of narrowed down by my experience in graduate school.

He noted that other factors also discourage breadth in graduate training: "You are on a timeline. You are being supported. They want you to finish. They don't want you to take time to take art history and other stuff." As he reflected out loud on the experience, he seemed unsure of whether graduate school had changed his way of thinking: "I think maybe I have rebounded. I don't think I was ever really narrowed. I just had to spend my time thinking about other things while I was in graduate school. But I don't know how much I have really broadened. I am teaching very disciplinarily." [Z]

A psychologist received a pep talk about the advantages of disciplinary specialization when he expressed his misgivings about graduate work to a favorite professor. True to conventions of specialization and depth, his mentor emphasized the development of mastery and expertise.

> When I was preparing to graduate from college and thinking about graduate school, I decided I would go into experimental psychology. I had a favorite professor in the humanities division of the college. . . . He was a philosopher by training and I respected him a lot. I went to see him one day on another issue and I told him that I was really feeling dismayed. I can remember the conversation. It went along the lines of: "I'm really feeling dismayed to be going off to graduate and I have been looking over what I will be studying and no matter where I go it's just going to be psychology from morning till night. And you know I really am not sure I'm going to be happy." I'd been studying all these different things, although I was a psychology major. And he said, "Don't let that worry you. It's really necessary that you go and spend four or five years, really, doing one thing, learning to be really good at one thing." "But," he said, "if your thinking is alive in these other areas, it will just be put on hold for a little while. Trust me, you'll get back to it after you're out. But you really do have to go through this experience. You can't be any good if you don't sit down and really master something, whether it's a foreign language or a discipline like psychology. Whatever, you've got to get really expert in one thing. That's what graduate school will do for you." So that made me feel better, I guess. [J1]

Informants described a variety of school experiences, from grade school to graduate school, that both encouraged and discouraged interdisciplinarity. For a few, interdisciplinary role models offered mentoring and support, but the lack of such support did not necessarily dissuade informants from pursuing interdisciplinary interests. Likewise there appears to be no correlation between undergraduate and graduate experiences and propensity for disciplinary or interdisciplinary work. For example, a professor of Romance languages who directed a women's studies program and categorized her research and teaching interests as primarily interdisciplinary described her graduate training as "not interdisciplinary in any sense" [K]. In comparison an informant who supplemented a traditional graduate program in economics with a year of research in an interdisciplinary institute now pursued an entirely disciplinary line of research. Teaching courses in an interdisciplinary program was his only interdisciplinary activity since graduate school. Although he had a favorable attitude toward interdisciplinary research and teaching, it had little effect on his own scholarship, his views of his discipline, or scholarship in general.

Drawing Disciplinary Boundaries

Labeling faculty according to their disciplinary affiliation can obscure important differences among faculty and lead us to a false sense that we know what and how a given individual in a particular discipline thinks. Faculty within the same discipline or field may have very different methodological preferences, pedagogies, and epistemological commitments. The palpable differences between counseling psychologists and clinical psychologists, between experimental and theoretical physicists, between advocates of quantitative and qualitative methods in sociology, to provide just a few examples, demonstrate the commonplace nature of these differences. Despite this researchers frequently aggregate what we know to be loosely knit groups of faculty into broad categories such as mathematicians, biologists, anthropologists, and so on. We reify the disciplines even as we acknowledge the depths of the divisions within them. It is with these inconsistencies in mind that I include a few examples of faculty members' contrasting constructions of disciplines and some examples of how disciplinary assumptions influence faculty members' understandings of interdisciplinarity.

Faculty often talked about the boundaries of their discipline—what it included and what it excluded—but they rarely *defined* their discipline. When informants drew different boundaries around the same discipline, it was a vivid reminder that the disciplines are socially constructed categories. I therefore use the word *construction* rather than definition when referring to informants' descriptions of disciplines and interdisciplinarity. As I expected, faculty differed in their perceptions of what constituted interdisciplinary research and teaching. What one informant labeled as interdisciplinary was dismissed by another as merely multidisciplinary or even disciplinary. Informants' constructions of their disciplines, opinions about what constitutes interdisciplinarity, and the perceived influence of disciplinary norms on scholarship were meaningful elements of informants' understandings of interdisciplinarity. In analyzing these accounts I found it helpful to separate research activities from teaching activities. Although the teaching-research dichotomy is problematic because it masks important connections between the types of scholarly work that faculty do, temporarily dividing scholarship into these two broad categories reveals both the unique and common elements of each type of work.

Some informants adhered to a definition of interdisciplinary teaching as team teaching. For these faculty any course that was taught with a colleague from a different discipline was interdisciplinary. Furthermore a course that was *not* taught by a team of faculty from different disciplines was *not* interdisciplinary. Other faculty, however, never team taught a course but still considered all or some of their courses interdisciplinary. Informants also constructed interdisciplinary research in different ways; some thought the disciplines were the foundation of interdisciplinary research; others did not. An example of conflicting constructions emerged during discussions with faculty informants who taught undergraduate courses in evolution at their respective institutions. Three of the four individuals who taught evolution, at two institutions, considered this course interdisciplinary. The individual who did not consider the evolution course interdisciplinary had nonetheless team taught the course with a faculty member from another department. She did not, however, consider the collaborative nature of the course proof of its interdisciplinary character:

> I teach a course in ecology and another course in evolution and those are mainline biology sorts of topics. I team taught the evolution course with [another faculty member] one year, but that is not really interdisciplinary—he does paleontology, which is evolution in the past. I do evolution in the present. There wasn't really any major melding of the disparate disciplines that was involved. [Z]

If paleontology is evolution of the past, and evolution is mainline biology, then paleontology, which is simply evolution in the past, is a subfield of biology, at least according to this individual. Compare this statement with that of another informant who also taught evolution:

Geology includes within it, by its definition, the study of the earth and the history of the earth. There are geophysicists who are essentially doing physics of the earth, geochemists doing chemistry of the earth, and paleontologists doing biology of the past and evolution. Those are all very different fields. Evolution, for example, is a field that has paleontologists and biologists. We talk about biological issues, but the paleontologists are the ones that have to extract the data from the earth itself. [L1]

He defines evolution as a field that requires contributions by both biologists and paleontologists; it is an interdisciplinary field. Later he pointed to differences in goals and methods that distinguished the sciences used in the field of geology:

There are many people here who consider the natural sciences as a discipline and biochemistry or geophysics is not what they mean by interdisciplinary. But . . . there are different methods that are used in, say, physics. Physics is not an historical science; geology is. We develop a narrative, often of a series of events in earth's history, and to do that we need to use the tools of physics, chemistry, and biology. So, I see there are fundamental differences in the way in which we work and our goals. [L1]

Answering the question of whether evolution is a subfield of biology or an interdisciplinary field is less important for my purposes than acknowledging the existence of multiple constructions of the disciplines and understanding why these different perspectives exist. One reason for the existence of multiple perspectives, even in fields where there is a high level of consensus on questions and methods, is that there are no indisputable rules for deciding what is and what isn't disciplinary. In the absence of clear guidelines, individual faculty make judgments by constructing their own sets of more or less restrictive boundaries. Sometimes boundaries intersect and disciplines share areas of overlap. These intersections also change over time, thus complicating the task of deciding what is and what is not disciplinary. The disciplines expand with advances in knowledge and in methods. Then they may contract as subfields break off, establish their own territories and boundaries, and perhaps become disciplines in themselves. Biochemistry is a case in point; once considered an interdisciplinary field of study, it is now often defined as a discipline with its own content, methods, research community, and norms of scholarship. Revisions of disciplinary boundaries are inevitable since the disciplines themselves are the products of human thought and imagination.

If faculty cannot be expected to agree about what is disciplinary, neither can they be expected to agree about what is interdisciplinary, particularly when most definitions of interdisciplinarity begin with presumption of a disciplinary structure. However, informants did not necessarily define interdisciplinarity in counterpoint to disciplinarity; some articulated understandings of interdisciplinarity in which the disciplines were not central. The more tightly bound that notions of interdisciplinarity were to notions of disciplinarity, the more interdisciplinarity was subjected to a critique that takes disciplinary knowledge as the model for all knowledge. For example, the informant who did not consider the evolution course to be interdisciplinary remarked:

> I don't call what I do interdisciplinary even though it uses other disciplines and it uses my own discipline—whatever those are. Interdisciplinary to me has a more contrived notion to it. Like you go out and break boundaries and juxtapose things that don't typically go together. And I don't think you have to work at it quite that hard. You should just go out and get what you need to know or ask the next logical question. [Z]

Despite allusions to the need for flexible disciplinary boundaries and methodological choices, this individual was concerned that interdisciplinary projects were often "silly," "cosmetic," and "superficial," "fluff" and "filler." The idea that one should just "ask the next logical question," however, is a distinctly disciplinary notion. In the natural and physical sciences, where knowledge is more often arranged sequentially and hierarchically, this is a reasonable strategy. Given this understanding, to "juxtapose" is to ignore the coherence of disciplinary categories. In the humanities and social sciences, however, knowledge tends to be relational rather than hierarchical and there often is not a "next logical question." An anthropologist could therefore describe her work as exciting precisely because of its reliance on "juxtaposing": "It's taking counterintuitive things and juxtaposing them. Not working inside conventional boundaries always, I think, always allows you to do that, but it's pulling and pushing the boundaries against one another." [H1]

Just as faculty informants had different understandings of interdisciplinary teaching, they differed with regard to interdisciplinary research. Like the biologist who described evolution as a disciplinary topic, an associate professor of chemistry was also reluctant to label himself or his work interdisciplinary. To me, as an outsider, his accounts of his research in biophysical chemistry appeared to be textbook definitions of interdisciplinary research: his work relied on substantial understanding of physical laws, chemical bonds, and biological functions. Despite the interfaces among disciplines, he defined his work as disciplinary and offered a very restrictive definition of interdisciplinarity— one that excluded his work from consideration:

> I would define interdisciplinary—and with my definition I probably don't fit—as somebody [sic] who actually publishes papers in very different journals. I don't. I publish in biochemistry and biophysics journals. I haven't published in any physics journal or in a virology journal, let alone history or something else. [Y]

This individual considered biophysical chemistry a subfield of chemistry and was therefore able to define his scholarship as disciplinary. This may reflect a bias in favor of disciplinary research; however, given his enthusiasm for interdisciplinary study, such an explanation is incomplete. In this case any disciplinary bias must be considered in tandem with his belief that biochemistry has attained the status of a discipline.

Other individuals were more eager to characterize their work as interdisciplinary. At least two of these individuals took a view opposite to that of the chemist just described. A geologist saw his field as an interdisciplinary mix of scientific fields.

> Geology is almost by definition interdisciplinary. What I do is a combination of chemistry, biology, and standard geology. To understand fossils I have to be a biologist; I have worked with living organisms, recently dead organisms to better understand fossil organisms. Yet I must be a geologist to place them in their earth history context. And I have to use chemistry to understand how various rocks are formed and their history through time. So of all the sciences, geology is probably the one that intersects with more fundamental sciences: physics, biology and chemistry. [L1]

A biologist working in the area of cell biology considered her field inter-disciplinary because it relied on a technology developed by physicists. Prior to the existence of a powerful instrument, the elements and processes of cells could not be observed; with the development of electron microscopy, it be-came possible to look inside the cell. Cell biology is now a well-established subfield of biology. Like the geologist this biologist argued that her discipline is interdisciplinary because it relies on contributions from other disciplines, in this case, the major contribution being a technological one. Although these claims are arguable, the geologist and the cell biologist both characterized their research as interdisciplinary. Yet each still defined interdisciplinarity largely in terms of disciplinary contributions of methods and content to their fields of study.

Other informants offered explicit or implicit definitions of interdiscipli-narity that attenuated the relationship between the disciplines and interdisci-plinary work. Among these faculty were several individuals who were unwill-ing to define interdisciplinarity for fear that it would limit the scope of their research and teaching. For example, two humanities faculty believed that a range of interdisciplinary approaches should and does exist. Their comments stand in sharp contrast to the restrictive and exclusionary constructions of other informants.

> I think trying to pin down the features that one would associate with inter-disciplinarity is just part of that general fear of "What is it? We've got to corral it and define it." I would feel much more comfortable maybe hold-ing off on a rigid definition because I think there's a great variety of inter-disciplinary efforts. [C]

> What is interdisciplinarity? I suppose interdisciplinarity is as many things as disciplinarity is. . . . I hope there isn't one theory of interdisciplinarity because that would seem pretty silly to me. [N]

An anthropologist lobbied for a commonsense definition:

> I'm not sure how to argue about interdisciplinarity. It means that you have to go to whatever is out there to help you explain what it is you're trying to

explain. If that information is not in your discipline as it's constructed, then you go somewhere else. [M]

Informants described a variety of interdisciplinary experiences and expressed a variety of opinions about interdisciplinarity. Although one of my goals in this study was to explore the complexity of interdisciplinarity, I also hoped to reveal some patterns in faculty experiences of interdisciplinarity that would help us better understand interdisciplinary scholarship, the faculty who pursued it, and their experiences in their institutions and disciplines. In the chapters that follow, I describe and make linkages across these categories of experience. First, however, I suggest how individual accounts of interdisciplinary scholarship reveal the limitations of previous definitions of interdisciplinarity.

Constructing
Interdisciplinarity

Most definitions specify the integration of different disciplines as the litmus test for interdisciplinarity. In contrast the definition that guided this study broadly defined interdisciplinarity as the interaction of different disciplines. This definition left the question of integration open and made it possible to explore informants' understandings of interdisciplinarity without making assumptions about what these understandings should entail. While a few informants proffered personal definitions or responded to definitions encountered elsewhere, I did not press for these; rather my strategy was to analyze informants' accounts of research and teaching for insights into implicit definitions of interdisciplinary research and teaching. This approach had two advantages. First, it did not assume that faculty who claimed to do interdisciplinary work agreed that *integration* of the disciplines was the defining characteristic of interdisciplinary work. For example, faculty might disagree as to whether the variety of disciplinary perspectives presented in an interdisciplinary course must be integrated. Second, it eliminated the possibility that informants might second-guess themselves, leaving out experiences they might have considered interdisciplinary had they not been asked for a definition beforehand.

Categorizing Interdisciplinary Scholarship

As I read and analyzed the words of informants, I could not avoid comparing their varied descriptions of interdisciplinary work. My first attempts to understand these differences were driven by the literature, which suggests numerous, often competing, schemes for classifying interdisciplinarity. After failing to adequately match informants' understandings of interdisciplinarity with conceptualizations from the literature, I concluded that a different way of thinking about interdisciplinary scholarship was needed. Eventually as my analysis focused on the catalysts that prompted interdisciplinary research and teaching, and I noted that informants seemed to think about interdisciplinarity as they thought about research design, that is, they let the questions or issues that they wanted to pursue determine their method for pursuing them. Different kinds of questions led to different kinds of interdisciplinarity. Classifying these resulted in the following typology of interdisciplinary teaching and research, which is based on the four categories of questions and issues that faculty in their study pursued:

Informed Disciplinarity
Synthetic Interdisciplinarity
Transdisciplinarity
Conceptual Interdisciplinarity

I labeled this a typology of interdisciplinary scholarship despite my belief that the first category, informed disciplinarity, as its name suggests, is more disciplinary than interdisciplinary in nature. Informants, however, consistently identified this form of scholarship as interdisciplinary and I have titled the typology in a way that is consistent with their constructions.

Despite the fact that informants' scholarship ranged over many different topics and disciplines, each one's work could be classified into one of these categories. Further study of interdisciplinary research and teaching might confirm that all interdisciplinary research and teaching can be categorized in this manner, but it might also suggest additional categories of interdisciplinarity not described in this study. In Table 4.1 the types of interdisciplinary scholarship are described in terms of the teaching issues and research questions that characterize them. With the exception of transdisciplinarity (for example,

Jantsch 1972; Miller 1982), these categories had not been previously identified or defined.*

In the sections that follow I define these categories and offer examples of each from informants' accounts of their research and teaching.

These categories are descriptive, not evaluative; it is not my intention to suggest a hierarchy by ordering the forms of interdisciplinary scholarship in this way. The major difference between these forms of scholarship is the type of question asked, not the extent to which different disciplines are involved or the merit or desirability of the forms of scholarship. All are accepted and useful ways of asking academic questions.

Defining the Categories of the Typology

Theorists contend that one of the things that distinguishes one discipline from another is the type of questions considered legitimate to ask. Similarly types of interdisciplinarity may be best distinguished by the kinds of questions asked. The suitability of a focus on questions rather than on the level of integration achieved in teaching or research process or products is supported by informants' comments as well. Several faculty noted how learning another discipline or disciplines had expanded the range of research questions that they could ask and answer. But these faculty did not simply learn to ask new kinds of disciplinary questions; instead they identified interdisciplinary questions.

> Learning about conditioning has allowed me to ask research questions that I would not have been able to had I not known about the techniques and ideas behind reinforcing and punishing things, etc. . . . . I basically used a conditioning procedure to look at how a bird without a hippocampus might or might not be able to use the sun to learn about space. In my current experiment I'm looking at how the bird uses the sun compass, which is an ethological issue. I am performing a brain manipulation,

---

*After this study was completed, Liora Salter and Alison Hearn (1996) proposed several new definitions of interdisciplinary research that aligned somewhat with the categories that emerged from this data. These are discussed later in this chapter.

Table 4.1
TYPES OF INTERDISCIPLINARY SCHOLARSHIP

Type of Scholarship	Teaching	Research
Informed Disciplinarity	Disciplinary courses informed by other discipline(s)	Disciplinary questions requiring outreach to other discipline(s)
Synthetic Interdisciplinarity	Courses that link disciplines	Questions that link disciplines
Transdisciplinarity	Courses that cross disciplines	Questions that cross disciplines
Conceptual Interdisciplinarity	Courses without a compelling disciplinary basis	Questions without a compelling disciplinary basis

which is neuroscience. And I'm using the conditioning procedure to look at that, psychology. . . . I would not be able to do that if I didn't have some expertise in psychology. [D]

In cognitive neuroscience, the questions are all about the relationship between cognition on one hand and brain on the other. I hadn't asked those questions previously. As a result of learning something about this stuff, the questions I'm asking have changed, moving in the direction of what's called neuropsychology. [G1]

I hope what interdisciplinarity does for colleagues and for students is that same thing it does for me, that is, opening minds and making the questions more important than the mode of answering them. When I think about graduate students, for example, I think that one of the things that interdisciplinary work can do for graduate students is show them that research is not about taking a particular way of analyzing data and making publishable articles out of it. It's actually about answering questions or about thinking about how you would go about answering questions even if you can't answer them. The questions become really, really important. [L]

The following definitions of the categories of the typology focus on the types of research questions and teaching issues that are central to each type of interdisciplinary scholarship.

Informed Disciplinarity

The teaching issues and research questions of informed disciplinarity are essentially disciplinary in nature; that is, they are motivated by a disciplinary question. In informed disciplinary teaching, faculty make use of examples from other disciplines to help students make connections between disciplines, but the use of these examples does not change the focus of the class from one discipline to another. In research, disciplinary questions may be informed by concepts or theories from another discipline or may rely upon methods from other disciplines, but these disciplinary contributions are made in the service of a disciplinary question. Mere borrowing of methods, theories, concepts, or other disciplinary components to conduct research or to teach a course is not sufficient for interdisciplinarity. Only when borrowing is motivated by an interdisciplinary question or issue does scholarship qualify as interdisciplinary.

Synthetic Interdisciplinarity

Synthetic interdisciplinarity occurs when teaching issues and research questions bridge disciplines. These bridging issues and questions are of two subtypes: issues or questions that are found in the intersections of disciplines and issues and questions that are found in the gaps among disciplines. In the first type of synthetic interdisciplinarity, the issue or question belongs to both disciplines, in the latter it belongs to neither. In both subtypes the contributions or roles of the individual disciplines are still identifiable, but the question posed is not necessarily identified with a single discipline. A synthetic interdisciplinary course might examine historical and legal perspectives on public education. A synthetic interdisciplinary research question might explore the biological and psychological aspects of human communication.

Transdisciplinarity

Transdisciplinarity is the application of theories, concepts, or methods across disciplines with the intent of developing an overarching synthesis. It differs from informed disciplinarity and synthetic interdisciplinarity in that these theories, concepts, or methods are not borrowed from one discipline and applied to another, but rather transcend disciplines and are therefore applicable in many fields. The disciplines do not contribute components, but rather provide settings in which to test the transdisciplinary concept, theory, or method. Miller (1982) defined transdisciplinary approaches as "articulated conceptual frameworks which claim to transcend the narrow scope of disciplinary world views and metaphorically encompass the several parts of the material field which are handled separately by the individual specialized disciplines" (p. 21). The disciplines therefore become subordinate to the larger framework (Klein 1990), subsumed under what Newell (1998) calls "superdisciplines," such as Marxism or general systems theory. Sociobiology, which applies the principles of natural selection and evolutionary biology to the study of animal social behavior, is an example of a transdisciplinary approach. A transdisciplinary course might examine how a cybernetic system (an open system with inputs, throughputs, and outputs of energy and information) could be used to analyze individual behavior as well as social behavior. Transdisciplinary research might be undergirded by a belief in structuralism, which assumes the interrelatedness of all things and searches for underlying formal structures.

Conceptual Interdisciplinarity

The final category of interdisciplinary scholarship, conceptual interdisciplinarity, includes issues and questions without a compelling disciplinary basis. These issues and questions can be considered either interdisciplinary or predisciplinary because they can be answered only by using a variety of disciplinary contributions. Conceptual interdisciplinarity often implies a critique of disciplinary understandings of the issue or question, as in the case of cultural studies, feminist, and postmodernist approaches. In some cases critique may be both the motivation and the desired end product of conceptual interdisciplinary scholarship. In other cases the critique may be accompanied by an equally important concern for integration of disciplinary perspectives. A conceptual interdisciplinary course therefore might focus on the role of reggae music in affirming the cultural and political identity of postcolonial black Jamaicans. A study of domestic roles in medieval England that examines constructions of class and gender utilizing contributions from history, political theory, literature, art history, philosophy, and religion is an example of a conceptual interdisciplinary research project.

Informed Disciplinary Courses

In describing their courses, faculty often talked about how they used examples from other disciplines to help students achieve a broader picture of the topic or phenomenon being studied. Some faculty explained that interdisciplinary examples were either necessary or useful for helping students make connections in discipline-based courses. Courses that introduced students to a discipline sometimes fell into this category of informed disciplinary teaching.

> I teach principles [of economics], which may be a little interdisciplinary in the sense that [the] students don't have any grounding in economics so you have to kind of pull out of the other things they know or things they already know about economics but don't realize that they know about economics. [W]

Similarly a biologist talked about helping students make connections between biology and physics by providing interdisciplinary examples:

> When our biology students take physics, they often don't understand why. The reason they don't understand why is that physics probably does little to transfer the physics back to biology and we do nothing to receive the physics back to biology to show it's relevant. . . . So, when I teach animal behavior and we talk about the echo location ability of bats and signals that are in kilohertz, we do a little physics. . . . [Recently] we have been talking about electric fish. . . . There are two kinds of electric fish: some

that had their batteries arranged in a series and some of which are in parallel, basic ideas in electricity, depending on whether they have a lot of voltage or a lot of amperage in their charge. And this has to do with whether they live in salt water or fresh water. So there is a biology [story] and a nice little physics story that go side by side. [F1]

The extent to which faculty used interdisciplinary examples varied considerably. Some faculty included a few examples in their teaching while others claimed to infuse their courses with interdisciplinary contributions. Typically faculty who said they made many interdisciplinary connections described themselves, as well as their classes, as interdisciplinary. For example, a historian saw his approach to history as inherently interdisciplinary.

I don't approach history as a separate and distinct discipline. I don't think you can. . . . I don't have very rigid categories of what is history, what is politics, what is sociology, and I couldn't imagine putting together a course and not picking the most interesting book on that topic. So even though I don't consciously try to put those things together in a course, I find myself using a history text if I am doing a survey course, but I will grab a novel, I will grab an anthropology book, I will grab a reader of primary sources. It just comes very naturally. [V]

A professor of Romance languages shared a similar viewpoint. She argued that students in her classes have to understand the political context of the literature they read. She provided this example: "I'll have them watch the debates going on Quebec independence, even though they are reading a poem, because I want to talk about nationalist discourse. You can't get it in the poem if you can't see what's happening up there on TV" [N]. It is important to note that these categories apply to particular projects, not to individuals or to their scholarship generally. This Romance languages professor also taught women's studies courses that would be considered conceptual interdisciplinary courses; the biologist team taught synthetic interdisciplinary courses. Faculty may use different approaches for different courses, or research projects, depending on the subject matter and their own goals.

Informed disciplinary courses may be liberally sprinkled with examples from other disciplines, but these examples are not central to the material presented. In the literature courses described above, students read literature, not political treatises or histories of Quebec, despite the importance of the political context. The disciplinary framework may be enhanced by the inclusion of interdisciplinary examples, but the focus of the course is still on the literature. One organizational clue to the disciplinary nature of informed disciplinary courses is that they are not cross-listed between departments.

Informed Disciplinary Research

While informed disciplinary courses were common, examples of informed interdisciplinary research were much rarer. This may be peculiar to the pool of informants chosen, but it might also reflect scholarly norms. As one informant suggested, the depth of understanding that one needs to teach an interdisciplinary course is less than that needed to do interdisciplinary research. Informed disciplinary research was therefore limited to borrowing of disciplinary methods to answer questions posed in another discipline.

A cell biologist considered her research interdisciplinary because the technology she used was developed by individuals from different disciplines and was utilized in different disciplines. Although the technology that she borrowed allowed her to ask more sophisticated questions, the questions and answers that she described were still solidly within the field of cell biology. She noted that the field of cell biology was not possible without this technology, saying, "It's not important to our field. It is our field. It's not dissociable." When she learned cell biology in graduate school, she used this same technology. "Microscopy is a well-respected, venerable, ancient tool in cell biology, so that's accepted interdisciplinary work. In fact, it is not even considered interdisciplinary anymore, the set of technologies" [R].

Heckhausen (1972) considered the borrowing of analytical tools, such as mathematical models and computer simulation, pseudo-, or auxiliary, interdisciplinarity, depending on the transitory or enduring need for the method. Here the strong association between the technology and the discipline suggest a form of auxiliary interdisciplinarity. This categorization, however, ignores the status of the field of cell biology and the fact that the borrowed tool is used in the service of a disciplinary question.

In the social sciences, where methods such as survey research, ethnography, and narrative are more often shared among disciplines, there were few examples of borrowed methods, but at least one informant, a political scientist doing research in area studies, described his research as a form of interdisciplinary outreach:

> My method is to choose, increasingly, a commodity and to look at the politics of that because the instruments that are used to affect production, distribution, and growth in production of a particular commodity vary from commodity to commodity. So my method is to learn about the commodity, the nature of the production, learn about the nature of the interventions and read in a parallel manner the general stuff about politics of the country and then look for the political explanation of why the interventions were done the way they were. The most important methodological impact on me has been economics. . . . There is a well-known book, published ten or fifteen years ago, by an economist who did his dissertation research in Zambia. He developed his technique into a method that drew very heavily on economics but applied it to politics. . . . I have been very influenced by that. [C1]

This political scientist's goal in applying this borrowed method was to understand the distribution of political power, a traditional concern of his discipline. As he explains, the economic data answers a political science question.

> When governments control prices or get involved in monopoly marketing or subsidize inputs, manipulate the exchange rate, so forth and so on, all these economic instruments have an income distributive effect. In places that don't have elections, they tell you a lot about the distribution of political power. That's the assumption. As a political scientist, what I do is I infer about the distribution of political power and the problems of changing the distributing of political power by watching what happens when economic instruments are manipulated in a certain way. It is kind of a roundabout way of saying I just use the economic data to tell me something about distribution of power. [C1]

Some informants clearly made a distinction between work informed by other disciplines and interdisciplinary work. An informant working in the area of cognitive psychology interpreted his own work in this way. He had attended seminars and institutes on linguistics and philosophy of mind that were related to the work he was doing in psychology. Despite his engagement with these disciplines, he viewed his early work as essentially disciplinary in nature; he argued that his later work, which related brain activity to performance on a cognitive task, was truly interdisciplinary in nature.

> Some of the research that I ended up doing, and I think this is true of others as well, was really straight cognitive psychology — but it was at least informed by these other disciplines. I think that's a worthwhile improvement, but it wasn't a giant change. Some of the work that I did in collaboration with an individual [who was very strong in logic and philosophy although trained initially as a psychologist] was more of a change. It was almost like a new kind of work, something more interdisciplinary. . . . I think some of the papers that we did . . . really were kind of true interdisciplinary papers and I was professionally very identified with the cognitive science movement. [G1]

As was true of teaching activities, individuals were not limited to pursuing one form of interdisciplinary research. Faculty moved back and forth among these types of scholarship.

Synthetic Interdisciplinary Courses

Faculty also described courses that linked particular disciplines. For example, an interdisciplinary program in urban studies was composed almost exclusively of courses in the departments of sociology, economics, and political science. Only two courses, an introduction to urban studies and a senior seminar, attempted to combine these three disciplinary perspectives. The introduction offered an overview of urban economics, urban sociology, and urban political science. The capstone course was intended to help students synthesize the contributions of these subfields:

> The senior seminar is not team taught; typically it rotates among the different members. Currently one sociologist, one economist, two political scientists are the core of the urban studies program faculty. We tend to

rotate that course among us. . . . In some ways, since one person leads that course and even in the intro course, the potential is there to get too much disciplinary bias. But, I think the people who participate in the program are sufficiently interdisciplinary in approach that that doesn't happen. I am the economist and I probably am more rigid from my discipline than sociologists and political scientists are in terms of the disciplinary approaches that we use, theories and things like that, but typically our interests are to maintain the interdisciplinary nature. [H]

Elective courses or advanced courses in a major program might link disciplines in a similar manner. The political scientist quoted earlier in this section hoped to help students make connections between his discipline and that of economics.

What is interdisciplinary about Third World Politics? I do a section on development and the reason is really because you can't understand Marxist or class-based analysis of developing societies unless you understand something about economic development. . . . Typically, I structure the class with what you might call a straight political science approach. We spend a lot of time reading political histories. Who was president? What happened? . . . Then I try to convince students that this is too superficial to understand why it is that certain changes occurred over time. I wind up with the political economy approach because I think it is a fuller understanding. I try to convince students that political science and economics are not really separate disciplines. [C1]

Another instructor taught a course that revealed the influence of his graduate training in both divinity and sociology:

The course that I teach on cults and sects is taught in the religion department, but it's probably taught much more like a sociology course than a course in theology and religion. And I make it clear when we are analyzing a particular phenomenon like participation or even leadership in a religious organization or group that a theologian might say something quite different about participation than a sociologist would say. . . . My intent is to get people to look at the problem from a number of different perspectives and to evaluate for themselves what insights are gained from one approach versus another. [U]

An economist who taught with a colleague from the religion department provided a good example of the influence of individual disciplines on a team-taught course:

We built a balance between theological arguments and economic ones. I was particularly interested in making sure that the students got grounded in the data of development so that they really understood empirically what it meant to call something underdeveloped or Third World or poor and how that was different from the United States. I spent some time talking about different kinds of models that economists had historically used to explain development and bring it about and to show why a lot of those had limited application because they didn't fit the right settings. At the same time, my colleague was doing similar kinds of things with theology. What we tried to do when we taught the course—although, by definition it almost has to be segmented—we tried to avoid the segmentation in the sense that we didn't want the students to say. "Oh, this week is theology and the next week is economics." [W]

In each of these examples, the disciplinary contributions to the issue under consideration are apparent, and faculty members represent their own disciplines in the classroom. Many of the courses described could be taught with different disciplinary foci. For example, to teach the course on religious cults, one might also call upon psychology and anthropology in addition to theology and sociology. Reliance on disciplinary experts to explicate particular aspects of a course often attests to the synthetic character of the teaching approach. Synthetic interdisciplinary courses, however, differ from the informed disciplinary courses described in the previous section. Rather than focusing on one discipline, they make substantial connections between two or more disciplines and thus have an interdisciplinary focus. Often such courses are team-taught and/or cross-listed between or among departments.

Synthetic Interdisciplinary Research

Several scientists identified the problems that they have worked on as sitting in the interstices between fields, and they borrowed theories and methods from other disciplines to answer their questions. The questions asked by individuals using synthetic approaches, however, were not framed within a single discipline. An anthropologist explained that his research was motivated by questions from different disciplines—and that had ramifications for the choice of method, the type of data generated, and the type of arguments used:

> The algorithms for determining who belongs to what race, what it means to belong to a race, differ dramatically from one culture to the next and from one historical epoch to the next, although in all cultures and all historical epochs people seem to believe that these enormously varying racial politics are grounded in the reality of biology. So, I started looking at these things and obviously it's interdisciplinary in the sense that's it's motivated by questions from different disciplines, it uses methods that come from different disciplines, as a result it uses data that are associated with different traditions and arguments about what's persuasive and what's not that come from different disciplines. So, it's almost by definition from the start, given the kind of problem that I'm looking at, interdisciplinary because it uses methods and concerns and theories from different disciplines and it also ignores the fact that there are gaps in method and theory in each of the home disciplines. [S]

His current research revealed a gap between the disciplines of anthropology and psychology.

> Anthropologists are not very concerned about how children learn about anything; the assumption being that it's a fairly straightforward process, kind of a photographic-paper theory of learning. You expose children to some patent variation, they have a way of recording that variation and then come to recognize it. Psychologists have long acknowledged that learning is a much more complex process than that. On the other hand, psychologists have not explored really at all what it means to be a member of a

human group and how it is that we represent knowledge about human groups, which is a starkly anthropological concern. [S]

Synthetic interdisciplinary research questions can also be explored using research teams composed of disciplinary experts. The disciplinary experts each identify a piece of the puzzle to solve; eventually the separate pieces are assembled to answer the synthetic question.

I direct a team of researchers based at five universities. Our project is to study the effects of elevated atmospheric CO_2 on whole ecosystems. We are simulating a doubling of CO_2 in the atmosphere at a biological station. . . . The team consists of five PIs who are all faculty members at different institutions. . . . There is a microbiologist, a soil invertebrate specialist, a root specialist, and a team meteorologist and a plant physiologist. And so we recognized from the outset that it had to be a very interdisciplinary approach. We are about to add some geochemists and hydrologists. . . . The research questions demand teams. There is no way an individual can be broad enough and have enough expertise across the range of disciplines. [I2]

All team-based research, of course, does not rely on multiple disciplinary experts. This model of interdisciplinary research, however, appears common in the sciences where research questions and methods are divisible. In this example the researchers have divided the ecosystem into its component parts to study the effects of elevated level of carbon dioxide on plants, microorganisms, and so forth.

Transdisciplinary Courses

Transdisciplinary courses focus on a concept, theory, or method that can be applied across disciplines. Informants did not provide any examples of transdisciplinary courses, although they did provide examples of transdisciplinary research. However, there is no reason to believe that transdisciplinary courses don't exist; they may simply be a rarer form of interdisciplinarity. Their scarcity may suggest that the departmental structure of U.S. colleges and universi-

ties discourages transdisciplinary courses that, unlike other kinds of interdisciplinary courses, have even more tenuous ties to particular disciplines and
departments than synthetic or even conceptual interdisciplinary courses. Alternatively the lack of examples may reflect the extent of interest in transdisciplinary approaches.

Transdisciplinary Research

Transdisciplinary research is driven by a belief that natural and social systems, such as those studied in economics, biology, and physics, have common
underlying structures or relationships. In this study two individuals described
transdisciplinary research projects in which they applied theories and/or methods across several disciplines, wherever they thought they might be useful.
A political scientist's early transdisciplinary leanings influenced his choice
of graduate programs. A math major, he looked for "a science to apply the
math to."

> Some of my interdisciplinary interests really go very far back. In high
> school I did a science project on computer simulations in biology. . . . In
> college I worked in an interdisciplinary group with the evolutionary biol-
> ogy. . . . Also, in college I had an interest in game theory, which is inher-
> ently—you know, the same tools are used in a variety of places—so it is
> kind of an easy thing to make interdisciplinary. [A]

Later, as a faculty member in a political science department, he pursued both
disciplinary projects in a well-established political science specialization and
transdisciplinary research projects involving mathematical models. He offered
an example of a transdisciplinary theory of cooperation that he eventually applied to evolutionary biology.

> I was interested in the Prisoner's Dilemma as a way of understanding how
> cooperation can evolve. . . . I originally conceived of this politically, for
> example, how to deal with the arms race, but I thought these findings
> would be important for biology, because . . . the rule that won was tit for
> tat, which is so simple, birds can use it. So I went looking for a biologist to

work with and make the applications. [Names colleague] was here at the time and he is one of the world's leading evolutionary biologists and he had a background in game theory. We were able to talk to each other, I knew enough evolutionary biology that I could talk to him on those terms. But, game theory was also a language that we could communicate in. So we wrote an article that helped establish the work in the evolutionary biology field.

This work, he contended, did not have a disciplinary basis at all and attracted the interest of economists, sociologists, philosophers, and mathematicians.

It doesn't look to me like I am borrowing like Darwin would borrow from Malthus. It looks to me like I am working on a fundamental problem and the way I have formulated it, such as when you can get cooperation from others, just happens to be abstract enough that the applications apply to many places. It is not that I got an idea from social psychology and I used it in biology. It strikes me as having more coherence than that. . . . In a way you might say it's nondisciplinary. [A]

A high energy physicist segued from physics to statistical mechanics to dynamic systems to times series analysis, applying tools and theories in the fields of economics, biology, and finance. He described an ongoing project in which data from simple physical systems was analyzed and understood using techniques based on the ideas generated by the study of non-linear dynamical systems. "These techniques, with modifications," he explained, "can be applied, seem to be applied usefully, to a wide variety of systems such as economic systems and some biological systems" [E1].

The individuals pursuing these projects argued that the decision to categorize their work as disciplinary, interdisciplinary, or something else was simply a reflection of the existing order of things academic.

So whether you call that disciplinary or interdisciplinary is not clear. Some of it, the techniques that are being developed, you could call disciplinary in the sense that "Well, that is applied math or that is statistics." Or you could call it interdisciplinary because it's applicable, potentially applicable, to lots of different areas. So it is a matter of semantics. [E1]

Similarly the political scientist believed that the difference between interdisciplinarity and disciplinarity was, in some cases, little more than a historical accident.

> It seems to me that it is not silly to say you could have a department of game theory . . . that [brought] together people of different backgrounds that were all using game theory to solve problems. And they would have as much to say to each other as different political scientists, some of who were game theorists and some weren't. It's sort of an historical accident that it's not because game theory didn't get established, fully established until the 1950s and all the other departments were frozen in already. But if somebody were starting a new place in England or New Zealand or California or something, there is no reason why they might not try that. Then you would say that somebody that was just doing game theory was disciplinary and somebody that was just doing political science was interdisciplinary. If you are driven by a certain subject, or you have a certain approach, whether the world organizes that with the boundary crossing through you or on the side, is kind of their problem or their choice. [A]

It is useful to consider how the examples of transdisciplinarity in informants' accounts compare to those suggested in the literature. Klein (1990) reports that the term *method interdisciplinarity* has been used to denote methods, presumably statistical techniques, computer modeling, or simulation, that can be used in more than one discipline. She specifically cites the use of game theory in evolutionary biology, mentioned here by one of the informants, as an example of this form of interdisciplinarity. What is missing from consideration of these terms and their definitions is the search for underlying structures or nondisciplinary theories that motivates the use of the method. The term *method interdisciplinarity* therefore only partially describes the type of interdisciplinary work performed by these informants.

Miller (1982) intended the term *transdisciplinary*, which he applied to approaches such as structuralism, general systems, and sociobiology, to connote a more comprehensive effort to identify connections or underlying similarities in natural and social phenomena. He suggested that although some supporters of transdisciplinarity hoped their preferred conceptual frameworks would replace existing disciplinary approaches, others saw transdisciplinarity as an alternative or as a source of coherence for interdisciplinary efforts. It appears that the two faculty quoted here take a similar stance to that of the latter group. The term *transdisciplinary*, despite its multiple connotations, is appropriate.

Conceptual Interdisciplinary Courses

Conceptual interdisciplinary courses assume that a variety of perspectives must be brought to bear on a particular issue or problem. Various disciplines are included in these courses as needed to explain the topic under examination. Organized topically or thematically, these courses often lack a disciplinary home. First-year seminar courses that introduce new college students to a variety of disciplines by exploring an issue or phenomenon are examples of such courses.

> You have to teach science and you have to teach religion in the Great Ideas course. It's set up to look at four or five of the most pivotal ideas of civilization, so it's radical in a very deep sense, I think. Not only breaking out of the discipline, but really looking at the core ideas out of which civilization comes. [X]

These courses can also serve the additional purpose of developing students' academic skills, such as writing or critical thinking. According to some informants, this focus on process, rather than discipline, is part and parcel of their interdisciplinary nature.

> A group of us started a course for freshmen on the creation and manipulation of images. The general thrust was to help the students understand what happens when you look at things from different perspectives. . . . That course eventually went from that general framework to a course that really emphasizes critical reasoning. [O]

Conceptual interdisciplinary courses may call on many disciplines, as the Great Ideas course requires, or a more limited number of disciplines, such as a first-year seminar that introduces students to methods of inquiry in the sciences. They may be offered as both lower and upper division courses, required or elective:

> Third World economic development, by its very nature, is an interdisciplinary course because it is impossible, at least in my view, to talk about issues of economic development without understanding a whole phalanx of things about cultural values, social and political institutions, religious structures—a whole range of things that shape the environment in which development takes place. [W]

A number of conceptual interdisciplinary courses were offered through interdisciplinary programs such as women's studies, black studies, and environmental studies. These may serve as electives for students in other disciplines or fields or as required courses for students in the programs themselves.

> Part of what I see my work as doing is really exploding how people think about black family issues. So in my marriage-and-family class we start off looking at how people think about family. What do people think family is and dealing with that really fundamental question and looking at all these kind of discussions about family over time and looking at all these images. Or saying, "What if we start thinking about culture?" Then they'll have a series of readings from different ethnic groups. "Well, what about context and class?" I'm trying to get them to say, "What if I thought about the world really differently than I'm thinking about it now. What if I really challenged some of the ways I think about family?" [T]

While synthetic and conceptual interdisciplinary courses both ask an interdisciplinary question, conceptual interdisciplinary courses are not arranged so that particular disciplinary perspectives or contributions dominate. In fact faculty who teach such courses typically explicitly critique the disciplines' answers to the question they ask; this is common in ethnic studies or women's studies courses. In most cases the answer to the question posed, and thus the course itself, has no compelling disciplinary basis. For example, it is very difficult to determine the disciplinary focus of the course on the black family described above. Many disciplines could contribute, and it may surprise some to learn that the individual who teaches this course, concerned with issues of class and culture, as well as family, is a psychologist by training.

Conceptual Interdisciplinary Research

Several informants in the social sciences and humanities rejected the widely accepted description of interdisciplinary work as borrowing and struggled for alternative ways to describe it. Some talked about the importance of theory or pointed to the lack of distinctive disciplinary questions. Overall they suggested that interdisciplinary thinking constituted a different way of thinking about intellectual problems and a different way of asking questions.

> Maybe I even wouldn't find the borrowing of the particular theoretical concepts from particular subjects what I define as true interdisciplinarity. I think that's borrowing from a discipline to illuminate your own. But I think of interdisciplinarity as the creation of new intellectual space that's neither—it's more than the combination of the individual disciplines. [C]

An anthropologist suggested that her version of interdisciplinarity was not defined by borrowed disciplinary contributions, but rather by a reliance on encompassing theories and the creation of new interdisciplinary spaces.

> I haven't ever thought that the historical work would *inform* my work. I think anthropology is sort of redefining what history is, even what constitutes history—what are the ways that we can know about the past. So it's not a question of what do you take from history, it's more what you take from social theory. . . . So, it's not the method, it's not like talking to an historian and they say, "Oh, I just love how you use cultural theory." It's more cultural studies and theory . . . and a whole sort of way of thinking about the past and the present, but that's not necessarily coming from the historians. [H1]

A political scientist talked about the lack of resemblance between traditional disciplinary questions and those that she typically asked.

My questions have never looked like political science questions. Some-times by the time I get to the very end of a piece of work, I can make it look like a political science question or a like a question that would fit into any other paradigm. My questions are generally pretty broad and up until that very end, it's kind of like my questions are "What's going on here? What's happening? How can we make sense of this?" [L]

She acknowledged that she had to package her findings so they were acces-sible to a disciplinary audience:

For example, you can say here are some ways in which we can take the sense that we made of this and put it into a context and then it looks more like a political science question. And then it can bounce off against other political science questions. But it's a long time between kind of the start of the research and getting to the point where there's an answer like that. Or a question like that. [L]

These comments suggest that one way of thinking about questions is to ask whether there is any compelling reason that they should be asked from a particular disciplinary standpoint. The questions described by the political sci-entist could be asked from a number of disciplinary standpoints, as she sug-gested:

I define what I do as organization theory. . . . Organization theory, for me, is a combination of political science and the study of bureaucracy and public administration, sociology, anthropology, and psychology. It could also be economics but my version of it isn't very much; there are a few economists whose work I use. One of the areas that I specialize in is deci-sion making. The psychology kind of comes in the individual decision making and issues of leadership. Sociology comes in when you're talking about social movements and such, and political science is kind of the pub-lic domain of decision making. That's probably where I use the most eco-nomics—the economics of information issues—and then anthropology comes in for me mostly in the way I study things, which is by doing ethnographies, mostly. So, I rely a lot on anthropological methods and concepts for kind of thinking about how to organize the world. [L]

Many of the humanities and social sciences faculty I interviewed had been influenced, to varying degrees, by feminist theory, cultural studies, or postmodernist theory. These influences might themselves be termed interdisciplinary, as one individual made clear:

> When I was writing the book that got me here, I came across cultural studies. Now it's a growing field, but when I started there was a center in Birmingham* and people publishing in England and some people in the United States publishing but not many. I discovered this whole world which brought together, at that time, some literature and anthropology and sociology and brought this together in a very fruitful way. So I kind of stumbled on an analytical way of thinking that was already interdisciplinary. [D1]

Informants with postmodernist or feminist orientations called upon different disciplines to create an understanding of the context surrounding the object of study.

> I was becoming fascinated by this whole new generation of women writers who were doing some very audacious things around notions of feminine identity. . . . If you wanted to try to figure out how to couch them, you couldn't say they were only psychological, only philosophical, only political. They were all of those things and they happened to be happening in this particular place, so that I then had to take those questions and then contextualize them historically and culturally. There was all this overlapping; if I was going to write about it I had to explain the interconnections, the sites of resistance to all of those things. So it meant that I—in my own head I had to constantly be separating out and decoding what I would call an interdisciplinary puzzle . . . and that also adds a certain kind of critical interdisciplinarity to it. [N]

*The Birmingham Centre for Contemporary Cultural Studies in Birmingham, England.

Although faculty who worked in an informed disciplinary mode also called upon different disciplines to contextualize information, faculty whose work was conceptual used context as a basis for critique, not simply as background.

> It's a model of exchange that leaves the way open for change of the original questions. I take a theoretical concept, I look at it in a new context, I don't try to make that context fit. I see the way the context also critiques the original concept. And I take it back to the first context and see what I can newly perceive based on how that concept has been changed. It's a process of change on both sides. Therefore the space is reconfigured and the space that I have taken the concept to is also reconfigured in relation. It's a kind of process that changes each original context and creates something new. [C]

Informants themselves perceived a difference between the integration of disciplinary perspectives and the critique that motivates conceptual interdisciplinarity. A biologist associated with both women's studies and environmental studies tried to distinguish the two:

> I am definitely attracted to a sort of meta-look at the disciplines. I am not sure that's the same thing, however, as putting together information and perspectives from different disciplines to arrive at something new. . . . A critique of a discipline, or a set of disciplines, or of disciplinarity is different from putting information and ways of knowing from two different disciplines together to arrive at new knowledge, to create new knowledge, or to look at things in a new way. [A1]

An economist agreed:

> There is no question in my mind that they are different kinds of questions. . . depending on what framework you choose, you are going to ask a different set of questions and they may not necessarily be the ones that you are particularly interested in or the ones that are particularly important.

Other informants argued that the questions and motivations behind conceptual interdisciplinarity differed in theory, but that in practice faculty often moved between forms based on critique and those based on integration. The associate professor of Romance languages suggested that critique and integration could both define interdisciplinarity:

> I think they [critique and integration] are part of the contradictions. . . . They are a microcosm of the world, for better and for worse, and the impulses I think are not as distinct and specific as that. You have some people in—if you want to call them factions or groups or pressure points or whatever—who are going to act most on the critique side. But then you have other people and approaches that are going to act more on the integrationist side. And they are not fighting each other. I think both of those sides are doing something to the middle—which is the status quo, which is the rigid boundary-driven thinking. And [people] will choose different strategies if they think they are going to be useful. I do that. If I think the integrationist argument is going to be more useful and compelling with a particular group of folks who are more traditionalist, that's what I use because the other one will be too threatening and you won't get anywhere. So the critique is useful when people can understand and take it. It's not useful when it alienates and then it gets you right back to where you are. [N]

Another informant argued that although epistemological foundations were "very open" for her, she was nonetheless striving for integration of the disciplines in her work. To do interdisciplinary work strictly focused on critique was "just not part of my experience" [P]. She and the Romance languages scholar noted also that at the time they were earning their graduate degrees, the discourse linking interdisciplinarity and critique had not yet taken hold.

> I think that that's a generational difference because I think increasingly that scholars are having to start from almost predisciplinary assumptions, the way interdisciplinarity has developed as a concept in the academy, but that option wasn't open to people of my generation . . . because we were so clearly anchored in our own imaginations, and in the imaginations of our advisers, in a discipline. [P]

In my own case, I think the complementarity part of it emerged first historically. But I think that young scholars and students and faculty educated in the late 1980s and 90s are coming to interdisciplinarity in a different way precisely because of . . . feminism's and postmodernism's critique, I guess we could call them academic metanarratives about fields. But we didn't have that kind of conceptualization back in the 70s when I was getting educated. [N]

Although the examples of conceptual interdisciplinarity cited here were taken from accounts of informants influenced by feminism, cultural studies, and postmodernism, it is not clear whether all conceptual interdisciplinarity is necessarily postmodernist and/or feminist. Faculty committed to traditional epistemologies may also do conceptual interdisciplinary work, but it may require that they supplement their disciplinary training. A botanist, for example, was writing a biography of an important ecologist. She had been interviewing "ninety–year-old botanists," doing archival work, and enjoying the "detective aspects" of the project. She reflected on the relationship between this work and her disciplinary training and knowledge:

I am not sure where I am going with it. It's very different—I mean up until now I have been doing science, even if it's been a little funky to my more molecular colleagues. . . . But this is clearly not science—although I am drawing on my knowledge of science. I don't think a nonscientist could do what I'm doing. I'm looking at the transfer of ideas from Europe to this country and the development of particular subfields of ecology, so it's calling on all my scientific knowledge, but it's a very different arena, I guess. [A1]

This informant had expanded her content area to included the transfer of intellectual ideas and had adopted methods, interviewing and archival work, that are not typically part of the disciplinary repertoire of biologists and botanists. Earlier, through her botanical work, she became acquainted with several different disciplines.

I am a plant ecologist and generally plant ecologists ask the question "Why do plants grow where they do?" . . . Ecologists among biologists are among the most interdisciplinary [scientists] and interested in connections. . . . I think I am not a very mainline scientist in that sense, even in my training and research. To do my work I had to really pull on a lot of disciplines and knowledge of languages and culture. I had to look at the human history of the landscape to understand why plants were in some areas and not others. [A1]

She also well understood the limitations of her discipline as typically practiced. Ecology, she contended, has traditionally been ahistorical. She, however, always had an interest in history and thus has always been a critic of the field. Her long-standing belief that botanists must create cultural and historical contexts in which to understand plants and her willingness to test and adopt other methods for gathering and understanding information suggest that she might be more open to conceptual interdisciplinary strategies than more discipline-bound colleagues.

Epistemology, Disciplinary Boundaries, and Interdisciplinarity

In this study informants in the sciences tended to pursue synthetic interdisciplinary research. Social scientists and humanities informants, however, appeared as likely to pursue one kind of interdisciplinarity as another. The types of interdisciplinarity, however, are not simply proxies for the disciplinary groupings. Rather than disciplines, it is the epistemological commitments of informants that are more related to an affinity for a particular kind of scholarship. One set of informants, including the majority of natural and physical scientists interviewed and a subset of the social scientists, adhered to traditional positivistic approaches to knowledge. Another set of informants was epistemologically committed to poststructural approaches to knowledge. Virtually all informants from the humanities disciplines and a majority of the social scientists were included in this group.

Lorraine Code (1991) terms these contrasting approaches to knowledge *regulative* (what I call positivist) and *constitutive* (what I call poststructuralist) principles. Regulative principles include objectivity, value-neutrality, rationalism, and "decontextualized, ahistorical and circumstantially blind" knowledge (p. 33). Regulative knowledge is also more hierarchical: theories are composed of concepts, which are composed of generalized facts. In the paradigm-like realm of regulative knowledge, current work shapes future work, and knowledge grows in a cumulative fashion. Constitutive knowledge, Code argues, is plural, relational, and situated and does not tend to grow by accretion. It allows the objects of study to speak for themselves, is nonreductive, and is concerned with understanding difference rather than dismissing it "as theoretically disruptive, aberrant, cognitively recalcitrant" (p. 151).

These different epistemological stances influenced the way informants asked research questions and taught courses. Informants committed to traditional positivist approaches chose theories and methods from different disciplines that were epistemologically consistent with their own ways of thinking and with one another. These scholars framed synthetic interdisciplinary or transdisciplinary questions in which content served as a link between disciplines or as a setting in which to test an application of theory or method. In conceptual interdisciplinary research, the contributions of individual disciplines were often so attenuated that the disciplinary source of the question was not clear. The critique of the disciplines that often predicated conceptual interdisciplinarity led both to questions and to answers that were not phrased within disciplines because disciplinary questions and answers required the exclusion of crucial perspectives.

Despite differences in epistemologies, informants from a variety of disciplines argued that disciplinary lines should not constrain the search for knowledge. They differed, however, in the extent to which they questioned the legitimacy of disciplinary boundaries. Individuals whose work could be categorized as informed disciplinarity, synthetic interdisciplinarity, or transdisciplinarity tended to be more tolerant of disciplinary boundaries than those whose work was primarily conceptual interdisciplinarity. Two individuals, each of whom had pursued synthetic and/or transdisciplinary research projects, shared the opinion that disciplines have an inherent logic.

I think there really are quasi-natural ways of subdividing the world of knowledge. . . . You call one thing biological science and one thing social science and yes, there is overlap and I am an example, but by and large it is not just a social artifact. It is reinforced by a social artifact but it is not just a social artifact that the disciplines are more or less the way they are. I think if you started over again, many of the same ones and the hierarchy would be recognizable. It would be different but it would be recognizable. [A]

The disciplines are historical conventions whose borders and boundaries can be explained, but like many cultural conventions, this one was widely adopted because it resonated with some things. For one thing, it resonated with the development of the hard sciences; it's not an entirely implausible division of explanatory strategies for understanding the natural world. I doubt whether there is a natural domain of things that anthropologists study as opposed to sociologists as opposed to psychologists, but in any event these disciplines have developed traditions and ways of interrogating the world that have a certain plausibility and have significant value and I am not sure we are going to come up with some alternative way of doing this that looks better. [S]

These two faculty, although trained in the social sciences, had long-standing interests in the life sciences and had adopted research methods in their interdisciplinary work that are often used by faculty working in the physical or natural sciences — mathematical modeling and experimental design. Their affinity for positivist paradigms and synthetic interdisciplinarity is reflected in their views of the nature of disciplines.

Most informants who pursued positivistic forms of inquiry accepted disciplinary boundaries as reasonable and useful, if not natural. Those who were most opposed to borders tended to work in interpretative social science or in the humanities. For example, another informant, one deeply committed to interdisciplinarity, challenged the boundaries of her own discipline.

It's sort of this clash, it's crystals just breaking apart — this thing that was anthropology is an artifice in itself, there's no one holding it together. It's not that I don't think that there are real tools of cultural analysis that can serve us well, but I don't understand what this discipline is. The something that's held it together is the study of man, the study of human development. Well, psychology claims that. What is all this cordoning off? What part of human development? Why are archaeology, physical anthropology still taught in the same department as discourse analysis, and as the childhood fetish in China in 1955? I mean it doesn't make a lot of sense. [H1]

Strongly influenced by postmodernist and feminism thought, she pursued conceptual interdisciplinary research and teaching. Her unanswered questions about the discipline of anthropology included those about what students in the discipline should learn:

> That's a battle right now, whether the four-fields approach in anthropology is still viable. Linguistics, physical anthropology, archaeology, cultural anthropology *always* had to be taught together. I'm not sure taking courses in physical anthropology should be mandatory—but I think it should be an option for students to be allowed to do it. But I am not sure that that's more critical than having a mandatory course in philosophy in which thinking about rationality and logic would underride how we can understand cross cultural analysis. We have to understand what we are comparing. We have to think of questions of relativity and rationality. The question is "What do you need, really need, to understand the human mind and its variability and its similarities and differences?" I mean, do I need a course in archaeology more than I need a course in logic or in philosophy or in ethics? [H1]

Informants with an affinity for conceptual interdisciplinary tended to regard disciplinary boundaries as social artifacts that bore little relationship to reality. An informant who held a joint appointment commented:

> I am not too tolerant of rigid disciplinary boundaries. I think they really stultify people's thinking. And I think they are all arbitrary anyway . . . they are rooted in particular historical times. That is how disciplines get formed. And they change, they change by virtue of people working on the margins. [D1]

She noted that the advantage of an interdisciplinary approach is that it enables the use of a variety of tools and prevents researchers from trying to shape problems to fit disciplines:

One reason why I value interdisciplinarity so much is that if you are work-ing on a problem you have that many more tools to apply to the problem. You don't have to be restricted to the tools of one particular discipline and have to shape the problem to fit a kind of mold as to what it should look like. [D1]

This informant also questioned the usefulness of quantitative social science methods, arguing that defining research variables so that they were amenable to statistical analysis often forced complex ideas into a disciplinary mold. For her, these definitions tended to lack validity; that is, they did not measure what they purported to measure.

Occasionally informants interpreted the imposition of disciplinary bound-aries as neither benign nor inconsequential. They contended that disciplinary boundaries, with their tainted histories, stand in the way of knowledge. The anthropologist who challenged disciplinary borders also talked about the need to reconstitute knowledge that had been fragmented by academic disciplines and disciplinary norms.

It's like bringing a story together again when it's all been sort of guarded as turf. There's another kind of story to tell. . . . I asked the archivist to go find this for me in this file, in this file, in this file. He said, I know you want this, but you'll never find it in there. I said no, no, no. I know it's there. He said no. And then he came back and there they were. The ex-citement of knowing that you are on the right track by cutting through what you are supposed to ask about and know! Those questions are part of the politics [of knowledge]. That's how knowledge is constructed, by cut-ting off those kinds of knowledge, by bracketing it out, bracketing it out. For me, that makes it a very political act. There's a quote of Foucault's that I love. He says critique is the art of reflective insolence. And for me, that's how I think of my work. [H1]

A sociologist who taught in a merged sociology/anthropology department argued that disciplinary boundaries reflect the ills of the society that built them.

I like to think that the disciplinary boundaries that we put around sociol-ogy and anthropology are really artificial. In some cases, flukes of destiny.

In other cases, products of deliberate racism on the part of Europeans who have this idea that disciplines, especially separating the sociology of us from the anthropology of *those* people, primitives, savages, out in the wilds. I think I am antiboundary in that regard. [K1]

Faculty who believed that interdisciplinary work required a disciplinary foundation tended to rely primarily on informed disciplinarity in their research and teaching and to adhere to scientific norms of scholarship:

I believe that people should be grounded in disciplines. I have no trouble being a member of a history department. . . . I think that people should be fundamentally grounded in a discipline and use that grounding to be able to adequately go beyond the disciplines and then to access information from other disciplines as appropriate. [V]

I think I've always thought the best interdisciplinary work comes out of people who really know their discipline well, but who are willing to accept the fact that it doesn't do everything, that there are boundaries to it. That's not the same as the person who never really mastered their discipline. They've never taken the word discipline in the literary sense. . . . So they are interdisciplinary by default because that's where a lot of wishy-washy stuff happens. [J1]

Informants who were willing to challenge the perceived hegemony of scientific modes of inquiry and disciplinary boundaries summarily dismissed the idea of disciplinary grounding as a necessary basis for interdisciplinary work and tended toward synthetic or conceptual interdisciplinary research and teaching.

I remember hearing the discussion, even at the liberal arts college where I used to be, about how you have to have training in a discipline because it makes for this logical structure. *Then* you can move out and engage with these other things, as though there was something right and true about the disciplines that you can then add on to. And I just think that is a just a bunch of horse crap. I really do. [D1]

I think good interdisciplinary work requires the ability to look at what you do from the outside and I think scientists in particular often lack that in their training. In our social sciences departments, for instance, there are courses in the history of the discipline or the history and philosophy of the discipline that count for the major as disciplinary courses. That's not true in our sciences departments. If somebody taught a history of science course, it would be considered a history course, not a biology course or a physics course. I suppose I think a good disciplinarian would also have that perspective on the field and I think if they have that, then they are in a much more powerful position to do interdisciplinary work. But I think a stereotypic disciplinarian, at least in the sciences, is one who doesn't reflect on his or her field and therefore I don't think is in a very good position to reach outside the field. And I think that they don't know it. [A1]

This statement about the lack of courses in the history and philosophy of the scientific disciplines reflects more than a concern for balance in the curriculum; it reflects this biologist's own perceptions about the knowledge she needed to pursue her version of botany.

Most informants were aware of the standard critiques of interdisciplinary scholarship. A faculty member who considered most of her work interdisciplinary acknowledged the criticisms of her colleagues and perhaps some of her own anxiety:

There are folks here who would resist interdisciplinarity entirely and say you can't do interdisciplinary work because you can't be qualified. If it's taken you all this time to get qualified in your own discipline and to get status in it, how can you ever be a biologist coming from social science? . . . I am not sure that being interdisciplinary makes you stronger as a scholar from their point of view. I certainly think that it does because it takes you out of your own presuppositions, offers new lenses through which to examine what you do. But I can see the other side, too. Fear, I think, of not being good at what you do. [M]

A Romance languages scholar in area studies also shared some traditional thoughts about doing good scholarship. However, she suggested that the real issue wasn't shallowness in interdisciplinary work, but the failure in some disciplinary work to make connections. This comment may reveal her feminist leanings.

> I believe in the dig-deep metaphor. I do believe that one of the elements of good writing and significant thinking is being able to explore a delineated topic—not necessarily a limited topic, a defined topic—deeply. But defining it and digging deep don't mean, necessarily, that you don't consider a lot of other factors. I think that sometimes that's what's understood by specialists. "I'm going to dig deep in the subject matter and I'm not going to try to think about the implications for social policy or the historical context of the problem, or how educators are going to deal with it." And that's okay. We need that stuff, we need the deep trough of information or analysis or whatever it is. But we also need to know what to do with it. Otherwise it really does become separated from the rest of what we're about. Everything we do is all interconnected. [N]

Even faculty who roamed freely among the disciplines expressed concerns about the quality of interdisciplinary scholarship. One anthropologist, thoroughly committed to interdisciplinary research and teaching, feared superficiality in interdisciplinary work.

> I think that there are real problems in an interdisciplinary gesture. One can feel revitalized by drawing on something from someplace else because (a) your colleagues don't know about it, (b) you don't need to know a lot about it, and (c) it feels new and you can sort of get off on it and there's no one to catch you on it. And that makes me very, very nervous and I think it happens across the board. I think it's the way anthropology invokes history. I think it's the way psychology and history invoke culture. It's sort of a grab bag. If you can't explain it by A, explain it by B. And so sometimes it can lead to very exciting discussions and sometimes the level of naïveté— you can hear someone invoking some other discipline and you say, "How could he do this? It's off the wall. It's just like picking out of a hat. [H1]

There is a contradiction between the claim that knowledge has no boundaries and that good interdisciplinarity requires a foundation in a discipline, and at least two possible ways of explaining that contradiction. One interpretation is that faculty have learned how to talk the interdisciplinary talk but not to walk the interdisciplinary walk. In this case comments about the usefulness of interdisciplinary research and teaching may be little more than trendy rhetoric. An alternative explanation is that, at least for some faculty, time is needed to reconcile disciplinary training and norms with interdisciplinary thinking and scholarship. Many of the faculty whom I interviewed described the persistence of disciplinary perspectives in their thinking. In a number of cases, individuals with the most consistent and deepest levels of interdisciplinary engagement were the first to confess that in many ways they still see the world through the lens of their discipline. Contradictions and inconsistencies may be clues to continued grappling with issues of interdisciplinarity and disciplinarity. Some individuals may eventually resolve such inconsistencies; others may never do so. Whatever the outcome, the grappling is a valuable process by which faculty articulate epistemological positions and commitments.

Is a Typology of Interdisciplinary Scholarship Necessary?

My interpretations of informants' accounts is the basis for the claim that there are at least three types of interdisciplinary questions:*

> *synthetic interdisciplinary questions* that bridge disciplines and therefore questions that cannot be answered completely by a single discipline;
> *transdisciplinary questions* that are applicable across disciplines and therefore transcend a single disciplinary identity; and
> *conceptual interdisciplinary questions* that have no compelling disciplinary basis.

This focus on questions contrasts with the majority of definitions of interdisciplinarity. These focus on the integration of disciplines in interdisciplinary projects, but they propose different levels of integration. They beg the question "How much disciplinary integration is enough integration?" In other words, when is a project cross-disciplinary? When is it multidisciplinary or in-

---

*Questions that are merely informed by references to other disciplines are not interdisciplinary questions, I contend, but disciplinary ones.:

terdisciplinary? A foolproof method for assessing the level of integration of an interdisciplinary teaching or research project has eluded researchers. Some have tried to measure integration by examining the processes by which interdisciplinary research is accomplished, for example, by noting how often researchers on an interdisciplinary project meet to coordinate their work. Others have attempted to judge the final product of an interdisciplinary project, typically relying on the judgments of participants or the researchers themselves. If interdisciplinary projects, however, are born, not made, that is, if they begin as I have argued, with interdisciplinary questions, then such attempts are misguided because we must look to the point of origin to understand interdisciplinarity.

Attempts to define interdisciplinarity have yielded a wellspring of terms to describe it. Some have been applied either to research or to teaching, some to both. Some, such as interdisciplinarity and multidisciplinarity, have achieved fairly wide usage. All, however, are poorly understood even though they may be frequently used. Many have multiple meanings, and there is little consensus on which should prevail. Examining the parallels and the differences between previous categories and my own further elucidates the typology and demonstrates how it improves upon previous schemes. In Table 4.2, existing terms are aligned with the terms of the new typology.

Informed Disciplinarity and Interdisciplinarity

Interdisciplinarity has often been described as borrowing. Research approaches that borrow methods have been called *method interdisciplinarity*, or *instrumental interdisciplinarity* (see Klein 1993, pp. 64, 86). Research and teaching approaches that borrow either theories or methods have usually been called *cross-disciplinary*, a term that is intended to be broader than either *method* or *instrumental interdisciplinarity*. Cross-disciplinarity, however, has been variously defined. Miller (1982) defined cross-disciplinarity as efforts to connect and combine across disciplinary boundaries. He cited research areas such as criminal justice and area studies as examples of this form of interdisciplinarity. In contrast Kockelmans (1979) argued that cross-disciplinary scholarship seeks to develop or discover "encompassing frames of reference" similar to those sought in transdisciplinarity (p. 141).

Both instrumental interdisciplinarity and cross-disciplinarity, it has been

Table 4.2
COMPARISON OF TYPOLOGY
AND PREVIOUS CATEGORIZATIONS

Informed disciplinarity	Instrumental interdisciplinarity
	Pseudointerdisciplinarity
	Cross-disciplinarity
	Partial interdisciplinarity
Synthetic interdisciplinarity	Instrumental or cross-disciplinarity that is motivated by an interdisciplinary question
	Multidisciplinarity
	Partial interdisciplinarity
	Conceptual Interdisciplinarity
Transdisciplinarity	Transdisciplinarity
	Cross-disciplinarity
Conceptual Interdisciplinarity	(True) interdisciplinarity
	Critical interdisciplinarity
	Full interdisciplinarity

argued, are not true forms of interdisciplinarity. Heckhausen (1972) considered instrumental borrowing of methods from another discipline to be *pseudo-interdisciplinarity*. Cross-disciplinarity, Jantsch (1972) argued, implies a "brute force" approach to "reinterpret disciplinary concepts and goals . . . in light of one specific (disciplinary) goal and to impose a rigid polarisation across disciplines" (p. 107). Newell contended that any approach that does not attempt to integrate disciplines or that draws insights from other disciplines while viewing them through the lens of the original discipline are forms of *partial interdisciplinarity* (1998, p. 533). In the typology proposed here, instrumental and cross-disciplinary approaches might be either disciplinary or interdisciplinary, depending on the nature of the question they ask. They may be classified as informed disciplinarity if the question asked is disciplinary in nature, since borrowing alone is not sufficient for interdisciplinarity. However, if a synthetic, transdisciplinary, or conceptual interdisciplinary question motivates borrowing, the resulting project would be considered interdisciplinary. For this reason, I have not adopted the terms *instrumental interdisciplinarity* or *cross-disciplinarity*.

Partial interdisciplinarity seems to be a more useful term since informed disciplinary questions are, in Newell's sense, forms of partial interdisciplinarity. Adoption of this scheme is nonetheless problematic. In defining *partial* and *full interdisciplinarity*, Newell (1998) focused on the integration—or lack of integration—of disciplinary perspectives. Integration, however, seems too narrow a term for other forms of interdisciplinary scholarship described by informants in this study. Transdisciplinarity, for example, is most often concerned with universal structures or relationships. Its goal is to transcend disciplines rather than integrate them. While some conceptual interdisciplinary projects seek integration, others are better defined as critiques of knowledge. Only synthetic interdisciplinary questions are implicitly integrated in the sense that they bridge disciplines and require contributions from more than one discipline.

Synthetic Interdisciplinarity

Synthetic interdisciplinarity might appear to be analogous with what has been called *multidisciplinarity*, since the individual contributions of two or more disciplines can be discerned in these kinds of research and teaching projects. However, multidisciplinary work also has been criticized as a *false interdisciplinarity*. According to Miller (1982), multidisciplinary approaches involve "the simple act of juxtaposing several disciplines" and make "no systematic attempt at integration or combination" (p. 9). Newell (1998) classified multidisciplinarity as partial interdisciplinarity because it only includes one element of interdisciplinarity, that is, the perspectives of more than one discipline. Like Miller he excluded such approaches from full interdisciplinary status because they do not attempt to integrate disciplinary perspectives. Kockelmans (1979) argued that since all education is "inherently multidisciplinary" the term multidisciplinarity "should not be used as an expression to be meaningfully applied to possible research projects" (p. 131). I did not adopt either of these definitions because both emphasize integration.

I found that synthetic interdisciplinary work could be divided into two types: it could be based on questions found in the intersections of disciplines as well as on questions found in the gaps among disciplines. In most previous categorizations, questions that belong to no discipline were likely to be considered interdisciplinary, while questions that belonged to more than one discipline were likely to be considered multidisciplinary. I propose that either type of approach can be interdisciplinary depending on the question asked.

Transdisciplinarity

Both Jantsch (1972) and Piaget (1972) conceived of *transdisciplinarity* as the ultimate coordination among the disciplines. Piaget imagined a "total system without any boundaries between disciplines" (p. 138); Jantsch envisioned an "education/innovation system" based on generalized axiomatics and "the mutual enhancement of epistemologies in certain areas" (pp. 105–106). On the other hand Kockelmans (1979) rejected such conceptions of transdisciplinarity, which presuppose structuralist forms, genetic epistemology, or general systems theory. But Kockelmans and Miller (1982) acknowledged that supporters of transdisciplinarity held a number of different epistemological views. One group worked to develop holistic, encompassing conceptual frameworks that would replace existing disciplinary approaches; another saw transdisciplinarity as one alternative, a potential linchpin in interdisciplinary efforts (Miller 1982); yet another was concerned primarily with the development of a unified worldview (Kockelmans 1979). The transdisciplinary projects described by informants in this study did not appear part of a greater effort to unify the disciplines or worldviews; they were instead designed to identify similarities in structures or relationships among different natural and/or social systems. This is a more limited goal but nonetheless transdisciplinary. It also greatly resembles the transdisciplinary mode of knowledge production postulated by Gibbons, Limoges, Nowotny, Schwartzman, Scott, and Trow (1994).

> A transdisciplinary mode consists in a continuous linking and relinking, in specific clusterings and configurations of knowledge . . . brought together on a temporary basis in specific contexts of application. . . . The transdisciplinary mode of knowledge production described by us does not necessarily aim to establish itself as a new, transdisciplinary discipline, nor is it inspired by restoring cognitive unity. To the contrary, it is essentially a temporary configuration and thus highly mutable (p. 29).

Conceptual Interdisciplinarity

True or full interdisciplinarity has been defined as a form of disciplinary integration that obscures the separate contributions of the individual disciplines. True or full interdisciplinarity in this sense resembles conceptual interdisciplinarity. In conceptual interdisciplinarity, however, it is not the seamlessness of the answer, but the kind of question that is important. The question is central and disciplines are important insofar as they serve to answer the question. Typically the conceptual interdisciplinary question implies a critique of disciplinary knowledge and the answer extends that critique. The use of the adjective *conceptual* acknowledges the preeminence of the origin of this form of interdisciplinary, the question that motivates it.

The phrase *concept interdisciplinarity* has been used to describe cases in which a model or concept has either supplemented or supplanted the models or concepts of another discipline (Klein 1990). In addition others have used the term *conceptual interdisciplinarity*. Lynton (1985) used it to describe philosophically driven searches for synoptic conceptual frameworks that unify knowledge. These include approaches such as general systems theory, structuralism, and Marxism and are contrasted with interdisciplinarity approaches that seek to solve practical or social problems. Like Miller (1982), however, I consider these to be transdisciplinary approaches. In their classification scheme, Salter and Hearn (1996) considered transdisciplinarity a form of conceptual interdisciplinarity. They also included critical interdisciplinarity, that is, interdisciplinarity that poses a challenge to the disciplines, under the category of conceptual interdisciplinarity. This choice obscures the epistemological differences between transdisciplinarity and critical interdisciplinarity. Transdisciplinarity does not overly critique the disciplines; rather it seeks similarities among disciplines that make the cross-disciplinary application of concepts, theories, or methods possible. Critical interdisciplinarity, as its name implies, purposefully challenges disciplinary foundations of knowledge. Although Salter and Hearn (1996) were clearly aware of this contrast, they nonetheless classified both forms of interdisciplinarity under the rubric of conceptual interdisciplinarity. I preserve the important epistemological distinction between the two forms by adopting the term transdisciplinarity and defining conceptual interdisciplinarity more narrowly.

Determining the type of question that is being asked in interdisciplinary scholarship is to some extent a matter of interpretation. The occurrence of gray areas between typology categories should signal the need to add or refine the proposed categories. The typology, after all, was generated from a limited number of accounts; as informants who are engaged in other disciplines and fields are interviewed, new categories may be revealed. This may be especially true when multidisciplinary, applied fields such as medicine, social work, education, and engineering are considered.

The advantage to this typology, however, is that we need not wait until the end of a research or teaching project to determine its disciplinary or interdisciplinary nature. Interdisciplinarity is not merely a process or product, but a defining element of a project. We can determine a project's interdisciplinary or disciplinary nature by looking at the question that has motivated it. Additional information about approaches and methods to be used to answer the question, the audience(s) involved, and the epistemological commitments of the instructor(s) or researchers(s) may also assist in making an initial determination.

Pursuing Interdisciplinarity: Research and Teaching Processes

I chose to interview faculty about *how* they engaged in interdisciplinary work because I believe that we can learn much about what people think and value by examining their everyday practices. The accounts of interdisciplinary research and teaching activities that I collected revealed explicit and tacit assumptions about what counts as scholarship and how it should be done. The interviews focused attention on how faculty prepared for and carried out interdisciplinary projects and included conversations about reading practices; collaborative projects; attendance at professional meetings; involvement in interdisciplinary forums such as seminars, colloquia, or workshops; interactions with colleagues on and off campus; teaching activities; interactions with students; and so forth. Taken as a whole, the interviews demonstrated that regardless of the type of scholarship they pursued—informed disciplinarity, synthetic interdisciplinarity, transdisciplinarity, or conceptual interdisciplinarity—these faculty used similar, and familiar, strategies to learn about other disciplines and to incorporate their learning into their research and teaching.

Engaging Other Disciplines through Reading

Preparation for interdisciplinary teaching and research projects generally began with reading and collegial conversation. Reading might be pursued individually, but it could also be a collective activity in which individuals shared thoughts about what they read with colleagues. Such conversations could be informal, such as discussions over lunch or through E-mail, or formalized, in the form of interdisciplinary reading groups or seminars that engaged faculty from different academic departments.

Every faculty informant claimed to read widely and portrayed reading as a major dimension of interdisciplinary work, although some were more explicit than others in their comments about the kind of reading they did or the role it played in their scholarship. Some read widely in many disciplines as would be expected of individuals pursuing conceptual or transdisciplinary interdisciplinarity. Others organized their reading in another discipline to pursue a particular topic in order to pursue a synthetic or informed disciplinary teaching or research project. Different reading strategies sometimes marked different kinds of interdisciplinary work. For example, a political scientist whose projects most resembled conceptual interdisciplinarity talked about her approach:

> I read everything I can get my hands on. I overbibliographize, my [dissertation] adviser used to call it. He was cautioning me against doing that, criticizing me for it. It is just so much a part of the way that I work that of course I wasn't going to take that advice. That is what I do. I get sources from sources. It's a snowball kind of thing. [P]

In describing her reading strategy for a particular research study she revealed that, except perhaps for the breadth of topics, it was very similar to strategies that might be used for a disciplinary project. She identified areas of importance to her work and explored them intensively.

> I was interested in social movements at the time, so I was well versed in the sociological-political science literature in social movements. But I wanted to read more history and about the history of communism. I also used a framework based on the work of an Italian theorist—I just read about everything that was written about him, everything that he wrote. It was a real soaking in, an immersion. I read about nation building in the nineteenth and twentieth century, about the French Revolution, because those themes kept coming up in the rhetoric of the movement leaders. [P]

In addition to exploring content areas, she read to help her confront methodological concerns: "I read about discourse analysis, about autobiography, because I bring in my own positioning in this process and examine myself doing the research, what it meant to me, why I was drawn to it."

Different kinds of interdisciplinary work seemed to require different reading strategies. For the most part individuals doing synthetic interdisciplinary work, that is, bridging disciplines in their research or teaching, tended to concentrate reading in one or two disciplines. A tenured psychologist interested in cognitive science spent a yearlong sabbatical leave studying neuroscience, moving into an office in the neuroscience department and taking a number of graduate courses to build his knowledge base. Others felt the need to read more broadly, pursuing a concept or a theory across disciplines rather than trying to learn more about a particular field of study. A tenured associate professor who had been pursuing an ethnographic project for some time was frustrated by her lack of success in developing an understanding of what was happening in her research setting by using standard political science theories. Eventually she stepped outside of her discipline for an appropriate theoretical explanation. She stopped writing about the project so that she could read extensively in anthropology and sociology.

> Starting with my sabbatical and until this last year, I guess, so maybe three or four years I did mostly reading and teaching and not a lot of writing because I wasn't ready to write because I didn't have the theories. I had these observations, but I didn't have the theories to make sense of them. [L]

Her work became a form of conceptual interdisciplinarity: the phenomena she studied, rather than her disciplinary affiliation, now drove her inquiry.

The longest interdisciplinary collaboration that I encountered involved an economist and a theologian who coauthored three books over a twenty-year period. The economist talked about how he and his colleague helped each other understand work in the other's discipline to sustain a synthetic interdisciplinary teaching and research collaboration:

> The kinds of things that are most useful for us to read in economics are things that economists have written for audiences wider than just econo-

mists, so they are not that difficult [for my colleague] to read. That doesn't mean there aren't times when I have to help him understand something or that he has to help me understand something on the theological side of things. The theory in both places can be fairly murky if you are not raised in that tradition. Even though I have been reading theology stuff for almost twenty years now, I still run across things or I look at it and say, "I don't have the faintest idea what they are talking about" and I have to have [my colleague] help me. The same thing happens with him. [W]

In general faculty claimed that interdisciplinary research and teaching demanded that they do more reading and thinking than disciplinary scholarship did. Many expressed dismay that some colleagues did not recognize the depth of their involvement. One individual complained that "departmentally entrenched" colleagues "fail to understand just how much some of us have worked and struggled over the years to understand different disciplines well. People think you have read one book about it. It's a little more complicated than that" [K]. Another political scientist who conducted transdisciplinary collaborative research with a biologist revealed the depth of his interest in evolutionary thinking:

Well, I started that before I started political science. In high school I was already doing modeling of evolutionary thinking. I was seriously interested in how you can get a computer program to evolve better things by selection, by throwing things out that don't work and trying again. So I had that idea very early. And then in college I read Darwin seriously, again before I read much political science seriously. So depending on how you want to count, it's twenty years that that's been maturing. So it is not the typical scenario, for example, that a chemist is trained in one thing and a they do a postdoc in somebody's lab and it takes eighteen months to learn how to do this and then they are a biophysicist. That is fine, but I don't look that way. [A]

The theologian and the economist could rely on one another when their reading took them into unfamiliar waters. Other informants did not have the benefit of a close collaborator but continued their explorations. A political scientist who worked in area studies wished he had done more graduate work in economics:

> If I were doing it again, I certainly would have gone much farther in economics. I would have gotten the formal training because there is just a lot of stuff that you can reason through and figure out, but any mathematical presentation or use of that notation is not something that I am capable of looking at and saying "Well, even if I understand what they are trying to do with this equation, is this equation right? What assumptions have to be made for this to work? What are the tolerances here? How big does this number have to be before I am really convinced that the implications they're drawing are correct? . . . I do worry about it. I worry about it a lot. I'm worried about getting sold a bill of goods. I worry about an inadequate understanding of different schools of thought within economics. What is a structuralist versus a neoclassicist? Do I accurately understand that tradition and the differences between them so I can use that to identify what I am reading? [C1]

A Romance languages scholar active in area studies was similarly concerned but recognized that those feelings subsided over time as she gained familiarity with other fields:

> I think the trap you can fall into—which I'm sure I fell into more than once—when you are a neophyte in another discipline is the tendency to read the book and believe everything in it. So if you stop with that one book and you say, "Okay, well, I know about the history of the French and the English, I understand what happened there and this is the way I am going to present it." Well, obviously that approach has a lot of flaws. Of course, there are people within the discipline that do that, too. . . . Early in my investigation of this topic, I was reading a lot of stuff from a nationalist point of view because one text would lead me to another; I would work from the bibliography. So I got the nationalist discourse down really, really well. Of course, I really wasn't looking at some other points of view. But I've since integrated those in a much more intentional way. [N]

Statements such as these are notable because they reveal informants' anxieties, as well as traditional disciplinary concerns, about interdisciplinary work. These informants worried that their colleagues often misunderstood their work and that they would be or were labeled dilettantes. Their discussions about the depth of their engagement with other disciplines suggest a desire to establish their careful and thoughtful pursuit of interdisciplinary projects; they did not want to be perceived as running willy-nilly through the groves of academe. Many individuals, even those successfully pursuing interdisciplinary research and teaching through sanctioned means such as joint appointments or interdisciplinary programs, acknowledged that, despite their attention to quality, their work would nonetheless be subjected to this critique:

> To the extent that you see interdisciplinary work simply as having read in various different fields and bringing them together, then to someone who is a specialist in a department and sees that as being the epitome, knowing everything about whatever, then you are always going to be accused of being superficial, of reinventing the wheel, of never knowing enough about any one discipline to actually be interdisciplinary. . . . That would be true if you had to know everything about a discipline in order to understand how it worked—and I don't think that is. [K]

Despite the difficulties encountered in reading outside their disciplines and the fear that others would judge them harshly by disciplinary standards, most of these individuals believed that their time and efforts were well spent. Each new project, one informant noted, required time to "gear up" and this could be overwhelming on occasion [D1]. For the most part, however, informants appeared to have found ways to cope with the task. A zoologist who used learning theory in his experimental research projects took a pragmatic stance:

> I rarely run into something that I read that I can't make at least some sense out of it. It's never a waste of time. I simplify it along the way. I'm not going to go through the equations of anything that involves a very complex mathematical formulation, but usually there's a narrative ex-

planation that tells me what all these Xs mean and that usually makes sense. The neural network models I encounter would be a good example of that. [D]

A philosopher with feminist commitments argued that interdisciplinarity requires one to renounce the typical mastery approach to learning that is encouraged in colleges and universities and replace it with a feminist perspective. In time, she argued, things usually became clear.

> I used to try and master [what I read in another discipline] and beat it into submission . . . and I finally realized that is ridiculous and what I do now is enjoy it. Learn from it. Try to make it accessible to other people . . . sometimes I can't figure it out but it's still pretty interesting and exciting and I just kind of put that aside for a while . . . and then I notice a whole bunch of things clumping together and gradually shifting from the corner to the center and it's like, "Ah ha! Now I see what that's for." I can put that together with this bit over here and now I am beginning to better understand the pair of them. [J]

Other strategies for coping with the volume of information to be absorbed when working across disciplines included one that closely resembled disciplinary specialization. Instead of attempting to learn a new discipline or disciplines from the ground up, a number of informants attempted to be interdisciplinary within a narrow scope, to delineate clearly what they were claiming for their work. An assistant professor of art explained that since he couldn't master all the material and read in depth in two disciplines, he decided "to work with people, with figures, within the same cultures and that begins to bring it together. So even though I have this philosophy side and this art side, I began to style myself as a Germanist. I was doing German philosophy and German art" [E]. In order to improve his language skills this informant studied in Germany for a year.

An English professor who considered herself a cultural critic and collaborated with an area studies scholar found that careful positioning and inclusion of experts enhanced the credibility of interdisciplinary projects. Her description of her strategy, however, depends less on the development of a narrow area of specialization and instead focuses on establishing a sense of positionality:

> I don't claim to be any kind of specialist in this area. I instead position myself as someone using theory to look at what I see. And I argue that precisely because people in this field are trained in that tradition, they are not able to see certain things that I am able to see and that I am just trying to write from a particular perspective. That seems to satisfy people. [C]

Still, she combined this strategy with others to ensure that her work was credible: "Of course, I have to be really careful that I am not making boneheaded, naive statements. I make sure that I check my work. That is why it is good that this current project involves someone who knows this area very well" [C]. While most informants either were—or felt compelled to be—modest about their abilities, one informant argued that reading outside her discipline was no more challenging than reading within it:

> Anybody who's gone through the 70s and 80s in literature has had to read a lot of theory, what we call theory. And theory is anything from, you know, Sartre on existentialism, way back in the 40s . . . to Baudrillard, Cixous, any of what we would call the fashionable literary poststructuralists, postmodernists. It's pretty challenging stuff so I've never found reading history or politics more challenging than that. I am not trying to downplay their significance, but it's pretty understandable stuff. [N]

Every individual I interviewed described reading as a major component of doing interdisciplinary work. For a few reading was the major form of interaction with other disciplines. Others combined reading with course work or conversations with faculty who shared similar interests. Some individuals read in depth in one or two other fields, guided by the needs of their research or teaching. They carried out synthetic interdisciplinary projects in this manner, selecting reading material directly related to the problem or issue involved. In these cases reading focused narrowly on the disciplinary content and methods involved. Other informants, individuals doing informed disciplinary or conceptual interdisciplinary research and teaching, ranged more widely over the disciplines in search of relevant theories and information. Individuals pursuing transdisciplinary topics seemed to pursue a combination strategy: guided by the desire to apply a theory or method to a particular discipline or field, they read more broadly than informants pursuing synthetic work, but they narrowed and intensified their reading in particular disciplines when pursuing a particular project.

Engaging Colleagues in Interdisciplinary Conversation

Conversation in academia takes many different forms. Some faculty consider any kind of engagement of mind with subject matter, whether it involves individuals or simply their writing, as a conversation of sorts. I define conversation more narrowly as a dialogue between two or more individuals. Such conversations can be informal talks between two colleagues over lunch, E-mail exchanges, discussions among faculty attending a seminar on a specific topic or a professional association meeting, or a more formalized collaboration. Nearly all the faculty I interviewed attended the annual meeting of their disciplinary association. Attendance, however, was often described as perfunctory. Individuals viewed these meetings as opportunities to connect with old friends and see what was happening in the field but not as exciting opportunities for scholarly stimulation. More often, smaller interdisciplinary or multidisciplinary meetings better served their interests.

The best discussions I have are at small meetings. The most fruitful, let's say influential, discussions I have are at meetings where I meet with colleagues from other places who work in the area I work in, psychologists and zoologists. I would say it's split fifty-fifty. . . . It's really a nice mix. It's a stimulating kind of situation to be able to talk with people with a variety of different interests since my research straddles two very broad subareas of both psychology and biology. [D]

I have stopped going to the big disciplinary meeting. I find it lacks any sense of intimacy where you can really talk about whatever it is. So the recent conferences that I have gone to have been the smaller regional conferences. If fact, I've narrowed down in political science and have been going to the ones that have more of a reputation of doing black and women's studies and thus it's much more interdisciplinary. [I]

Attendance at the annual disciplinary meeting, although roundly criticized as unnecessary, can be a persistent disciplinary norm. Since it is easy to abide, many faculty seemed willing, if not eager, to take part. One biologist attended multiple meetings as an information-gathering strategy.

A lot of people belong to these organizations, but not to my particular constellation. I belong to the Entomological Society of America because of the value of finding information or feedback about insect biology and that isn't necessarily in a context that I want, but I can apply. When I go to those meetings, for instance, there are very few papers that work on what I work on. If I go to an animal behavior meeting, I see very few papers that work on what I work on with insects, but between the two I can find a lot of interaction. So I belong to kind of a wide range of them to get little pieces from each. Within those organizations, do they particularly foster interdisciplinarity? No, I would say that most of them are fairly narrow. [F1]

Workshops and institutes focused on specific topics were particularly useful to faculty with interdisciplinary interests. Here, faculty could make professional, as well as intellectual, connections. A political scientist interested in transdisciplinary research regularly attended meetings at an institute on complexity:

That has been helpful in the sense of providing me with a national community that is interested in computer simulation. It's not mainstream social science and it's not a large field in the social sciences. I keep in touch with those people and learn from them and get feedback from them, things like that. And the last three years, they have provided funding for my work in computer modeling here. . . . They have provided more generous funding than I could have gotten otherwise on one of the topics I really wanted to do. And I don't feel I have to bend myself out of shape, which I would have to do for the NSF [National Science Foundation] so the [review] panel would understand what I was doing. [A]

This community appeared to be an "invisible college," that is, a small network of individuals working in a highly specialized research area (Crane 1972). Such networks are usually developed by personal contact and sustained by the exchange of written material and the occasional specialized colloquia. Informants with long-standing synthetic interdisciplinary interests also used specialized meetings and institutes to learn more about a topic and connect with like-minded colleagues.

In some cases attendance at an institute marked the beginning of interdisciplinary interests and scholarship. An economist vividly illustrated the effect that learning about interdisciplinary theory and research had on her thinking.

After I got tenure a friend of mine suggested I go to an institute on feminist theory and pedagogy. That was about 1981. I said "All right, I'll spend three weeks doing that." . . . Of course, what they call theory and what [economists] call theory just weren't the same. If it didn't have equations, to me it wasn't theory. That kind of changed my whole way of thinking about economics. . . . [Later] when I was doing some research on female executives' compensation, I did some seminars on research on women. We met every month for a year. I was exposed to some of the top women doing that kind of research. It really gets you thinking about economic modeling and what modeling is all about, how narrow the model that most economists use really is. How if you accept that as the real world— rather than just a very narrow definition of the real world—it really limits what you can think about. [B]

For other informants meetings served a more generalized function—stimulating ideas and revitalizing the mind. A biologist found that meetings were avenues to creativity. Although he admitted that he could not trace particular creative acts to particular conversations, he believed the interdisciplinary interactions were more stimulating to him than isolated study. A Romance languages scholar active in area studies expressed a similar notion: that the best encounters were the ones that resulted in learning. She also enjoyed the opportunity to think about "something different" for a while.

> A lot of people who go to the meetings of this area studies association say that they go even though it's in addition to their regular discipline offerings—and you know that there's not a lot of money for travel these days, so it's a hardship—because it's interesting, because it's fun, because they don't just go to all the literature sessions, because they go to a political science debate over something, because they hear a great paper about contemporary music. They want to know more than just their own thing that they teach because they want to keep learning and they want to be excited and they want to be renewed and when it starts getting dry and dull, you know, that's when we all want to check out. [N]

Faculty seminars, a mechanism for facilitating local conversations, served similar purposes for faculty who wanted to share their ideas on topics with campus colleagues. At one institution several informants pursuing conceptual interdisciplinary projects attended the same seminar. An anthropologist commented on the connecting thread: an interest in critical theory.

> I've been involved with a particular faculty seminar in various successful ways and unsuccessful ways over the last five years. . . . We talk to each other because we are all coming from similar places in critical social theory. So we are reading the same material, though we're all covering sort of circles that overlap in certain areas. What happens is we get a lot of energy from what is being brought in from those outer edges. Sometimes you reject them because they are too far out, but sometimes they are exactly what opens you up to a whole new thing. [H1]

For scholars with nascent interests, the seminar was an opportunity to test new ideas and receive feedback from colleagues.

> It was an important moment in my life because it was the first time I had ever presented my work to an audience other than literature people. It was an amazing moment because I gave this paper and people in history and anthropology had things to say to me. . . . It was great! One person who

works in feminist anthropology helped me think through some of the feminist dimensions of the paper, gave me some excellent references and
helped me think it through theoretically. Another person whose theoretical origins are in Marxism helped me think about those parts of the paper
that bordered on Marxist issues. [B1]

For this associate professor, an interdiscplinary seminar deepened and refined
her interest in critical theory and eventually brought it closer to the center of
her academic life.

Campus-wide forums also served interdisciplinary interests. A biologist described a seminar that connected individuals interested in ecological issues
from across the campus and generated research opportunities for the faculty
involved:

We began talking and it very quickly became a forum for people interested in related issues. It began with about fifteen people and two years
later there were about sixty attending two-hour sessions each week. Engineers joined. Atmospheric scientists joined. Ed school people joined. A
whole bunch of us discovered that there were lots of people at this university we didn't know who were doing related kinds of research. We
also discovered we liked talking to each other and we saw all kinds of research opportunities, particularly if we worked in a truly interdisciplinary
way. [I1]

A psychologist used a variety of means to build his understanding of cognitive
science. In addition to attending campus seminars on psychological approaches to meaning—"what a person knows when they know the meaning of
a word"—he took graduate courses on philosophy of mind and participated in
a summer workshop on artificial intelligence and another on linguistics [G1].
Individuals used these forums as ways to gather information, to learn what
others were thinking about the same topic, and to crystallize their own ideas.
They valued the opportunity to present their ideas to colleagues and the feedback they received. Like meetings of professional associations, seminars, institutes, and workshops often served multiple purposes. For one anthropologist,
whose research interests had taken him far from his home discipline, a graduate seminar offered a regular opportunity to connect with students.

The seminar is not hugely central to my empirical research, but it's extremely central to my place in the university. My first couple of years here I had a lot of students, got involved with a lot of graduate training, but entirely with students in psychology. There'd been this desperate need to have someone who spoke psychology but was in anthropology and I got swamped by the number of dissertation committees I was on—but all in psych. The seminar has allowed a coterie of students in anthropology to develop and that's very exciting for me. [S]

At all the institutions that I visited, faculty considered such local colloquia and forums to be important meeting grounds. Most belonged to at least one interdisciplinary faculty group; a few were serving or had served as directors of these groups. Where annual disciplinary meetings fell short, institutional colleagues with similar interests took up the slack. One faculty member described her efforts to put together an interdisciplinary seminar based on the work of twenty faculty members from across her campus as a desire for community and a "fishing expedition" to see "who was out there and what might happen." For faculty who pursued individual interdisciplinary projects, such forums were useful sounding boards for new ideas. For those separated from departmental colleagues by research interests or intellectual impasses, these meetings and forums also offered colleagueship.

Delimiting Expertise and Authority

During the 1970s and 1980s, researchers conducted a modest number of studies of interdisciplinary research. These focused almost exclusively on team-based interdisciplinary research in both academic and industrial settings. While a few included teams with social scientist members, the objects of most of these studies were interdisciplinary projects in the applied sciences and engineering. The literature therefore leaves the impression that interdisciplinarity can be achieved only by collaborative means, and indeed it was often suggested that there is no such thing as an interdisciplinary individual (for example, Taylor 1986). About half of the faculty whom I interviewed had collaborated on interdisciplinary research and roughly half had team taught at least one interdisciplinary course. Informants who did not collaborate across disciplines did not necessarily eschew collaborative activities altogether. In fact several had collaborated on a number of projects with colleagues in their own discipline but had pursued their interdisciplinary projects solo. For others who wanted to collaborate with colleagues outside their disciplines, it was a matter of finding someone interested in what they wanted to do.

Most of the participants in this study taught interdisciplinary courses ranging from informed disciplinary courses to synthetic or conceptually based topical courses without the aid of collaborators. In fields such as women's studies, interdisciplinarity is a way of life, and individuals often teach courses that require substantial interdisciplinary knowledge. In feminist circles willingness to relinquish the role of classroom expert for the more collegial position of colearner is considered part of the effort needed to redress the power imbalances of the typical classroom. The experience can be trying, but it is not particularly unusual.

> You read a lot and you pray a lot and you hope that you're not going to look foolish in front of students who are, in many cases, likely to know more about a particular interdisciplinary area than you are. The first time that I prepared for the intro course, I can't tell you the number of times I shook my head and said, "How did I ever get myself into this?" [G]

This faculty member's experience of being asked to teach a women's studies course mirrored the experiences of many others in the study: "they asked me to do it and I said, 'Yeah, I'll try.' It was probably a naive response because I had no clue about a lot of the stuff that goes into a course like that . . ." [G].

Interdisciplinary work was a constant reminder of the limitations of one's knowledge. Most informants realized that they could not claim the same level of expertise in their adopted discipline or disciplines as they did in their home discipline. For individuals in this study, this meant they had to live without the comfort of expertise.

> One of the reasons why I think interdisciplinarity is always fighting an uphill struggle is because it is not only multivocal, it's not only less certain, but has a softer feel about it. People who have a narrow disciplinary focus are able to say things they think with great confidence. What can interdisciplinary people say with great confidence? [F]

An economist who regularly taught interdisciplinary courses argued that the "desire to understand and appreciate the breadth of what's out there is different than the ability to do it." He believed that he had learned to make use of experts, "as opposed to being the expert in everything. Or even claiming that you're expert in your own discipline" [O].

Experienced and inexperienced informants alike talked about the pedagogy of interdisciplinary courses, arguing that interdisciplinarity demanded a different attitude toward instruction. Once again informants discussed the need to abandon notions of mastery:

> Teaching gives me a chance to try out some of the new ideas, to work them through for myself as well as introducing them to students. It's a whole philosophy of teaching that doesn't proceed from mastery; it proceeds from an ongoing effort to be learning and to translate that to students. [C]

> I've done certain things that the students haven't done yet, but I'm not going to set myself up as this expert or try to assert my authority as a way of covering up what I don't know. I'd much rather play master of ceremonies and have this back-and-forth thing. Try to summarize every once in a while, but not assert my personality and knowledge base because I can learn so much from my seminars. When you create a situation where it's really active learning, people get so much more involved and it's much better for everybody. It's precisely people bringing in their individual perspectives and knowledge bases that makes it exciting, makes it possible for everyone to contribute. [E]

Traditional academic concerns about the depth of knowledge permeated these interviews. Individuals seemed to feel compelled to qualify their comments about other fields with a confession that they lacked expertise in the area. They claimed that they still felt they did not know enough about other disciplines in which they were working, and they were eager to provide evidence of the quality of their engagement. Although these concerns arose in conversations about both teaching and research, they seemed to be more troublesome in research activities. A French-language scholar who served as a director of a women's studies program acknowledged the need for greater depth in research:

I guess the only kind of authority that has ever interested me is the authority of knowledge. And maybe that was the one time, when I first began to teach women's studies, when I thought, "What do you mean you are going in there and talking about biology or going in there and talking about the problems with this statistical data?" I had to get over that. And certainly there is a level of expertise on which I might draw in an introductory women's studies class that I would never draw on in my own work. It's simply too superficial. [K]

An anthropologist studying social and religious rituals pointed to a collection of biology and physiology texts on her bookshelf, as if to demonstrate that her words were backed by actions:

> I'm doing anatomy and physiology right now because my own research is requiring me to understand the production of the amino acids and how that's created by particular kinds of foods that we use in ritual. It's really important to know what's actually going on. I'm wading through that. I'll never be a biologist, you know, but it's really interesting. I've pretty much figured out what kinds of amino acids are created with what kinds of foods, but that has required me to make appointments with the nutritionist at the hospital. . . . So what I needed to understand, was the ritual food and it seems to me there is a strong reason to look at what the properties of that food are and how the definitions of the food are given through time. [M]

The psychologist who spent his sabbatical year studying neuroscience in a graduate department of his university contended that his knowledge of biology was still not adequate for the work he pursued: "I still don't know enough because I have very little background in biological work. . . . I don't know it as well as the students do" [G1]. A political scientist was also careful to dispel any ideas that he might be an expert in agronomy:

> You need to know something about the technical processes of producing rice, for example, if you are going to do research on a rice society, because you have got to know something about, for example, the wet season, the dry season, what kind of rice grows when, the impact of the Green revolu-

tion. I mean it is not a detailed understanding, I certainly don't want to put myself forward as someone who could do research to improve yields of rice or palm oil or whatever it is. But you need to know something about [it] — so I also sometimes end up reading things about the technical nature of production; usually if I start a new commodity that is where I begin. [C1]

A number of individuals talked about reconciling themselves to the idea that interdisciplinarity precluded the desire to know everything about a subject. A philosopher, in particular, seemed content with this conclusion rather than resigned. She spoke enthusiastically about interdisciplinary work while recognizing her own limitations.

I think as I become more mature, I am less ego-invested with a very highly defined sense of myself as a moral or other expert. I am more willing to acknowledge how poorly educated I am. And you know just how exciting some of this other stuff is. It's just an amazing new series of worlds that makes very credible connections with my work . . . and it makes my work seem much more rich. I consider myself being about as thrilled giving up interdisciplinarity as going on a starvation diet. I think of it as becoming a scholar and less a technician. [J]

Throughout these interviews, informants seemed to stress their limitations rather than their strengths. In some cases, these kinds of statements may reflect a sense of personal or scholarly inferiority. Often, they reflect socialization into disciplinary communities where depth of knowledge is emphasized and breadth of knowledge more often criticized. Even faculty in liberal arts colleges, where general education and breadth are valued components of higher education, assessed their work using the traditional standard of depth. In the case of some women informants, comments about limitations also reflect the feminist perspective that all knowledge is partial and that mastery or authority is illusory. Still, on occasion, the requirement of humility wore thin. A biologist suggested that faculty crossing disciplinary lines were forced to take an overtly and overly modest stance, so as not to offend their disciplinary and interdisciplinary colleagues. He described his conversations with a physicist on his campus.

We both still sort of act like, "Oh, but you know, I really don't understand the muscles," or "Please, I am not worthy, please be tolerant with the fact that I don't understand cells." Now this is a very smart woman. She is a great physicist. If my students, in a day's time, can understand how these muscles work, certainly so can she. But why do we continue to act as if we are doing this weird sort of dance about that? Why not be embracing of each other's disciplines like this? Can't we be confident to try and talk in each others discipline? Maybe make a mistake? [F1]

This biologist also provided a example where he chose not to join the dance: "I teach writing in my classes and I think I do it well, but I can tell that when I talk about it with members of the English department, for instance, it is like, "This is not your area. We will give you advice on how you should teach writing to your students in science." He argued that when he does not play the expected part, he is perceived as arrogant and that this stymies interdisciplinary conversation. His final comment on the subject can be interpreted as either defeatist or accepting: "Perhaps if I want to have the interaction I need to play the game" [F1].

Collaborating with Colleagues

One common strategy for compensating a perceived lack of expertise was to collaborate with those with the needed expertise. Most informants described collaborations of two or three faculty from different disciplines. Few had participated in large team projects; in this study only a few psychologists and biologists had experienced the kind of team interdisciplinary research that has been the focus of empirical studies of interdisciplinary research. A biologist interested in global change had the most team experience and was currently director of a group of principal investigators from a variety of disciplines on a long-term, large-scale project. A few individuals team taught a course with three or more colleagues, but this was the exception rather than the rule.

The process of identifying colleagues to share teaching and research responsibilities was rarely a systematic process. Finding a collaborator was more frequently accidental than planned. Only a few faculty sought out individuals with the particular purpose of collaboration in mind; most simply met like-minded individuals along the way. Faculty described these meetings as impromptu discussions of shared interests that blossomed into collaborative teaching or research projects. One political science professor described an interdisciplinary course that grew out of a guest lecture on obscenity given in a colleague's art class: "The students really appreciated having that information and she appreciated me doing it because she couldn't have done it; she didn't know that stuff. It was a very positive experience and we said, 'Gee, this was really fun and really interesting. . . . Well, gee this would be fun to do a course on this'" [I].

An opportunity for an interdisciplinary research collaboration arose when another political scientist gave a lecture on his work for campus colleagues.

> I had a theory of alliances that was based on the simple idea that you tend to want to work with people you are compatible with and you tend to not want to be in an alliance with people who you are incompatible with. And I applied this to nations to predict the alliance structure of World War II. . . . In one of the presentations I made here, some people in the business school had come to hear the talk. They came up to me afterward and they said, "This is great. This applies to business alliances." And in particular, they had an example. . . . [After hearing their idea] I said, "That sounds neat. Let's talk about that." So we talked about that. They brought in a graduate student and another faculty member . . . and I had a graduate student doing the programming and the data work for me. The short story is that it worked. You could use exactly the same theory with different notions of what makes for compatibility, obviously. That is being published in an organization science journal that is mainly read by economists. [A]

An associate professor of English literature and women's studies who often collaborated with colleagues on research and teaching projects explained that these activities had many origins. One teaching collaboration resulted in the decision to write up the experience that appeared innovative. Another grew out of a friendship. In contrast to expectations that collaboration results from a rational search for complementary expertise, this individual argued that the personal connection was the more important ingredient in her collaborations: "It's not as if I would have an idea and approach somebody at the university who I didn't even know, because of the discipline they were in" [C]. She looked for an analogy that would reveal the motivations for her collaborations:

> It's a little like falling in love, it really is. You have a kind of simpatico going on there. Sometimes it's because I admire someone . . . and I want to find out more about who they are and what they think, what they might have to offer me. It's almost like a teacher-pupil relationship there. A lot of times it just grows out of the conversation.

Opportunities for collaborative projects presented themselves during lunches, after committee meetings, following presentations, or as a result of attendance at seminars. Serendipitous meetings of the mind were particularly common in the liberal arts colleges I visited where the small size of the faculty and campus facilitated cross-disciplinary conversation. The political scientist quoted above noted that she often offered to guest lecture in colleagues' classes, not only because she liked doing it, but also because the small size of the college made it possible to know what colleagues in other departments needed. A geologist also noted that size and proximity created opportunities.

> He's just across the hall. I don't know if we would have collaborated—I'm sure we wouldn't have—if the philosophy department didn't move into the geology building. The building was renovated and that added some space. So they moved here. That has been great. It has worked out very well. Both departments have a considerable amount of interaction. We've learned a lot about each other and our disciplines that way. [L1]

An informant interested in questions straddling anthropology and psychology talked about coming to the university as a new professor and happily finding a ready-made connection to an individual whose work he admired.

> One of [my collaborators] is someone whose work I had long been inter-ested in and when I came—this was entirely accidental—it turned out that he was married to someone in the anthropology department. So it was easy for me to meet him. We had a numbers of interests in common and we ended up doing a conference together and editing a book together

and writing a couple of things together. There is another psychologist here and, again, he was somebody whose work I knew. He had a lot of interdisciplinary curiosity and we became quite close and worked together. Once I started, the connections with other people in psychology were fairly easy to make. [S]

An economist told a complicated tale of how he came to see connections between development economics, liberation theology, and social change, while on a sabbatical to study energy economics in the 1970s. The conduit was a series of lectures on liberation theology given by a priest at a local church. The lectures helped him think about the ways in which social change occurs and how it can be organized: "For me, that was the missing ingredient in economic development theory; I couldn't see how to get social change to work" [W]. When he returned to his home institution six months later, he found himself sitting at a lunch table with a colleague from the religion department.

I kind of innocently said, "Gee, is anybody in your department doing anything with liberation theology?" He said, "I just finished writing a book about liberation theology." So we started to talk about how I got interested in it and why I thought it was an appropriate topic for an economist to look at. We decided that day that we had the makings of a course. The next fall we taught the course for the first time. [W]

While serendipity played a large role in collaboration, some of my informants purposefully sought others with similar interests for collaborations. A biologist who specializes in entomology first searched for interdisciplinary connections through the literature and, after finding them, sought individuals who could help him follow through on his ideas. His collaborations often resulted from his overtures to individuals with the ability to answer a particular question: "The collaborations with the folks like the person in the optics lab, that kind of stuff, is one where I bring them a question and they help me with a technical solution. I get to learn this area and I learn a lot of theory, too" [F1].

In other cases the nature of the research required a team approach. One psychologist, who worked almost exclusively on research teams, enjoyed the experience.

I should say everything I do is collaborative in some sense, from either just the genesis of the project to writing. Almost all of my publications are multiple authors. I think that happens in part because when you do interdisciplinary work, it's bigger. Everything's bigger. I mean you're trying to look at more things, you're interested in the interconnections between more things and you need more expertise and you need more manpower to pull them off. When I had the postdoc in public health, they were really oriented collaboratively, so you have centers: you have epidemiologists, psychiatrists, etc. And it's a model that I really like. I like that better than the kind of individual soldier model out here. I just feel like you just learn so much from talking to someone else about what you are doing. [T]

Another faculty member working in the natural sciences similarly sought out collaborators to do "the mechanics" of research: "the relationship that I have with my colleagues tends to be more focused on the mechanical aspects of the research. The intellectual, the ideas behind it, the writing, etc., I tend to do that by myself" [D]. He confessed that he was not the "kind of person who is going to sit down and work together in terms of generating ideas and interpretations." For him collaborators were useful for the technical knowledge they brought to his experiments involving brain manipulations on animals and because they "keep me from getting bored." Another individual trained in electron microscopy was the source of technical expertise for chemists at her university.

We do some work with one of the chemists who makes little tiny balloon-like vesicles out of the membrane lipids. I think the chemists' thrust is to encapsulate something in those artificial membranes that they can then introduce as a chemotherapeutic or something. It's something so far from what we're thinking about that I don't even know what the application is. But the vesicles are so small that they can't see them with any other method except the electron microscope. So . . . we have the apparatus and the methods and the machines and the films and all the things they need to do this and . . . their role is to bring a drop containing the vesicles and our role is to look in the microscope. So it's just a combination of expertise that from such diametrically different parts of the thing the chemists and the biologists have to do it together. [R]

A psychologist described a collaborative research project with a teaching physician. Despite their differing goals, they were able to work together successfully.

I'm interested in doing this to answer basic questions about knowledge organization and problem solving, simply using this research setting as the vehicle, the content domain. I mean it doesn't matter to me; I could do this research in any setting. But for this person, it's more than that. This is what he does. [Q]

Other individuals described incidents where differing disciplinary goals impeded the success of a collaboration. A psychologist who had collaborated with a philosopher on a number of projects recounted one failed project:

We drafted out a paper, a coauthored paper that never got published. We had a first draft; I wrote part of it and he took pieces out of his dissertation, which had never been published, so we married it with the stuff I had written and we sat down together and we tinkered with the whole. We really spent a long time talking through the ideas to the point where we both were comfortable with what we wanted to say. But then the paper didn't get worked on for a while. In the meantime, he's got some papers coming out with some of these same ideas, I've got a paper coming out with some of these ideas and then last fall we agreed to abandon it because each of us by then had gone farther in our thinking on the issue and second of all, basically we said what we had to say. So I think what may have gotten in the way there were disciplinary constraints on how you publish. For me, it's different audiences. I wanted to target the paper to psychology, the cognitive science people. He was more interested in targeting the philosophy of science. Again, those are our disciplinary bases, but I think that's part of the problem. [J1]

Individuals who had not collaborated with colleagues on interdisciplinary projects often indicated their willingness, but a lack of opportunity, to do so.

Right now, I don't have time to do anything except stay afloat. . . . I can't even conceive of proposing to teach an interdisciplinary course here because my responsibilities are to provide courses in the major for majors. As much as I think it would be great fun to teach a course on plants and history, the role of cotton in world history, there is no way in my life that I will ever have time to do that. [Z]

Time pressures were a particular concern. An experienced collaborator commented: "You can't sit down and say here is this project and we are going to work on it and we are going to be done with this project three months from now. You have to recognize that there is a long time frame before these kinds of things come to fruition" [W]. A director of a black studies program embarking on his first collaboration with a colleague from a different discipline anticipated that extra time would be needed to familiarize himself with the material from another discipline, as well as with his new collaborator:

You can't sort of walk into the situation with the anticipation that whatever you write and whatever perspectives you take are going to immediately ring a bell or be familiar to the other person. So it takes a lot more effort. In fact what we have done in order to prepare for this—we hope [it will become] an article, and I don't know maybe if it works out maybe we can go further and write a book—but we have assigned each other books out of our area to read and articles to read. So, yeah, it takes a lot more lead time and preparation. [U]

Similar preparation issues surfaced in discussion of interdisciplinary teaching. The director of black studies talked about the extensive discussions he and a colleague had before they developed a team-taught course.

If you are team teaching a course it is very helpful to have a good bit of lead time. . . . The last course that I taught was with someone in the English department. We spent a semester plus a summer simply talking before we even put the course together. Then we met every week, sometimes two or three times a week, making sure that we understood where the other was coming from and trying to bring some coherence to the material. [U]

Disciplinary courses, a biologist explained, could become rote after time; even a new disciplinary course could be created from familiar materials: "If you are teaching within your discipline you can fall back on something that you know very, very well. Even when I teach a new course in this department, big hunks of it are things I have taught before, so I don't have to think about it—I know the best way to convey something" [A1]. In contrast interdisciplinary courses took more time because they made different demands:

It's a lot more work because you have to make explicit assumptions that you don't have to make explicit when you are in control of your course. I've taught both within the department and outside and I think it's been much more satisfying outside, much more enjoyable. It's much more of a stretch. . . . And, of course, with interdisciplinary, team-taught courses, chances are there's not a textbook because it's in some new, developing area. [A1]

While collaboration is clearly an important part of interdisciplinary work, it is not all of interdisciplinary work, as the empirical literature suggests. For some informants collaboration defined interdisciplinarity, and they worked for long periods of time with a single colleague. Others were serial monogamists who collaborated with different individuals in a given field in order to answer interdisciplinary questions. Still others, mostly those who had team taught a number of courses, worked with faculty in a number of different disciplines. About half of those interviewed had not collaborated at all across disciplines, but most did not rule it out. Only one person purposefully avoided collaborations, comparing the search for a collaborator to the search for a mate and enumerating her expectations for such a relationship. She viewed her research, which I categorized as conceptual interdisciplinary, as a very personal creative process:

Because there are no models, doing interdisciplinary work is kind of seeking inspiration. It's a feeling that you generate in yourself, this instinct to see things in a broad way and get ideas. . . . It's making all kinds of connections that other people might say, "What? This is insane!" . . . It's a very private matter. It's a conversation that you have with yourself and the outside world, but kind of privately. [P]

Time has always been a valuable commodity for faculty, and informants deemed it crucial to interdisciplinary work. Whether they worked individually or in collaboration, individuals needed time to gear up for interdisciplinary projects. Reading and learning the language of other disciplines took varying amounts of time, depending on the distance or proximity of the neighboring disciplines. Once informants began teaching an interdisciplinary course or conducting interdisciplinary research, they did not necessarily stop reading and talking with colleagues. However, these activities became secondary as informants entered the classroom or began an inquiry.

Teaching Interdisciplinary Courses

Many informants described a type of teaching that could be categorized as informed disciplinarity because it focuses on helping students see phenomena through different disciplinary lenses. Faculty from the liberal arts colleges were especially familiar with this kind of teaching, perhaps because they often taught general education and service courses to undergraduates as part of their teaching load. However, advanced courses could also take an interdisciplinary turn and often went beyond informed disciplinarity to synthetic or conceptual interdisciplinary forms. An anthropologist from one of these small colleges questioned the worth of specialized approaches to teaching, criticizing them as a "very American, western idea":

We think you really need to be superspecialized. Well that's a very American, western idea. I teach a course on magic, witchcraft, and religion which looks at the sacred from sociological, psychological, and anthropological perspectives. When you think about all the different ways people can define that, all the different ways people can experience that, I just

don't understand how you can say you can only do one. It just—that's not
what human life is. That's not what life is. We can't pretend to understand
it all anyhow. [M]

Informants often asked the question "How can you teach ___ without considering ___?" An English professor who taught a course on episodes of genocide
around the world was adamant about the need for an interdisciplinary approach:

How can you understand the literature of genocide without understanding all those other disciplines? That would be immoral as well as intellectually dishonest to try to do that. You can't take a disciplinary approach.
You can't go through and look at the way different elements work in the
text. You could do that, I suppose. It would be interesting. But the students would have these questions about why were all these people bystand-
ers? What motivated the Nazis? [X]

Faculty practiced interdisciplinarity to help students see the connections
among disciplines. A zoologist helped students see the relationships between
biology and physics by teaching them about the electric fish that he kept in an
aquarium in his laboratory. He recounted how his physics colleague loaned
him her oscilloscope and equipment for a demonstration in his biology class.
She, in return, asked if she could borrow his fish. Using examples, information, and perspectives from two or more disciplines allowed these faculty to
help their students develop a complex understanding of the object of study.
The zoologist explained how this approach challenges students:

My students ask me why this class was so hard when high school was no
problem. I say, "Well, in high school they gave you the hammer and the
screwdriver, this piece of wood, and a saw." And they said, "Memorize
what these things are supposed to do." We are evaluating your ability to
use these tools by saying build a house. You have to use them in a way that
is integrative. It seems like the more tools that are in the box, the more
choices you are going to have. So looking at these questions from several
different angles or looking at them from a physics point of view versus a

biology point of view, or seeing the connections between them might make the world less mysterious. They might be looking down fewer tunnels. They are seeing through more than one window at a time. [F1]

Many of the liberal arts college informants were attuned to the discomfort that students could experience in interdisciplinary courses. They acknowledged that these approaches could be unfamiliar to students, even counter to what they have previously learned about the disciplines: "We are asking them to do things and to think things that we didn't do. And we talk sometimes about stopping and looking at each other and thinking, what if I had to do this? Could I do what I am now asking them to do?" [K]. Another informant commiserated with students who must read across disciplines. Describing a course he cotaught with a group of colleagues from other departments, he admitted his own discomfort with the assigned material:

When it was time for me to listen to the other faculty present, I had to read in their areas and that was much harder. I think that everybody who does this—who studies under somebody else—understands how hard it is for students. Here I am experienced at reading and studying and all I've got to do is participate in this class discussion—as a student for the most part. The reading is slow going and it is complicated at times. I had to sneak off and ask the faculty, "You know, I don't get this at all, can you explain this to me?" Come in and say to them, "I'm lost. I really need some help with this." [C1]

Informants also talked about finding ways to achieve their learning goals for students in spite of the obstacles interdisciplinarity presented. Several informants aided students in interdisciplinary courses by explicitly discussing and reiterating the difficulties they should expect to encounter and the challenging nature of the approach on a regular basis during the class. They encouraged students to ask questions about things they didn't understand. They also suggested that interdisciplinary courses highlighted the importance of faculty's being conscious of students' needs, slowing down, providing more examples and illustrating points, increasing office hours, and adjusting evaluation systems as well.

I realize this is hard for students. They come in and they don't know what to expect. I start talking about political science stuff and the political students feel, "Oh, I understand this, this feels okay." The others are anxiety-ridden. Then I am talking to the black studies students and the political science students are anxiety-ridden, they don't think they are going to get this information. So I tell them just at the outset that this is an interdisciplinary course and we have three different majors in here. I want to meet all of your needs and similarly you're going to have some anxiety about whether you are successful or not. So to reassure them, I had many more feedback mechanisms then I do in a regular class. For example, exam measures and other things like case briefs, or articles to respond to, so that I can give them feedback: "Yes, you're doing fine; you're on the right track." [I]

A philosopher who typically worked in a conceptual interdisciplinary mode talked about the difficulty students experienced in dealing with the complex, real-life problems that she presented in a course on medical ethics. She reminds students in her classes of the arbitrary nature of disciplinary divisions, noting "the world is very different from the world you saw in school. You will not find any little nicely drawn lines any place in the world." She also stresses the need to learn how to use information from different disciplines: "You're just going to have to solve these really complicated problems that have all these things put together and if you can't manipulate them, you aren't willing to try." She suggested there is no room for argument: "And you know I just give them really complex interdisciplinary problems and I say, 'Welcome to the real world. Now we're going to learn to cope'" [J].

Concerns about depth and coverage often arise in disciplinary classrooms and can implicate an entire interdisciplinary curriculum. One challenge is ensuring that students understand the fundamentals of both disciplines:

Ideally a course like this should be taught to seniors who have had three science courses and three philosophy courses. Then we would have greater depth to explore. These students [who took his interdisciplinary course] have had neither philosophy nor science, so I would have to consciously slow down and emphasize the examples more because that drew the students in: "Why did they think about this in this way?" Once they start asking these questions you can proceed on those, but it was very hard to just introduce basic science and basic philosophy and then try to draw that interdisciplinary synthesis. That is hard. [L1]

A faculty member who once taught in women's studies complained as well about the depth that can be achieved in an interdisciplinary course: "I think part of the problem with women's studies programs—this is why it was a long time before we went to the major—is that everything is at an introductory level. You're starting over all the time" [K]. For an anthropologist the introductory theory course in anthropology encapsulated the difficulties created by her belief in interdisciplinarity:

> What do you teach? To be an anthropologist in 1995, you have to read Foucault, you have to read David Harden. You have to read a range of things that *never* have been considered part of the anthropological tradition to be an anthropologist. But to be an anthropologist, you also have to know what was narrowly defined as anthropology, those disciplinary sort of great men, or you're going to end up reinventing the wheel. . . . But you still have a semester, two semesters, to teach students what anthropology is. So what do you do? What are your choices? Do you give them Marx and Weber and Foucault and not give them Evans Pritchard and Radcliffe-Brown? I mean what do you do? And we [the faculty in the anthropology department] all are confused about it. And the students are confused about it and they're confused about what anthropology is at all anymore. [H1]

For a number of informants, the conflicts presented by interdisciplinary work were not simply obstacles for students and faculty to surmount, but rather teachable moments. The faculty member's responsibility was to teach the subject matter *and* also to teach the conflicts presented by the subject matter. One might expect individuals with conceptual interdisciplinary interests, which typically include a critique of disciplinary limitations, to be particularly attuned to conflicts, but instructors pursuing all types of interdisciplinary courses adopted this strategy. Often these informants engaged students in explicit conversations about interdisciplinarity as a method of inquiry. An anthropologist working on synthetic interdisciplinary projects commented on the goals of courses in an interdisciplinary graduate program.

Well, the idea is to try to get them to grapple with the issues that interdisciplinarity addresses, that is, the limits to the traditional ways of knowing about a problem and dealing with the problem. So, for instance, psychologists are no less concerned with culture or cultural interpretation than anybody else, they just ignore the fact that they're doing it. It's as if culture was not something that was shaping the way white college sophomores were responding to pencil and paper tests, but in fact, it is. And the issue is to try to bring that cultural interpretative dimension to the fore. . . . [S]

Other faculty used disciplinary conflicts to model critical thinking for students. A team-taught course provided an economist and his colleague with opportunities to disagree publicly and thereby to encourage students to express their own opinions.

[My colleague] would just as soon get rid of markets. He thinks markets are basically evil and I just fundamentally disagree. I think markets are very important. I think that the problem with markets as a tool in the context of development or anywhere else isn't that the market is a weak tool, it's that we build all sort of constraints and boundary conditions around the market that leads the market to satisfy the interest of a small elite group rather than satisfy the well-being of a society. We fight about that issue all the time, especially in front of the students. We are convinced that good interdisciplinary pedagogy demands that the students see the thought process going on and see the conflicts. Otherwise they are never going to participate in the process. But as soon as they see me criticize him or they see him criticize me, then they feel free to jump in also with their own objections to the kinds of things we are saying. [W]

This strategy of public debate was common in team-taught courses; informants believed it offered students valuable learning experiences. A political scientist commenting on a synthetic interdisciplinary course that she taught with a colleague from the fine arts department argued that her own inability to accept a particular viewpoint helped students acknowledge the possibility of multiple perspectives on a topic.

What I began to appreciate more was how the artist needs just to get un-
conditional funding. That's the way the arts stay free. I can appreciate that
need on the part of the art community, but on the other hand the art for
art's sake, which is one of the major debates that we had in the class, I
never could quite understand that. For me, art has to have a purpose, a
message. This is what challenged me the most. Everyone in the class understood—this is one of things I thought was good for the students—they
understood I didn't get it. I just plain didn't get it. I saw the world differently then the art people saw it. And I thought that was a healthy thing. [I]

An informant from an English literature department noted that at the graduate level, conflicts between disciplines become first-order experiences for students as they *experience*, rather than simply witness, them. The methodology
classes in the women's studies program had a reputation, she observed, for
producing confrontations among students from different fields: "it's first-year
graduate students who are . . . trying to establish themselves in their discipline
and they come into this women's studies class and they're asked to throw that
out. That class is known as a place where the students sort of learn to define
themselves" [B1].

A few informants considered content to be, *primarily*, a vehicle for teaching students how to think. A professor of history claimed, "I am less interested
in teaching students factual information than teaching them a set of thinking
skills, a set of reasoning skills—sort of critical inquiry" [V]. Similarly a professor of economics commented:

What we ought to be doing is trying to get students to understand how to
think a little more clearly. . . . That's the foundation upon which all my
teaching now is built. To me, part of the critical reasoning concept is that
you constantly have to be looking at alternatives, what's not being told,
different perspectives.

Rather than exciting students by helping them understand the specifics of an
economic model and overlooking its weaknesses, he argued that students need
to look at the different perspectives and goals underlying them: "if you really
want to understand the richness of economics and why there are these diversi-

ties of thought, then you got to understand it's not that this side is right and that one's wrong. But they're coming at this thing trying to achieve different goals" [O].

Other informants also suggested that exposing students to multiple perspectives enhanced their learning, but they did not phrase the need for multiple perspectives in terms of critical thinking. Informants working on conceptual interdisciplinary projects typically assumed the existence of multiple realities and different contexts. A political scientist provided an example from an undergraduate class she taught.

> Most students come in with a classic, kind of rational approach to decision making and I think it's very important for people to understand that if that notion of decision making fits any decisions, it's a very, very narrow set of decisions and that if they are going to be thinking about decision making in their public life or their own decision making in organizations, that they need to have a much broader context for understanding it. They need to understand things like incrementalism and they need to understand how important context is, and they need to understand that goals don't always precede choices, sometimes choices get made and then goals emerge. Most of them still think that that's *bad* when they leave my class. My version of it is understanding that that's not bad, that's part of life. But at least, even the people who come away from it thinking that's it's bad, at least now understand that it happens and I think they'll do much better in life if they understand that that happens. [L]

One individual trained as an economist later adopted a feminist standpoint. She found it possible to teach traditional economics courses, but she also asked students to be wary of neat, disciplinary questions and answers and cognizant of how contexts influenced those answers. Another informant offered an example from a seminar in the history of art. In this graduate course students were often the source of differing perspectives.

> I tend to focus on readings that are diametrically opposed. I like to get a debate started around some topic and give people the feeling that they can disagree, both with what they've read and with *me*. And, so really give people a sense that they are all contributing perspectives on an issue and

trying to broaden our treatment of the subject as much as possible, you know, and eventually try and come to some consensus on it, but really use seminars to build out on an issue and look at the various ways something can be treated and get graduate students very, very involved. [E]

Learning theorists and others have argued that conflict promotes learning (for example, Carter 1988, Trimbur 1989, Graff 1992). Hill (1990) contends that both learning and writing require dissonance, turbulence, and perhaps fear. Advocates of postmodern curricula, such as Doll (1993), suggest that disequilibrium produces a learning environment that challenges students to personalize their learning and thus intensifies the experience. This kind of experience may not produce depth as it is traditionally defined, but, Doll argues, it is rigorous in its careful and critical exploration of underlying assumptions, multiple perspectives, and possibilities. Students who explore opposing points of view and who move between disciplines develop new ways of thinking. Informants who adopted the idea of acknowledging and discussing conflicts in interdisciplinary courses appeared to subscribe to similar theories.

Interdisciplinary teaching created its own set of challenges for faculty, but informants who taught in merged departments or in a discipline other than their own were especially conscious of the ramifications of interdisciplinary instruction. In one liberal arts college, an anthropologist in a merged sociology/anthropology department was required to teach sociology to undergraduates and to guide them through independent study projects.

> This is only our second year as a combined soc/anthro department and we're still trying to fill positions . . . we're looking for just the right person who can cross both and can work with anthro or soc students in their independent studies because you have to do that. So I have learned soc because I've had to, because I've had to work with anthro and soc independent studies. At the beginning when I was the only one, I really had to become as much like a sociologist as I could right away because I didn't have any of my own majors and that's what they needed. [M]

Similarly, a political scientist hired by a university sociology department found that teaching courses in that discipline was more difficult than either she or her colleagues anticipated:

I spent a lot of time training myself in sociology because it turned out that sociology and political science weren't as similar as we thought. When I was hired it was assumed that they were basically similar graduate trainings and they really aren't. They emphasize different things, there are different heroes and villains, and different rubrics. So I also spent a lot of time training myself in sociology and sociological language, and terms and theories, and just studies and learning the names. And who's where and who just got divorced and who just bought a house and you know, it's something you learn as part of the discipline, the gossip as well as the theoretical and intellectual stuff. [P]

These retooling experiences occurred in the liberal arts colleges as well as the universities in my study and in the sciences as well as the social sciences and humanities. One informant, a zoologist, described being hired as a post-doctoral researcher in a university psychology department. He credited his ability to do interdisciplinary work in the sciences to teaching general psychology to undergraduates during his postdoctoral work, a task he reluctantly accepted. In this and numerous other cases in this study connections between teaching and research activities were catalysts for interdisciplinary projects.

In their reconceptualization of scholarship, Paulsen and Feldman (1995) argue that integrative work can occur not only in research and teaching, but also in service activities. An interdisciplinary program committee is one example of this kind of service. A biologist who served on a committee that created an environmental studies program at her college recalled that initial conversations among committee members representing a variety of disciplines required considerable discussion of individuals' assumptions about the field.

The provost . . . invited a group of us to talk about what shape the environmental studies program should take . . . This provost's field was English and she felt, as I think the chemists did, that anyone going on in environmental studies should have very strong technical proficiency. They should be able to measure pollutants in landfills, that was the essence of environmental studies . . . whereas I and some others in social sciences and humanities who were at this meeting argued that what is needed is to understand the context of environmental problems and that the solutions aren't scientific ones for the most part. [For students, being comfortable] with science was important so that you couldn't be buffaloed—but breadth was much more important and that problem solving in general and interdisciplinary thinking was more important in environmental studies than anything else. [A1]

Once these early issues were discussed, the biologist realized how helpful her earlier experiences on other interdisciplinary program committees had been:

We tried to understand how—questions like how to get depth in a program for students without having a lockstep curriculum. How to have the equivalent of advanced courses in environmental studies when you weren't sure that you would have a cohort of students that would have all had similar backgrounds by the time they took that course. So, those questions were very similar to ones in women's studies when they developed a major there—and in fact I felt very well prepared having gone through the whole thing years before with women's studies. I was the only person, really, on the environmental studies committee that had had experience developing an interdisciplinary program and wrestling with these questions and it was very helpful to look at it with a whole different set of constraints and assumptions. [A1]

A political scientist played a similar role as a member of a committee that created an interdisciplinary undergraduate program spanning political science, economics, and philosophy. His comments on that experience focused largely on the teaching aspects of that work: the committee read students' proposals for programs of study and advised their senior theses. He noted, as did the biologist quoted above, the occasional political maneuvering as faculty tried to use interdisciplinary programs to generate greater enrollments for their courses. These, however, seemed to be minor annoyances rather than divisive issues among faculty from different disciplines.

Despite the challenges that interdisciplinary teaching presented, most informants welcomed the responsibility. Informants were able to empathize with their students as they guided them through unfamiliar waters, often as they themselves were learning to swim. The experience encouraged them to reflect on their pedagogical styles and philosophies. Interdisciplinary teaching also seemed to require that faculty recognize and accept multiple and sometimes conflicting perspectives. A few informants, particularly — but not exclusively — those working in feminist and poststructuralist modes, saw interdisciplinarity as an opportunity to consolidate research and teaching interests. An associate professor of English became director of an interdisciplinary program, in part, because the position offered this option:

> I really wanted to leave my department, though, because the kinds of courses that I could teach there were too narrow and I wanted to be able to bring together my research and teaching. That's one of the ways I stay sane: being a person who is interdisciplinary means that you get pulled in many different directions, and to integrate teaching and research is great. [C]

Doing Interdisciplinary Research

Research questions often distinguish the disciplines from one another and disciplinarity from interdisciplinarity. Disciplinary assumptions and preferences are often revealed in research projects and must be negotiated to ensure successful collaboration on interdisciplinary research projects. Informants who pursued individual interdisciplinary projects often conducted these negotiations internally. An economist discussed her choice to explore other ways of conducting inquiries in her field:

> I find myself becoming increasingly disenchanted with mainstream methods because I think they [explain] so many things away to fit things into nice neat mathematical boxes that there are lots of important questions that don't get answered or even asked. In work that I did . . . I came down really hard on neoclassical approaches to technology and neoclassical approaches to understanding women's position in the labor market because they take everything out of institutional context. And I think that that makes no sense when you are studying either technology or women, or certainly the relationship between the two. So I mean my bottom line there was, I don't think you can *do* this. I don't think you can answer *these* questions using this particular method. I think you have to open up a lot and consider institutional context, social forces, the way that interacts with

women's work, and the development of the computer and other kinds of technology and all that stuff. [G]

Her explanation of her position on economic modeling and statistical approaches revealed her epistemological commitments and also the effects that the development of these commitments had on her approach to research. These commitments influenced ways of doing disciplinary and interdisciplinary research.

It's important, to me anyway, to emphasize that even if you can't mathematically model it, it doesn't mean you can't build a model that makes logical connections between things. And it *doesn't* mean that you can't empirically test hypotheses because I see a real big difference between doing statistical analysis and doing mathematical modeling. I think there are lots of questions that you could answer, questions that I think I did answer, at least partially answer, using statistical analysis in my work. Did I have a formal utility-maximizing model of firms when they pursue technological change? No. Because I think that there is too much stuff that is going on in that decision-making process to put it in terms of a mathematical model. I just don't think you can do it. [G]

Another economist reconsidered economic theory as a result of his research interests. Like the majority of U.S. economists, he was trained in the neoclassical paradigm; however, it didn't seem to help him understand development in developing countries. Eventually he refashioned himself as an institutional economist.

The key piece of institutional analysis is the argument that says the way any economic system really functions and really accomplishes its goals of allocating scarce resources is shaped by the institutional arrangements. Institutionalists contend that there is no universal economic theory, that there can't be. A universal theory would imply that the institutional arrangements were the same everywhere and they are not. In every different setting you have to have at least some marginal changes in the theory in order to understand what is going on. That was very helpful to me because it removed my guilt. My guilt came from rejecting the neoclassical paradigm in the context of all these Third World development issues that I was looking at. The institutionalists were telling me, that is good, you should reject the paradigm because it doesn't fit that setting. [W]

Faculty who pursued interdisciplinary work in the sciences or in social science fields that operate in a scientific paradigm, such as cognitive psychology, often encountered differences based on disciplinary assumptions and methods. A physicist who ventured in the statistical analysis of economics data offered the example of financial models:

A received wisdom in economics and in finance has been for many years the efficient markets hypothesis. This is the notion that financial markets by and large are efficient in the sense that price movements are unanticipated and random and that the system is sitting in some sort of equilibrium. So if you analyze a price series, you will see movements that are kind of randomish, unanticipated. . . . [E1]

He noted that the natural reaction of a physicist to this state is that the system is not in equilibrium:

The physicist looks at it and see all these guys on the trading floor, you know, in the pit, yelling at each other and doing hand signals. All this information is coming in all the time, and there is lots of stuff going on, there's lots of dynamics. The natural way for a physicist to think about this is as a dynamic system. It is a system that has its own internal dynamics and maybe some of these jumps and wiggles are just because of the internal dynamics of the systems and it is not at equilibrium. Now, these are very, very different ways of looking at the same phenomena . . . from the outset you come to this with a much different view of how you analyze the system. [E1]

Problems like the one recounted above were resolved, if resolved at all, only after much discussion. Informants often argued that the key was for collaborators to understand and respect the assumptions of each other's disciplines.

If you are going to go and work in another field or try to bridge across to another field, it is not productive to forget where you came from. It is also not productive if you are too dismissive about it. You really have to try to get into the mindset of the people who work in that field, try to understand their concerns, which are legitimate and which you may be able to help push. And it is not a trivial thing to do. It takes some time. You have to strike a balance between sort of maintaining your intellectual integrity and your own intellectual history and the tools that you have and visions that you have and striking some posture of intellectual humility. It is not productive to put on your white hat and ride in like the cowboys to save Dodge City because it just doesn't work like that. You can end up really falling flat on your face. [E1]

A psychologist echoed the opinion that openness is needed but that interdisciplinarity should not require a researcher to renounce his or her disciplinary knowledge: "If you're good at what you do, you'll never let go of what you do. It will always be in the back of your mind, but you really should immerse yourself in it, just completely. Until you start to see it a little through their eyes" [G1].

Informants engaged in all forms of interdisciplinary research had to negotiate, albeit to varying degrees, disciplinary assumptions and methods. Those pursuing conceptual interdisciplinary work typically centralized disciplinary conflicts by including explicit critiques of disciplinary perspectives and philosophical justifications for interdisciplinary approaches. Those working on synthetic and transdisciplinary projects treated disciplinary conflicts as pragmatic issues to be wrestled with and overcome. With the exception of economists, who talked extensively about disciplinary obstacles to interdisciplinarity, faculty informants in the humanities and social sciences were least bothered by the notion that disciplinary assumptions would hinder collaborative efforts with colleagues in other fields. These individuals typically attributed the success or failure of interdisciplinary projects to personality factors, such as preferences for collaboration or control of the inquiry. Among the disciplines economics is notable for its strict assumptions and specific methods. Unlike faculty in other fields who could adopt methods from neighboring disciplines that were consistent with their beliefs about how knowledge should be pursued, economists in this study faced conflicts about basic epistemological and methodological commitments when they considered theories or methods from outside their discipline. The conflicts between existing and new conceptions of economics led to a modification of their central disciplinary commitments. More flexible models and theories replaced previously held economic tenets.

Faculty most often described the process of doing interdisciplinary work as a learning process. Even when they were not attending classes or seminars, they still perceived themselves to be students of other disciplines. Two individuals who had postdoctoral appointments in disciplines other than those they studied as graduate students used their appointments as opportunities to learn new research techniques. One commented on this experience:

> In many ways this was a fundamentally important time because I was publishing some of the stuff from my thesis, thinking about what I was going to do, and the postdoc at least gave me some experience with people doing experimental studies. The big turning point came when I applied for money to do some experimental studies. I turned the thesis and its claims into the basis for a set of studies which I then kind of designed on my own without any real understanding of how experimental psychology worked. I did these studies which were awkward and clumsy and much more time-consuming than they should have been, but it ended up being all right. I published them as experiments and they were a major learning event. It was an opportunity for me to develop some of the skills as an experimentalist for which I never had any training. [S]

Others engaged in reading programs that improved their understanding of different disciplines. Still, after five years of reading anthropology and sociology, a political scientist admitted she was "still learning" and attempting to make sense of insights from these disciplines:

> It's an ongoing process. In some ways I will always be learning it. But now I am moving in a direction where I am able to look at the observations [I've made in my studies] and I'm able to be true to them. I think that is what is important to me, rather than kind of pick and choose and analyze them into appropriate categories so that they're squished down in some way. [L]

For individuals who collaborated on research, the learning process was a two-way street: both parties needed to learn something about the other's discipline(s).

Our collaborators at the medical school are in nuclear medicine. They've learned a little psychology. Now psychology's a lot more transparent than neuroanatomy, so it's easier on them than on us. But they get into it, they definitely do get into the psychological issues and we try to get into their kinds of issues. I think that's essential. And then of course, it helps to have similar standards about what you think of as good work, things like that. [G1]

Although many informants had spent substantial amounts of time learning about other disciplines, few went so far as to agree with the psychologist who spent his sabbatical year studying neuroscience.

I think this idea that you can pick up another person's discipline just by conversations just won't work. It's just not serious. You've got to be serious. In his autobiography, Herb Simon—I mean he's a truly interdisciplinary writer, a renaissance man—he estimates that in order to do interdisciplinary work, at an absolute minimum, you have to immerse yourself for one year in the other discipline where that's what you do. I didn't quite put in that much time—close—but I think that sounds about right. That basically if you want to do interdisciplinary work, you should wait till your sabbatical or get a year's leave, get out of your office, and become the equivalent of a graduate student and that's all you should be doing. [G1]

Collaboration on interdisciplinary research and teaching projects requires shared standards. While agreeing to disagree might work well in an interdisciplinary classroom and provide a valuable learning experience for students, in research, agreement on methods is essential. The psychologist quoted above referred to the need for "shared problem space," but also focused on methodological and epistemological consistency.

If I had to make one simple generalization, it's that the major way disciplines differ is not content, but in method. One of the reasons why our work in cognitive neuroscience has gone so well is that we are hooked-up biology types. They totally believe in experimentation just the way we do. My other efforts in cognitive science—almost inevitably they're all people who are big believers in experimentation. Philosophers obviously are not. Linguists rarely do experiments and their methodology is all in the form of "Is this an acceptable grammatical sentence?" It's the only method they really use. They find psychology experiments often trivial. In artificial intelligence, the methodology has to do with the construction and design of computer programs and they think we rely too much on experimentation. So there's always a clash about the methodology part. There's less of a clash with neuroscientists about this. [E1]

In some cases collaborations we built with the knowledge that individuals would bring different strengths to the project. One psychologist who conducted a study with a physician talked about the contributions each made to the effort.

He certainly deferred to me on issues about research design and data analysis and statistical inference. His previous research had been more or less to develop a model of how his students should approach problem solving. He would instruct them in that model, would illustrate the model, and I think his sense of evaluating the effectiveness of that model was just pragmatic. I'm very sure he never did any kind of a study with any kind of comparison groups or control groups or any kind of longitudinal pre/post test. He would just try to intuitively understand how students were using the model and which types of students were better able to and which were not. I think he's very good at doing that, but that would be his sense of research. He could not design a study in which certain precautions are taken to enhance validity and reliability and so forth. I think we did a pretty good job on negotiating and compromising on our different needs in this study. [Q]

Crane (1969) suggested that the success of interdisciplinary collaboration might depend on the amount of cognitive reorganization it required of its participants. A need for extensive reorganization might stop a project in its tracks; participants might simply refuse or be unable to make necessary cognitive changes. Barmark and Wallen (quoted in Rossini and Porter 1984) suggested that disciplines may be more permeable than paradigms; interdisciplinary research involving individuals from different paradigms therefore might be more difficult than research involving individuals who share similar ways of thinking about the world. According to this perspective, the easiest, and perhaps only, route to interdisciplinary research, is collaboration with those who share cognitive space.

In keeping with metaphors about disciplinary borders that so often characterize writing about interdisciplinarity, observers have focused on the barrier that disciplinary languages present to interdisciplinary scholarship. Similarly study participants often likened learning a new disciplinary language to learning a foreign tongue. Learning the lingo was considered an important step in building a successful collaboration: "You have to find out enough about this other discipline so you know the lexicon. You've got to know what they're talking about" [G1]. Scientists, who typically use more technical terms and particularistic concepts than faculty in the social sciences and humanities, vividly described the problems related to differences in specialized languages. A physicist who had explored applications of statistical analyses through a number of interdisciplinary projects provided some concrete examples:

> You realize how much vocabulary matters, the sensitivity that you have to the words that are used and to the difficulty of the vocabulary. For example, at the second meeting [of our group], I volunteered to give a little talk on some work I was doing and I called it state-space methods. . . . I started and someone said, "This isn't state-space methods." I said "Of course it is." This guy said, "No, state-space methods means this." The same phrase means something different to people in statistics than the meaning I used. And I can give you another example. There is another commonly used term, *stationary*, a time series is stationary. This group of people in this project includes a guy in biostatistics, a mathematician, and me and we spent a long time trying to figure out what each of us meant by stationary. We really mean something rather different. It is really important to be able to understand the right vocabulary. [E1]

A biochemist recounted his difficulties in publishing a paper, demonstrating that these were traceable to language issues.

It just turned out that the people working in viruses used a totally different term to refer to the [junction] structures, and when I did literature searches I never came up with it. But I happened to give a talk at another university, in a very medically oriented biochemistry department. The first guy I talked with was a biologist who works with viruses that have those junction structures. It's an integral part of the virus. I asked him what he called them. He called them something that just didn't make sense to me. I said, well, we call them three-way junctions. [Y]

Earlier I introduced a zoologist who had completed postdoctoral work in psychology and taught general psychology classes at the university level. He claimed to be fluent in psychology as a result of this experience. However, even he acknowledged his limitations. He suggested that the appropriate goal for interdisciplinary explorations was learning, not expertise:

I speak both languages so I get a long quite well actually. I can survive. Every now and then I'll stumble but I have no problem about embarrassing myself. In other words, if I say the wrong thing I don't really care. I'm more interested in learning. If I make a mistake along the way, that's fine. I speak enough of both languages where I could function quite well with both of them. . . . There's a book sitting on my shelf which has always influenced me. It's a book written by zoologists who studied a certain phenomenon in animals called foraging theory. They literally wrote the book pointing out the relationship between words zoologists and psychologists use to describe the same phenomenon. The words they use to do it would be entirely different—how could one group possibly understand what the other group was talking about? I was struck by that. That was given to me when I was a graduate student. I was really struck by that. [D]

As might be expected, faculty working in the sciences and those collaborating with individuals from fields with very different paradigms were most attuned to issues of language. In the social sciences and humanities, where terms are often familiar to individuals in a variety of disciplines, the language was less often considered a substantial barrier to interdisciplinarity. The influence of disciplinary training, however, could be persistent; even individuals who had been reading and working in other disciplines for extended periods of time continually confronted language problems.

> Whenever we are discussing a topic, we both start out using the language of our disciplines. Then, every time he or I come up against something we don't understand we say, "Explain that because I don't understand what that means." I think what we do is break down the jargon. If you read the things we have written, you will find a relatively small amount of jargon in there. Most of it has been converted to English. The only place the jargon still shows up is in professional papers that we present at meetings. [W]

Learning disciplinary languages is a necessary step, but successful collaborations require participants to expend the requisite energy:

> Part of writing together is writing off of each other. [My colleague] will have an idea and he will write eight or ten pages about his idea. Then I will look at it and say, "Well, I see some ways in which I can fit in the economics here" and I might take what he has written and I might rewrite it and write into it some economics so that when it is finished you can't tell who wrote it. Our students always have a hard time with that. They always say, "[Professor], why did you say this?" He says, "I didn't say that, that is his." [W]

Beyond the iterative writing process, this economist argued that a certain attitude was also needed.

> We spoke at the very beginning about the importance of burying your ego. That is part of how we learned to do that. We began to say that if anybody is ever going to publish this book, it can't look like here is the chapter the theologian wrote and here is the chapter the economist wrote. There has to be something that makes the integration with theology and economics make sense, but somehow it has to be written together. As we began to do that we did begin to bury our egos and say, "You know you are right, that stuff I wrote sounds like shit. Let's fix it." [W]

166 CREATING INTERDISCIPLINARITY

Bakhtin (1981) described learning as the struggle for a new language. This analogy may resonate with many faculty who do interdisciplinary research. However, learning a new language does not always require extensive changes in the way we think. As many informants in the sciences suggested, collaborations may be successful to the extent that collaborators can agree on content issues and methods. The learning that occurs in these collaborations resembles "assimilation," the term Strike and Posner (1985, 1992) used to describe new learning that does not require individuals to make major adjustments in existing cognitive frameworks. In contrast, the economists quoted earlier, who rejected the neo-classical model, seemed to have undergone a process of "accommodation." Strike and Posner contend that this is a more radical way of incorporating new conceptions, requiring an individual to alter deeply held commitments.

Characterizing Interdisciplinary Processes

Informants prepared for and conducted disciplinary and interdisciplinary research and teaching in similar ways. The difference was often one of degree. Informants claimed to read more widely when doing interdisciplinary work than they did for disciplinary work. They argued that interdisciplinary research and teaching required greater preparation time. Collaborations, they suggested, also required more patience and longer timelines so that disciplinary bumps could be smoothed. In general, however, informants pursued typical academic activities—reading, talking with colleagues, and collaborating— when pursuing interdisciplinary projects.

Reading in other disciplines was universal among the faculty informants, although reading strategies varied. Some individuals were more selective in their reading than others. Informants doing synthetic interdisciplinary work that combined two or three disciplines generally claimed to limit their reading to these disciplines. Individuals pursuing informed disciplinary and conceptual interdisciplinary work generally read more broadly. Regardless of the type of strategy, however, faculty talked about lengthy engagements with the material of other disciplines. Reading was almost always supplemented by conversations with campus and off-campus colleagues. Informants valued specialized meetings, institutes, and campus forums as sources of information and contacts and as sounding boards for new ideas.

About half the faculty interviewed had collaborated with one or more individuals from other disciplines on teaching or research projects. These collaborations were more often serendipitous than planned, although informants in the sciences more purposefully sought collaborators with particular disciplinary or technical expertise. Informants in the social sciences and humanities rarely suggested that they used this strategy. Individuals in research collaborations negotiated issues of content and methods before agreeing to collaborate; fundamental beliefs were therefore not contested. In the classroom faculty need not agree with collaborators; instead informants acknowledged conflicts and multiple perspectives, discussed them with students, and used them as a teaching tool.

Faculty informants grappled with similar issues in interdisciplinary and disciplinary teaching—how to evaluate students, how to motivate students, whether to introduce a new text. Interdisciplinary scholarship, however, appeared to sensitize faculty to disciplinary, epistemological, and pedagogical issues that they might have overlooked in purely disciplinary work. Both interdisciplinary research and teaching could force faculty to confront their assumptions about knowledge and the ways in which it is pursued.

Abiding Interdisciplinarity:
The Impact of Academic Contexts

Chapter

Much of the rhetoric of interdisciplinarity concerns perceived indifference or outright hostility to interdisciplinary scholarship, resulting from skeptical disciplinary colleagues, rigid departmental structures, traditional promotion and tenure systems, and inflexible budgeting practices. Undoubtedly disciplinary structures can impede interdisciplinary scholarship, and faculty are sometimes dissuaded from pursuing interdisciplinary work by fears of unfavorable reviews from colleagues (see, for example, Birnbaum 1981a and Hurst 1992). Yet interdisciplinary teaching and research happens. What impact, then, do departmental and institutional environments have on interdisciplinarity? How does support or a lack of support for interdisciplinary scholarship influence faculty and their work? What role, if any, do administrators and colleagues play in encouraging or discouraging interdisciplinary efforts?

In interviewing informants about institutional and departmental settings, I learned how they assessed these environments and how they believed the settings affected their work and academic lives. The overall picture is a complex one. Some informants gratefully acknowledged administrative support for interdisciplinarity while others enumerated institutional policies that hindered interdisciplinary teaching and research. Many complained of suspicious departmental colleagues, and some felt compelled to look outside their institution for the colleagueship of like-minded people. Others praised colleagues who supported their work and who advocated for interdisciplinary teaching and research projects. Some informants also perceived strong attitudes toward interdisciplinary work within their disciplinary communities and discussed how disciplinary associations created a national or international context that influenced perceptions and conduct of interdisciplinary scholarship. As I analyzed informants' narratives about departments, institutions, and disciplines, I searched for patterns in perceptions of departmental, institutional, and disciplinary contexts and the extent of interdisciplinary engagement. The evidence suggests that while individuals recognized collegial and structural impediments, these did not alter their willingness to participate in interdisciplinary activities, teach interdisciplinary courses, or conduct interdisciplinary research. Had I interviewed faculty in general about participation in interdisciplinary activities, I may have found individuals who were discouraged by structural and/or collegial barriers. Other research, however, does not necessarily support this idea. In their review of the research and theory on motivation in college and university faculty, Blackburn and Lawrence (1995) argued that faculty do what they believe they are good at doing: intrinsic motivations and rewards often override external influences.

The Academic Department as Context

If the typical story about interdisciplinarity portrays academic departments and colleagues as obstacles to be surmounted, the informants in this study offered a more nuanced, even favorable, picture of departmental life. They recognized that some colleagues looked askance at interdisciplinary research and teaching but found others supportive and encouraging. A few described stressful tenure experiences with dismay and surprise, but the same individuals praised colleagues who supported them during trying reviews. Although research and experience suggest that disciplinary cultures typically adjust to fit the local circumstances (Austin 1990), observers of interdisciplinarity have rarely looked closely at these specific contexts to understand their influence on individuals and on interdisciplinary scholarship.

According to informants, particular institutions had reputations for openness or resistance to interdisciplinarity. These reputations were often validated as individuals within the same institution offered similar assessments of the climate for interdisciplinarity in their departments and institutions. At the research university informants regarded their departments as open to interdisciplinarity; they felt colleagues both tolerated and appreciated different interdisciplinary perspectives and innovation. A tenured political scientist commented:

> One of the things that makes this department really good for somebody who does interdisciplinary work is that it's always been rated as one of the top departments [in political science] and I think as a result has felt less constrained by the norms of what it is that everybody else is doing. It felt more free to say, "Oh, that's interesting work. We'd like to have one of those." [L]

A new assistant professor who depicted himself as "not particularly radical" happily described the welcome he received from his departmental colleagues. His appreciation of various perspectives—"I believe in traditional stuff as much as I believe in contemporary methods"—appeared to work in his favor:

> This department is fairly traditional in its approach, but it's also fairly large and very broad based. The department is careful to have people who represent different perspectives. They want students to be trained, conventionally, but they also want students to be open to more cutting-edge things. They felt they could talk to me—they mentioned this was one of the reasons for hiring me. It's very collegial, it's very supportive. . . . I feel that we are working together and it's not "Okay, here's the weird, cutting-edge interdisciplinary, theoretical person. We need to have him, but we don't have to talk to him." [E]

Department chairs were credited with the ability to encourage interdisciplinarity and sometimes served as champions of individual faculty. A professor of psychology intensely involved in interdisciplinary research in neuropsychology praised a succession of departmental chairs as "wonderful" and "terrifically supportive of interdisciplinary work" [G1]. Similarly an untenured informant acknowledged the crucial role that a supportive chair played in her hiring and in convincing members of the department that interdisciplinary scholarship was a worthwhile pursuit:

Probably if there was someone else who was the chair of the department who didn't have this particular orientation, then . . . [trails off]. It's so decentralized that whatever the particular vision of the chair is really has a really strong impact, I think, on the direction of hiring in the department, even though areas do a lot of subhiring. So it would really depend, at least for a person like me; either the department has to have that strong focus or some central people have to really push that focus. Otherwise I'm really too much out of step with the main program. [T]

As a junior member of the department, she felt particularly vulnerable and in need of validation from senior colleagues:

If you don't have a chair who's really pushing [interdisciplinarity], then there needs to be some senior person somewhere that tells somebody, "Oh, this is good. This is right." Or someone who can interpret. Because it's very difficult, I think, as a junior person to articulate those things. You can't validate yourself to other people who are more powerful than you are, that's part of the problem. [T]

Several informants perceived the departments at the university as committed to an academic ethic of civility and tolerance; members seemed able to work collegially despite differences in perspectives. Ruscio (1987) argued that there are a few core academic values that are common across disciplines and sectors of higher education. These commonalties are the result of the scholarly socialization process that creates a common ethos across significantly different disciplinary cultures. Ruscio writes:

However broadly "knowledge" is defined, disciplines impart a respect for it. They also establish such procedural expectations as the sharing of information among researchers, the importance of disinterestedly reviewing evidence, and the privilege—indeed the responsibility—of exercising self-regulation. . . (Ruscio 1987, p. 363)

At this institution, most informants believed that a deep respect for academic work in general seemed to override disciplinary biases against interdisciplinarity. But there were, of course, exceptions. Informants who had joint appointments were positioned to see more than the typical faculty member does. These appointments, although they required approval by the faculty in both departments, were not always comfortable arrangements for those who held them. A tenured professor perceived substantial differences in attitudes between her two departmental homes, sensing that one department was "more genuine" in its appreciation of her work than the other. This department was composed of individuals who "do theory" and borrow from disciplines and perspectives such as anthropology, literary theory, Marxist theory, and cultural studies. Their eclectic nature made them "very, very open to interdisciplinary work." This department, she noted, was also remarkable for having a large number of joint appointments with fields in the social sciences and humanities, including faculty working in perspectives such as literary theory or cultural studies. That was fitting, she believed, because the discipline had allied itself theoretically with different disciplines at different times.

In the other department she noted some strain. Some colleagues conceptualized the discipline very narrowly. Others did not "like people who dabble too much in literary theory." She felt she shared some interests and common ground with some of the faculty in this department, but she concluded, "there is nobody that I can really just talk with." She compared the different perspectives on scholarship that characterized the two departments:

> Recently, [one] department has been all concerned with the standards for tenure and how you make judgments of people's work. And I know that one way they judge people's work—and I don't agree with this—is whether it's published in particular journals. So, I am thinking, "I don't publish in those journals. Maybe I ought to. . . ." And I have to work hard to resist that desire to be accepted. . . . In the other department, they don't worry about that at all. It's not something that ever gets discussed. . . . They sit and read the work and talk about its quality and there doesn't seem to be an agenda that people bring to people's work. . . . They're wonderful. [D1]

The atmosphere of the former department left her struggling to decide whether the faculty there really liked her work. She underscored her confusion as she thought aloud about her experiences:

> I think people genuinely like my work there. I feel like I am very accepted
> in both departments to be honest with you. In fact, I wish somebody would
> reject me a little bit. That is not true, I wouldn't want to live in a place
> where I felt rejected, that would be awful. But I feel—as a person—I feel
> like people accept me pretty much in both departments. How they feel
> about my work, it's hard to say. I would like to be respected. [D1]

At the other three institutions represented in this study, informants' assessments of departmental climates varied. Some sensed their departmental colleagues accepted their interdisciplinary work; others found the atmosphere
uncomfortable. Several thought their departments were divided on the question of interdisciplinary scholarship. The director of an interdisciplinary program noted that while there was a healthy degree of support for interdisciplinary work in his department, there was also some opposition.

> There are also significant numbers of faculty who are put off by interdisci-
> plinary collaboration. There are people on our faculty who feel that
> the integrity of the discipline is compromised by the fact that we have all
> these joint programs. I am sure that you will find that throughout the uni-
> versity. [S]

At another institution a tenured professor of psychology suspected that many
of the members of the department disapproved of both his interdisciplinary
research and his service on dissertation committees in an interdisciplinary humanities program.

> Some colleagues [in the department] have problems with it. They haven't
> a clue what I'm up to when I move into these committees or when I tell
> them what I am doing researchwise. And a lot of my colleagues think that
> what I do is quaint, probably silly. They don't say that to my face, but that's
> my sense, that I'm not a serious scientist. [J1]

Several other informants were similarly troubled by colleagues' responses
to their interdisciplinary activities. An economics professor was both saddened
and angered by colleagues who refused to acknowledge her feminist research:

"For the most part, the people in this department do not acknowledge my re-search: 'Oh, great you got a book published. How wonderful!' Nothing. I don't think they probably have a clue what is in it and probably don't care" [G]. Like this economist a biologist felt isolated in her department, and she wondered whether she would have ventured outside her department if the atmosphere had been more engaging:

> I have sort of been driven outside of my department to look for people to interact with because my colleagues are not interested in interacting. [That] is my perception. . . . If I came into a department where people were interested in interactions among biologists, I may never have set foot outside the department. It's hard for me to tell. But this is — of depart-ments — one of the worst in terms of people interacting with the rest of the campus. Most of my colleagues are not known — even people who have been here for thirty years aren't known to the rest of the campus. [A1]

An associate professor of philosophy also sought colleagues outside her department, in part because she was the only woman faculty member in the department for many years.

> Despite the fact that we allege ourselves to be an applied department, we are really pretty traditional and pretty analytical. So, in the last ten years I have really had to work to make connections with colleagues across other disciplines. My clinical work takes me all the time to clinical scientists, health-care providers, researchers. My connections with women across the campus necessarily took me out of here but because for the better part of eight years, I was it [the only woman faculty member]. So I wanted to find out what on earth was going on with everybody else — I have a kind of survival instinct and wanted to find the rest of the barge and see what was happening to other people. [J]

A junior faculty member noted some tensions related to the power structure of her merged department. One of the disciplines in the department comprised three junior faculty, the other three tenured individuals: "So there are, inevita-bly, some tensions there." These, however, were not insurmountable.

Sometimes the areas we have problems with are around defining [my dis-
cipline] sometimes. They might use a . . . text that I feel doesn't represent
my discipline well. They might feel the same way about the . . . text that I
select. . . . I think they would listen to me; they are open to hearing things.
I can't say they don't listen to me, they do. [K1]

Institutional emphasis on research appeared to influence the degree of
concern that faculty expressed about their interdisciplinary work and its impact on their academic careers. A tenured professor with a distinguished chair
at his university commented that his productivity eclipsed that of his institutional colleagues. Under these circumstances he did not have to be constrained
in his research: "The fact that I do a lot is adequate unto itself. . . . Some of my
colleagues want to sneer at that kind of [interdisciplinary] activity and see it as
dilettanteish, but they are prevented from doing so by the fact that there is
huge output compared to theirs . . ." [F]. At the same institution another professor considered his colleagues to be rather self-concerned and somewhat
oblivious to extradisciplinary matters. She thought her work was not so much
accepted by colleagues as ignored: "Well, almost everything is okay [here] . . .
people don't check up on me and vice versa" [R].

Becher (1989) noted that individuals within the same field often have more
in common with individuals in other departments than their own departmental colleagues; specializations within fields can be very different in terms of
epistemology, language, method, and focus of study. These variations can constitute important differences, even in traditional departments, as several informants confirmed. A political scientist described his department as "kind of a
holding company" and explained why he and his departmental colleagues did
not necessarily see eye to eye on teaching and research issues. His statement
clearly illustrates Becher's observations about differentiation within disciplines:

My colleague next door is a theorist who has a lot more in common with
the philosophers than I do with him. My colleagues down the hall are
Americanists who do constitutional law, and the presidency, Congress,
American government kinds of stuff. I have more in common with my
colleague who does Soviet politics, essentially in area studies or international relations, than I do with either of those. And I probably have more

in common with my friends in econ who do international economics and development economics than I do with any of these people. So it's hard. What is political science? We argue about this—or we discuss this—in departmental meetings all the time, especially in the context of doing assessment. How do we assess whether a major in political science has really learned political science or achieved the goals of what this political science department thinks a major ought to? . . . It is very, very difficult, a very, very difficult enterprise. [C1]

Faculty turnover also affects departmental cultures. An associate professor of English talked about having fought "the promotion battles" in the past but expressed gratitude for his current cadre of colleagues: "I think I have a very special group of colleagues now. I haven't always had that here" [X]. Changes in departmental cultures were most apparent when they were accompanied by changes in the standards for tenure. Two full professors at the doctoral institution claimed that less stringent tenure requirements facilitated their entry into interdisciplinary scholarship. As the standards for tenure tightened over time, they argued, the environment for interdisciplinary work became less hospitable. A psychologist noted, "I came here in 1970 and at the time there was pressure to publish, but it was not as intense as things generally are now. They did expect you to publish, but the tone was more, "We don't care what you do, just do it" [J1]. An economist felt lucky that he was able to do interdisciplinary research as soon as he wanted. He attributed that to the fact that few of his departmental colleagues were doing any research at all: "As a consequence of that context at the time, I was able to just move to interdisciplinary activities very smoothly" [F].

An associate professor of English at the same institution also thought that tenure concerns could impede interdisciplinarity. Having achieved tenure based on her disciplinary research, she speculated that her recent interdisciplinary work might not be so well received today.

[This book is] much more experimental and innovative . . . and I guess I feel at this point I have the luxury of being able to do that. I am not under a tenure gun anymore. I can take a few chances and play around a bit more. It's safe now. I did publish a book in my discipline—even though it uses a lot of postmodern theory, it's about a respected writer, a single-author study, and in some ways it's very traditional . . . so I sort of paid my dues. . . . If I had tried to get tenure on the basis of this new book, it would have been very problematic. [C]

Many informants across institutions shared the opinion that junior faculty should concentrate on disciplinary research and teaching before tenure; only after tenure was it safe, as one informant put it, to make interdisciplinary research and teaching a major scholarly focus. Most believed that the rules changed once tenure was achieved; only then, they argued, were faculty free to pursue interdisciplinary scholarly work. A university physicist described how he had started "moving out" of his field before tenure and the problems that ensued. He offered this advice to junior faculty:

If somebody came to me and asked me for advice about this, I would tell them to keep their nose clean until they get tenure because it's a risk, it's really a risk to go between fields or even between, sometimes even between areas within the same field. But certainly, to go outside of your field is not a safe thing to do. The climate could be changing, but I don't know. I still say it is a risk to do that. [E1]

A sociologist who did interdisciplinary research and who taught religion and black studies courses in one of the liberal arts colleges offered a similar perspective.

One has to be aware how scholarship is evaluated. It isn't necessarily important to me because I'm tenured, but it was before. One has to be concerned about how the institution is evaluating the scholarship because most scholarship is looked at in the context of a particular field. And so outside evaluators become crucial. . . . So that's always a concern with interdisciplinary scholarship in that junior faculty also have to think about their careers—promotion and tenure, that kind of thing. [U]

Not all informants, however, believed that their interdisciplinary work would stand in the way of tenure or promotion. An untenured university anthropologist was confident that his tenure bid would be successful despite—or perhaps as a result of—his forays into other disciplines.

> There are expectations that the university and the department have for somebody to be tenured and you can meet those using any number of styles. I don't think that being an interdisciplinary person is going to preclude meeting those things. The department is a diverse, but friendly department, and a fair amount of care has gone into hiring and finding people that are not—that can get along with one another. [S]

Working in a research university that vocally and financially supported interdisciplinarity no doubt influenced his opinion. A colleague in another department was also confident, although to a lesser extent, about his prospects for a successful tenure review. A recently hired assistant professor, he was banking on the fact that he clearly fit the position for which he was hired. Nonetheless he felt the need to market his work carefully.

> In the back of my mind there's this little worry: I could get caught between disciplines, each discipline saying "Well, he's not really what we do." But I definitely fit the category that my job was advertised as. And the university, also, has developed lots of interdisciplinary institutes, so [it] seems to be a fairly interdisciplinary place. . . . I think I have to publish stuff that is either theoretical/methodological questions of aesthetics and theory or I publish stuff in twentieth-century Germany and I try not to range outside of that. I think the horror stories I've heard about not getting tenure is they think you are too diffuse—and I think I have to focus on that. [E]

Opposition to interdisciplinarity can be painfully apparent in hiring and tenure decisions. An assistant professor of psychology revealed that when she finished a postdoctoral appointment, she wasn't certain she still wanted an academic career, "in part because of my graduate experiences and in part because it didn't seem like I just strongly fit anywhere." At her postdoctoral site the researchers did not all understand "what I was doing, or what it was about, or why it was important." Despite having a powerful ally in her corner, the appointment ended, and no continuation was offered.

> I took [a] two-year appointment at a university with the understanding that we would explore opportunities for a tenure-stream appointment. The

psych department there was a much smaller department, a much more mainstream department. There was a chairperson who was trying to push them my way, but they went with someone who was more sort of traditional mainline. I think the consensus of the department was what I was doing was not psychology at all and it wasn't really relevant to the questions psychologists were asking. So I left. [T]

This informant's next position was in a tenure-track position. After celebrating a positive interim review at her current institution, she was now taking great care to present and explain her work to departmental colleagues who would soon vote on her tenure case.

One of the things that I have to do is be more explicit about why this is relevant to whatever three or four disciplines I'm in. I certainly recognize the importance of doing that. I'm more willing to do that and less willing to approach my work in a way that doesn't seem natural because I don't know how to do it that other way. [T]

This work was time consuming, she argued, but necessary. She too felt the key to acceptance was positioning her work and linking it to recognized work in different fields.

Unfortunately, what I find is that if people don't understand what you are doing, they decide that it's wrong, that it's not right and worthy as opposed to the norm, because no one wants to say "I don't really understand what you are doing." . . . It just means that you have to do so much more additional work framing it and linking with all the right people and all of that. There still are people who say, "Well, yeah, that's interesting, but why is it important?" and so I just think that's an ongoing struggle. [T]

A tenured associate professor at the same institution also took precautions before her review but abandoned these once she had achieved tenure:

I was coming up for tenure and so I wrote some papers to tell people what I had been doing all these years in the field and some of them were accepted. The journals asked me to make some revisions and resubmit them.

And once I had tenure I quit all of that because I knew it was just to get tenure. [L]

The strategies of playing by the rules, or at least making it look like they were, pushed informants to define carefully an area of interdisciplinary research. Most attempted to simulate the depth of specialization perceived to be the basis of good disciplinary work. These tactics were intended to allay colleagues' fears about interdisciplinary work by packaging it in accordance with disciplinary norms.

Informants' comments about interdisciplinary scholarship reveal the presumption that such work poses a risk to faculty. Still, untenured informants pressed on and tenured individuals recalled similar actions and attitudes during their first years as faculty. A biologist claimed to have known that his interdisciplinary work was a concern during his tenure review but believed a supportive provost would serve as a safety net. Another informant claimed to be more daring.

> I think it's about two years, give or take some, that I got tenure. The weird thing is I decided I would do this before [I had tenure]—recognized that [it] could be grossly self-destructive, at least in the sense of the powers that be, and I am so stubborn I just said "I don't care if I get tenure or not." Or more to the point, I did care but you know I'm going to fight you if I don't get this. I think I have earned it and I will present myself [for tenure review], but I will be damned if I am going to turn myself into you along the way. I'm going as myself or I go in flames. [J]

A number of other informants also expressed a disregard for the common wisdom about refraining from interdisciplinary work before tenure. Now tenured, they either beat the odds, or they provide evidence that departments and institutions are not as opposed to interdisciplinarity as is often reported.

Tenure reviews were not always uneventful, and a few provided unwelcome surprises. Two informants in different fields at the same university were awarded tenure despite departmental colleagues' critiques of their interdisciplinary scholarship. One informant had pursued clearly disciplinary work until shortly before her tenure review:

> I came up for tenure this year, which I got, but it's that my newer work
> met with some resistance in my department . . . the commentary that was
> passed on to me from my tenure committee was that they felt that my new
> project didn't really seem like me, that it seemed like it was sending me
> out in directions I shouldn't be going. [B1]

She was surprised by this reaction, having considered her home department
very hospitable to feminist work because it had sustained "a long working relationship with women's studies." She struggled to understand this perceived
contradiction between the response accorded her work and openness to feminist scholarship.

> I feel like there's a kind of lag time between people's genuine interest in
> interdisciplinary work and intellectual or conceptual commitment to it. I
> guess it's a lag time between people's commitment to something in some
> sort of ideal sense and what happens when issues of evaluation and terri-
> tory emerge. . . . I have wonderful colleagues who totally support what I
> do, but it's when the institution has to do the things that it does, then that's
> when I think the conservatism comes out. [B1]

To exonerate her departmental colleagues, she suggested that the real source
of trouble was the administration and structure of the university.

> We are in this strange position right now where universities, up to the top
> level administration, give a lot of positive lip service to the idea of interdis-
> ciplinarity but the systems of evaluation that we all have to go through are
> still very bound in traditional disciplinary concerns. [B1]

Another informant described her tenure battle as openly acrimonious. She
had been hired by a department that was populated by a number of highly
regarded individuals doing interdisciplinary work: "They said, 'You would fit
right in here because we're all sort of working across disciplines and we're really excited about that.' That's why I chose this place over the other offers
around the country" [P]. But when a few key individuals in the department
left the institution, "the balance of power" shifted and she and other new, in-

terdisciplinary hires were left to fend for themselves: "I was just increasingly miserable because I really felt they were not accepting the kind of teaching I was doing and the kind of research I was doing" [P].

Many members of the department, she said, responded poorly to her interdisciplinary research:

> A lot of my colleagues didn't recognize some of the things I was citing and they were angry that I wasn't citing standard texts. [These] were woven in to some extent and I was also studying a [topic] that was [disciplinary]— but to them, it was too way out. They just didn't recognize what they were reading because it was innovative, because it was bringing to bear a lot of different sources that they weren't familiar with. [P]

Her case divided the department, and although she had strong support from a subset of departmental colleagues, the intervention of colleagues elsewhere in the university was needed to seal the decision to award tenure. With the support of the administration, she renegotiated her appointment and joined another department at the university.

Regardless of their experiences and their concerns about departmental relations and responses to interdisciplinarity, these two informants praised their institution on the whole for fostering interdisciplinarity. Institutional and departmental contexts at this institution, however, were clearly in conflict. Encouraged by administrative rhetoric, by collegial encouragement, and by financial incentives for interdisciplinary work, these individuals were blindsided by the negative reactions of departmental colleagues.

Whereas tenure and promotion decisions might not be as troublesome in smaller institutions where standards for tenure are based as much (or more) on quality of teaching as on research productivity, faculty in the liberal arts colleges had their own set of concerns about the impact of interdisciplinarity on colleagues. In these institutions interdisciplinary teaching created financial and personnel problems for their home departments and, occasionally, for the faculty member who wanted to teach a course collaboratively.

> If I team teach a course with another faculty member, my department is missing a faculty slot. And I have heard grumblings in the past about

whether we could afford to do that if we are to maintain a certain effort per student. [F1]

College policies on team teaching and course loads affected departmental colleagues who had to pick up the slack. One informant worried about the implications of team teaching and concluded that most people on his campus chose not to burden their colleagues.

> These days with shrinking resources, it becomes more difficult to do that and my guess is that a lot of people would do it as an overload. I can't speak for them, but if the opportunity arose I would not say I'm not going to do it if I don't get release time. I would say, "Gee, that sounds like fun." [C1]

Faculty members themselves are scarce resources for interdisciplinary undergraduate programs. At least four informants were recruited to teach courses in women's studies programs in their institutions. A political scientist was recruited to teach in an interdisciplinary public policy program. A zoologist was asked to teach undergraduate psychology courses during his postdoctoral appointment. Although these informants were not trained in these areas, they acceded to the requests. Most were solicited for interdisciplinary teaching stints early in their careers, before they had been awarded tenure. For most their first course marked the beginning of a continuing relationship with an interdisciplinary program or a commitment to interdisciplinary work in itself. Mirroring the often accidental nature of interdisciplinary collaboration, these invitations were also serendipitous opportunities that prompted interdisciplinary scholarship of various kinds.

Two professors of economics at different liberal arts colleges were asked to teach courses about women and economic issues through the women's studies programs on their campuses.

> People said, "Oh, gee here is a woman and she is in the economics department. Why don't we see if. . . ." And, interestingly enough I had no training in that area, so that all of my women's studies stuff is kind of self-taught, you know, get involved in the program and see what you can do. [G]

When I came here my areas of expertise were money making and industrial organizations, and when I got here they wanted me to teach women in the labor force. My dissertation was on the . . . distribution of income, which is a macro problem, but it really has nothing much to do with labor force participation. They gave me money to kind of prep for that. Then I started teaching women in the labor force. [B]

Institutions occasionally acknowledged the challenge associated with preparing interdisciplinary courses. An associate professor of English literature obtained departmental funds for course development, but such resources are not common and they may be particularly difficult to obtain in the case of interdisciplinary courses.

Women's studies was a hospitable place for me to develop an interdisciplinary course. They enabled me to do this not only by being enthusiastic about the course and feeling like it fit into the curriculum, but by also providing me with certain kinds of resources. I don't think this is secret, but it's so wonderful that I've never really gotten over it—I think this dates back to the time when nobody was trained in interdisciplinary studies, nobody was trained in women's studies, and it was seen as a kind of extra burden on faculty to teach women's studies because it was always taking them out of their primary field. Here, every time you teach a course in women's studies you get research money to support the development of the class or whatever you want to use it for. [B1]

These funds allowed her to hire a teaching assistant. Teaching this course, she noted, resulted in ongoing research on the subject. She was in the process of writing a book that was "very interdisciplinary in its method and its scope."

Interdisciplinary programs do not always have the power to hire their own faculty; many borrow faculty from disciplinary departments to provide courses for students in the program. For the directors of such programs, negotiating for faculty time is a constant activity and a constant concern:

There are a number of people who have taught in the program over a rather lengthy period of time—for well over twenty years—and they've done that on a regular basis, contributing at least one course, and sometimes two courses a year and more. . . . But then there are people that are on the margins—who if their department would say, "We can't afford to have this course taught this year because we need something for our majors and we need you to do it"—then there is that tug and pull. And particularly if they are individuals who don't have tenure. . . . It hasn't been a huge problem, it's just always a concern, always something that we are aware of and have to anticipate and be prepared to address. [U]

This program director claimed that the need to negotiate for faculty rarely escalated into a real problem at his institution; at another institution, however, directors and program faculty related contrasting experiences. One informant with an appointment in an interdisciplinary program chided her institution for marginalizing interdisciplinary programs with unfavorable personnel policies.

The bureaucratic order, the way the power channels are structured, is so hardbound, so disciplinary. They're departmental powers and the interdisciplinary programs lack the power to hire, fire, tenure, and everything else and we borrow all our personnel from departments who have to give us up as a grace gift, which understandably they're not thrilled to do. [J]

The former director of an honors program at the same institution described what he perceived as pressure to make the program less interdisciplinary and to recruit more faculty from the departments to teach honors courses.

While I was director, and I have to kind of assume that the same pressures are out there now, there was a constant drumbeat to make the program more disciplinary-based from sources around the university—partially [from] departments not willing to give up their faculty to do interdisciplinary things: partially [from] faculty themselves either not knowing what interdisciplinary work was or not wanting to do it, partially coming from higher administration saying that the real thinking goes on in discipline. While I was director—and I'm pretty sure it's still going on now—that push to make it interdisciplinary is constantly resisted. The attempts to get interdisciplinary courses in the program I think are still there, but it's bucking all these other trends that are out there. [O]

Another informant actively involved in interdisciplinary teaching and research activities confirmed the difficulties of the former director. He argued that the university administration gave lip service to interdisciplinary programs but withheld budgetary and other forms of support.

> Ever since I have been on this campus, there have been numerous verbal statements of support for interdisciplinary teaching by administrators. It seems to be something ceremonial, it's a kind of ceremonial cant that they exude. They think they're supposed to say it, they say, "I'm completely behind you." But then something is missing that would be an indicia of whether they are completely behind you and that is budgetarily—first, you're lucky if you have a budget, there is almost zero support for you budgetarily—that would be a sine qua non; you don't have budgetary support, you don't have support. Secondly, you would be able to recruit faculty from departments without having to beg—"Please could we possibly, once every five years, have a faculty member"—because departmental chairs would then know that this is something that is smiled upon. In the interdisciplinary programs I have been involved in on this campus, the director is a beggar and frequently takes the remains that the department doesn't want to use. [F]

Support, he continued, did not only mean budgets and personnel, but recognition as well. "Very little of that," he complained, happened on his campus: "on this campus and on many campuses that I visited, a few dedicated, wonderful people are really carrying the banner of interdisciplinarity while everybody else watches, hoots, and hollers quietly sometimes from the sidelines" [F].

A tenured associate professor serving as the director of an interdisciplinary program talked about her choice to direct this program rather than to stay in her home department. That department, she felt, had become a claustrophobic environment.

> There is a real fear of disciplinary encroachment on the part of the department. This department does not collaborate well with others. It feels resentful when its faculty want to teach in interdisciplinary programs. It discourages people from taking different theoretical approaches to the

discipline. . . . So I guess one of the reasons I wanted to be director is not just my commitment to the field, but because I wanted to get out of my department because I felt as if they were stifling me. It was just so restrictive. [C]

Academic departments can have profound influences on the lives of the faculty working within their confines. Through their attitudes and actions, departmental colleagues and chairpersons can discourage or encourage interdisciplinarity and those who would pursue it. Regardless of how they interpreted colleagues' attitudes and actions, the informants in this study engaged in interdisciplinary work: the absence of favorable environments or the existence of openly hostile ones did not deter them. Although a few had ceased affiliation with particular programs, none had abandoned interdisciplinarity completely. Even untenured faculty, who stood to suffer considerably if colleagues discredited their work, continued apace and developed explanations that would satisfy departmental colleagues and external reviewers who would influence their promotion and tenure. Every college and university faculty member, of course, may not be willing or able to ignore unfavorable opinions and disheartening actions from their colleagues, and there may have been faculty on each campus who were dissuaded from doing interdisciplinary work by the fear of disapproval or sanction. These individuals were not included in this study because they could not comment from their own experience on interdisciplinary research and/or teaching.

The Role of the Institution

Although we often describe higher education institutions as monoliths with sets of prescribed characteristics based on their status as research, baccalaureate, or other types of institutions, each institution comprises a set of departments with distinctive cultures. It is therefore difficult to generalize about an institution without flattening important topographic details. However, when describing the climate for interdisciplinarity in their home institution, informants typically generalized a commitment to interdisciplinarity—or lack of a commitment—from institutional policies and practices. Where manifestations of institutional support were obvious, for example, in the form of joint appointments or special funding, informants deduced commitment; the lack of institutional support was interpreted as a lack of interest or as resistance to interdisciplinarity.

At liberal arts colleges, where the standards for tenure favor teaching over research—informants typically described a sixty-forty split in emphasis—faculty often commented on how administrative policies influenced the willingness, or ability, to do interdisciplinary teaching. At the research university, where research was weighted much more heavily than teaching for promotion and tenure, faculty more often discussed administrative policies that affected research activities. The faculty informants at the doctoral university talked about the influence of the institutional climate on both research and teaching but tended to comment more often on interdisciplinary research policies.

Perceptions of the institutional climate were moderately consistent at three of the four institutions. Faculty at two institutions, the research university and one of the liberal arts colleges, perceived their institutions as particularly supportive of interdisciplinary efforts. At the other liberal arts college, there were fewer comments about support from the institution or colleagues. Faculty at the doctoral university offered varying assessments but tended to see the university as apathetic toward, rather than supportive of, interdisciplinarity.

Perhaps because it is hard to generalize about the institutional context of a university with numerous schools and thousands of students, the research university informants tended to talk very generally about the institutional climate for interdisciplinary work, occasionally citing administrative policies to support their assessments.

> This place is clearly more encouraging and supportive of interdisciplinarity than any other major institution I can think of. [S]

> People work across disciplines, across departments a lot more than they do other places, so I've felt more comfortable here than I have in other institutions. [T]

> . This is one of the most interdisciplinary places I've ever heard of. The fact that you can come and have a joint appointment makes it much easier to do the kind of work that I do. [L]

> I just found that [this university] fosters, in the social sciences, the ability to work across groups, across departmental structures. . . . You'll see a lot of people here who have joint appointments. [A]

> People have always collaborated a lot here. People have always had joint appointments and played with their different [appointment] fractions in interesting ways. [P]

A few individuals talked specifically about the university administration and its role in supporting interdisciplinary work. A full professor with varied interdisciplinary interests noted that finding support for seminars and new programs was often an uphill battle, but he recognized the complex and competing influences on administrators:

> It takes real leadership from department heads and deans and executive offices to recognize and nurture interdisciplinary work, to see when it is valuable and when it is just garbage, to be able to support it in spite of institutional structure which is very discipline oriented. Having worked several years to start an interdisciplinary program here, I can tell you that it is no trivial task to have convinced the administration, or some part of the administration, that something is of value and should be nurtured even though it doesn't fit neatly into the disciplinary structure. Mind you, that is despite the fact that the institution's public posture is to encourage interdisciplinary work. There are still many barriers. . . . We live in an era of constrained resources and because of that there is a push to become much more conservative and much more focused and narrow. [E1]

Another informant, also directing an interdisciplinary program, was grateful for the administrative support this research was presently receiving, but castigated the administration for its conservative attitudes toward new ideas.

> Even though the university favors interdisciplinary work, I don't always find that the administration is really willing to go out and do something about it. They've been very good to us lately—they've been great to us lately—but it took about four or five years. I think [the] administration is

> extremely conservative and doesn't view their role as helping to bring new intellectual directions into the university. They view their role much more as trying to make sure that bad things don't happen and not that good things do. But lately that's been changing. [The work we have are doing] has just been very successful and so we've had really good luck with the administration on that one. We're getting outside grants and stuff, but this is very, very expensive research. [G1]

One professor was surprised by her success in attracting the administration's favor, but she acknowledged that other colleagues may not have found the same administrative support for their interdisciplinary efforts: "It is interesting because a lot of my colleagues complain that we are not getting support, that we need more support. I have felt personally that all I have gotten is support for every single interdisciplinary gesture I have made" [H1].

Conservatism regarding interdisciplinarity is reflected in the tendency for funding to beget more funding. At least one informant argued that the university administration was reluctant to fund unproven ventures. Particularly when research projects are very costly to run, as was the case with this informant's work, the university looks for outward signs of success before committing its own limited funds for interdisciplinary research. For this reason the university always appears to be a step behind in terms of funding for cutting-edge research. External catalysts such as foundations, rather than universities, often spearhead innovative research programs. With so many projects in line for institutional support by the university, only those with a very high probability of success are funded.

Although a few individuals at the research university felt that the administrative policies and practices could be improved, most believed the university offered an encouraging context in which to pursue interdisciplinary work. At the doctoral university, informants' perceptions of the institutional climate for interdisciplinary research and teaching were more varied.

An associate professor with a long history of involvement with several interdisciplinary programs on this campus detected some support for interdisciplinarity, although he admitted it was less than he would liked to have seen.

> I think a lot of [interdisciplinary research] happens. It would be hard to say the university encourages interdisciplinarity. I think it supports it, but I

think that a lot of us who do it would like to see more support for that. But we recognize that there are other interests that are competing for limited dollars. [X]

Another associate professor with a history of involvement in interdisciplinary programs took the opposite view, contending that the university actively discouraged interdisciplinary programs and efforts.

> I think the university just resists [it] hammer and tongs . . . [when you] establish a community like women's studies that is by definition interdisciplinary because all the channels of power and privilege and advancement are disciplinary. People have been systematically penalized for their participation in these kinds of ventures and because they're not stupid, they tend not to do this unless they have other goals. [J]

At both the research and doctoral universities, informants called for greater sensitivity to the needs of faculty who pursued interdisciplinary work. An assistant professor at the research university who had difficulty finding a mentor during graduate school because of her interdisciplinary interests was now concerned about nurturing interdisciplinary faculty:

> I think generally for someone who has interdisciplinary interests in either traditional departments or even nontraditional departments, it's very difficult to get mentoring. . . . [Y]ou have all these people from all these disciplines, but they're being psychologists, or they're being historians, or they're being sociologists, so they're not necessarily interdisciplinary in their work. Perhaps this is changing in some programs. I don't know. [T]

An informant who also served as an administrator in the doctoral university commented on mentoring as well as other forms of support for "career interdisciplinarians."

> If we are thinking about the career path of someone who truly wants to be an interdisciplinary scholar and teacher, maybe we're going to have to make some allowances. Maybe we're going to have to say "Well, this person is maybe going to have to do a little bit of reading and thinking and

work here and maybe we're going to have to provide some on-site support.
Maybe they're going to need two or three different areas rather than just
one in their home department." You have to think about working differently. And that's where I think mentoring across departments, across programs, is really important because the traditional notion that you get
mentored in your own program, in your own department, isn't sufficient
for someone who's working across the disciplines. You need something
else. [N]

Perhaps because of their long engagement in interdisciplinary teaching and
research and their interest in conceptual interdisciplinary research projects
that tended to be least understood by colleagues, these informants were particularly attuned to these special needs.

As they did at the university sites, informants' perceptions of the environments at the two liberal arts college differed considerably. Informants at one
college were generally happy with their institutional lives and the attitude of
colleagues toward interdisciplinary work. Interdisciplinary activities at this institution had a long history of administrative support and there were several
well-established interdisciplinary programs. A number of informants at this
college commented on the conducive atmosphere created by college policies.
Informants who taught in interdisciplinary programs as well as in their home
departments were particularly appreciative. A biologist who was instrumental
in the development of two interdisciplinary programs on her campus talked
about the interdisciplinary atmosphere that attracted her to the college:

When I came here to interview . . . they took me to lunch at the student
union. And we sat at a table and we were joined by faculty, just by chance
I think, by faculty from other departments and the thing that made me
accept this job was the conversation that happened at that lunch. It was
like being an undergraduate again and having friends come back to the
dorm who were majoring in all different things and talking about what
exciting thing had happened in their class or lab that day. And that has
stayed true. A lot of the intellectual excitement of this place, in my experience, happens outside of my department. I have had very regular contact
with people outside the department since I have been here and that's taken
different forms. I've team taught seven different times with people in eco-

nomics, anthropology, and English, [those] are the primary fields. I was involved in helping develop [two interdisciplinary] programs. [A1]

A sociologist acknowledged that same atmosphere as a reason for staying at the institution:

I am lucky to be at a place that has been comfortable with interdisciplinary programs and activities over a long period of time. So it's fairly easy for me to work here having the kind of focus and orientation I have than it would be at some other place, I think. [Doing interdisciplinary work is] important for me personally and *then* if it's reinforced by colleagues and the institution, that even increases its importance. [U]

Because teaching is the primary activity at this institution, interdisciplinary teaching was a frequent topic of discussion during interviews. Informants were generally pleased that they had opportunities to teach such courses, but a few expressed mild concerns. A political scientist worried about the quality of teaching in interdisciplinary courses.

We all recognize that we have problems in teaching interdisciplinary courses. In fact, the overall evaluations for people teaching in interdisciplinary programs here are lower; the courses get lower evaluations from the students. But there is no sustained record to try and address those issues. I think the programs might be open to holding teaching seminars on how to do them. We have a teaching forum here where they have devoted sessions, some of which I have participated in as part of the panel, for example, on how to teach controversial texts or whatever. So the campus is committed to interdisciplinary studies and to try to make it work. I don't question that. But there is a big difference between saying that, providing a few opportunities, and really understanding the kind of difficulties that someone faces when they're trying to do that job. I think *that* struggle is pretty individual and there hasn't been a collective effort. [I]

Another informant, a biologist, worried about the preparation time associated with interdisciplinary courses and implied that an alternative would save faculty and departmental time.

Team teaching is not done here like I have seen at other places. Some schools, for example, do their introductory biology courses in large lectures and multiple faculty trade off doing lectures, but they each have a lab section. So, they sacrifice the personal involvement in the lecture level but they still retain it at the lab level. And the faculty reduce their preparation time by only having to do part of that class. . . . I would love, for instance, to teach an interdisciplinary course with a geologist or some other faculty member. But the department can't afford really to let me go to do that. That's the constraint more than anything else is. [F1]

Although the administration appeared outwardly supportive, he suggested it was also responsible for discouraging interdisciplinary teaching. He argued that while the administration claimed that the most important thing to consider was not the teaching load, but students' educational experience, "someone is calculating that class as half a class per faculty member."

Still, informants at this institution more often praised the administration for supporting interdisciplinary teaching than chastised it for not doing so. An economist considered course development funds provided by the administration to be critical in encouraging interdisciplinary teaching: "That was an important thing, that we could get funding, because you wouldn't ordinarily think of [faculty from two very different disciplines] at most institutions and getting any support for doing it together" [W]. This individual often traveled to other institutions to describe his institutions' unique economics curriculum. He commented on the critical need for incentives for curricular change:

Whenever I go to other institutions . . . and help them think about curricular matters in economics or teach about our lab program in economics. . . . I am very careful to point out to people that if they want to bring about change and they really want it to be successful then they have to make an institutional commitment that supports faculty as they develop their ability to do different things and move in different directions and become interdisciplinary . . . you gotta have some support and this college was good in two ways I think. Number one it supported us financially. [My colleague] and I have probably had four or five summer grants over the years. Usually that happens when we are either at the beginning or at some critical stage in the process. [W]

The other way in which the college supported interdisciplinarity was by recognizing and rewarding interdisciplinary research:

> [The college] has been very willing to recognize interdisciplinary work, particularly research, as having value at the time of contract renewal, promotions, tenure. That is important because if you want to create an environment where people do that kind of thing, then they have to know that when they get to those important crossroads in their career, somebody isn't going to say "Well, you haven't done any traditional economics" or "You haven't done enough traditional economics." [W]

An associate professor of political science echoed the belief that interdisciplinary research was considered as legitimate as disciplinary research.

> The quality of publication can be an issue here, but it is not a disciplinary concern. In that respect, I don't have the problems that I would have at an institution where someone might say, "That is a good journal, but it is . . . one of those squishy interdisciplinary kind of things." That could be a concern somewhere. Never here. [C1]

A professor at the same college was not convinced that interdisciplinarity was always viewed as legitimate scholarship. Having relied on the backing of a strong provost during her tenure review, she argued that the present administration was not as committed to interdisciplinary scholarship.

> I think it is much easier to evaluate work in traditional disciplines and I think it takes a lot of courage on the part of a department and on the part of an institution to really look carefully at what people are doing and evaluate it. It's much easier to look at where they are publishing and to look for—the provost and president use words like trajectory—a research trajectory. They've backed off from that but they did at one point make a public statement that what they were looking for was a sense of development and building blocks and a direction that somebody is going in. I think that's kind of the instinct of the administrative animal and of people who don't think very much about these issues. Yet I think to make any

progress you do need people who make a sharp left turn at some point or do branch out in some way. [A1]

This informant's comments are a reminder that just as departmental contexts for interdisciplinary scholarship change as faculty move in and out, institutional environments can also be transient. Strong positions for or against interdisciplinarity are more often the result of strong leadership than an established institutional mission, although there are a few U.S. institutions that do have such interdisciplinary missions. This suggests that individuals who are able to exert strong leadership may have a considerable impact on the lives of faculty within an institution.

At the other liberal arts college, informants were much more critical of faculty and administrative attitudes toward interdisciplinarity. One informant claimed that the administration was asking too much of faculty by encouraging interdisciplinary teaching and research efforts. She believed the administration's position on interdisciplinarity was ill informed.

I think the college speaks with a forked tongue sometimes. They would like a lot of things from us. There is still a basic set of stuff that they want, which is that we have to teach well and obviously you are more comfortable doing that if you are in your discipline, at least it is going to be easier if you are in your discipline. . . . But at the same time, I felt like the way I am going to get judged in the end has to do with . . . if I can do that and be interdisciplinary or show lots of boundary crossing kinds of activities as well. . . . And in some senses I think the college sometimes pats you on the head for stuff that's pretty silly or looks eclectic when in fact it is really sort of filler . . . . It seems the college is satisfied with superficial interdisciplinary stuff. [Z]

Another faculty member, a geologist who considered all his teaching and research interdisciplinary, took issue with what he perceived as a narrow definition of interdisciplinarity on the part of the administration as well as other colleagues:

What always has bothered me has been that the concept of interdisciplinarity has had a different meaning across the street, in the nonscience realm of college, than it does here. It used to be on our evaluation forms. We would have to describe the interdisciplinary efforts that we made. I would write I teach [a course I consider interdisciplinary]. I knew that didn't count. What counted was that interdisciplinary course [I taught with a colleague from another department] and it was one of the few courses that combined a scientist and a nonscientist. That was the view of interdisciplinary. We have many courses taught by two scientists, or scientists using two different scientific disciplines; those didn't count. I would like to see that broadened out so they do count. It's just as significant if a physicist and a chemist collaborate as a sociologist and an English professor. In many ways, some of the same kinds of barriers and cross-fertilization take place. [L1]

Others also complained about discipline-oriented colleagues. An associate professor who was a member of a merged program was exasperated by reactionary colleagues.

There are factions as in any institution. I think there is probably a group of folks who do not believe you can do interdisciplinary work no matter what you think you're doing and would resist it and do resist it whenever that topic comes up. . . . I guess that there's a cluster of folks on this campus who never cease to surprise me in what they think because it is so opposite of what I think. [M]

A professor of economics claimed that some colleagues masked deeper concerns about interdisciplinarity by developing a pragmatic viewpoint against it:

not necessarily everyone agrees that what you are doing in an interdisciplinary framework should be done. Some people see it as taking away from the department's resources. There is much sensitivity to that. Here, for example, we have contractual agreements with programs to supply faculty. . . . [Then] there are people who would say, "We don't value this kind of teaching experience and our involvement in the program does not help us in any way professionally." It's not just a resource argument. [H]

Informants at this institution continued to teach interdisciplinary courses and do interdisciplinary research, although they sometimes felt their commitment difficult to maintain. While supportive departments sometimes mitigated the lack of a facilitating institutional atmosphere, personal preferences may have been the real motivating force. A number of faculty I interviewed suggested that what they appreciated most about their institutions was that they did not dictate the type of research that was acceptable. As one informant stated: "So I see something interesting and no one else seems to be working on it, I can work on it. . . . I can stop doing something, too, if it becomes boring. I can say, yeah, this is boring and I can just not do it and go do something else" [L1].

While policies, practices, and pedantry might have dissuaded informants from interdisciplinary research and teaching, other institutional characteristics seemed to encourage interdisciplinary interactions. According to informants at the liberal arts colleges, the small size of their institutions fostered interdisciplinary conversation and collaborations.

Think about the economics department at a big university. There are, what, fifty faculty? The people that you talk to, that you have lunch with, that you go to the restroom with, are all economists and that's got to make a difference. It seems to me it has to make a difference. Here we certainly get thrown together a lot more by virtue of the smallness of the place. Just looking at this hall, we have economists, we have classical studies people, we have historians, we have a French person down the hall and that makes it more natural to get into this kind of thing. But my guess would be that it happens more easily and you have to work harder at it at a bigger institution. [G]

I will always tell people that I learned a lot by being here and interacting outside of the discipline as opposed to inside it—most of my contacts are focused in this wing [of the building]. It's not like your own floor or your own building so that your disciplinary colleagues are the only people you see. I like it here. I think I have learned a lot by being here that I wouldn't have if I were somewhere else. And I like it. Other people would not. [H]

Even at the smaller of the two universities, an informant suggested that the size of the university had an impact on the frequency of interdisciplinary conversations and research.

> I think it's an environment that fosters interdisciplinary research because it's small. . . . You meet [people from other disciplines] on a daily basis . . . because of serving on committees, interdisciplinary programs. I meet them because they come to use [my lab equipment], and so forth, there are a number of mechanisms. I think probably a larger number of mechanisms for mixing up the disciplines [exist] here than there are at larger universities. [R]

While departmental and institutional barriers were often difficult obstacles, they were not insurmountable. Determined informants pursued interdisciplinary research and teaching with or without the help of their colleagues, their departments, or their institutions. They welcomed some assistance but did not necessarily see it as essential.

Higher education theory suggests that institutional type is a powerful influence on academic life. In this study, however, institutional type seemed less important to informants than the perceived climate for interdisciplinarity. The kinds of institutional support for interdisciplinary scholarship that informants found helpful—for example, funds for course development, faculty seminars, or research programs—were not reflections of institutional type but rather of administrative philosophy. Clearly, however, structural and funding supports for interdisciplinarity provided incentives for interdisciplinary research and teaching, and institutional needs could motivate interdisciplinary scholarship. Interdisciplinary programs such as environmental or women's studies, and merged departments such as sociology/anthropology recruited informants to teach interdisciplinary courses and advise undergraduates. Even less malleable characteristics of an institution, such as its size, facilitated interdisciplinary interactions.

Disciplinary Boundaries and Border Crossings

Despite the perceived resistance of departmental and institutional colleagues, several informants thought their disciplines were turning in the direction of interdisciplinarity. Some felt that they had anticipated this trend with their work, others thought they were "catching a wave," and still others were surprised at the slow pace and continuing opposition. Several informants identified specific moments when their disciplines appeared to open their doors to different kinds of scholarship. Not all faculty informants commented on the disciplinary environment for interdisciplinary work; some chose to focus on other, presumably more immediate departmental and institutional environments. As might be predicted, informants from the research universities discussed disciplinary contexts most often, perhaps because the opinions of these colleagues were important in determining who gets published, who gets funded, and who gets tenured. Informants at the liberal arts colleges and doctoral university, however, shared concerns about the state of one discipline, economics, where resistance to interdisciplinary work was gauged to be exceptionally strong.

An anthropologist talked about being in the vanguard of interdisciplinary work in her discipline.

> I was doing historical anthropology and its nexus with anthropology before it became the hottest thing in anthropology, before the historic turn. So in a sense the work was an opening to where anthropology went. The difference is that when I applied for my first job about ten years ago, some people were uncomfortable that I wasn't doing anthropology. Five years ago, another institution came after me *for* what I do, in interdisciplinary terms. That was a shift that you could see. [H1]

This informant argued that changes in society necessitated changes in the way anthropology was done; in essence, the discipline followed along.

> It's a whole shift in the world economy. Who anthropologists are going to study is no longer as clear as it was when there was certain governments backing certain kinds of work—when peasants were peasants and when

the Third World was a place that you could identify as a place. Whereas if you look at the sort of transnational economy right now, the Third World has come home. Europe is dealing all the time with its former colonized populations. So it's a really different set of problems. [H1]

Another anthropologist contended that the debate about interdisciplinarity in anthropology was still raging, citing a series of articles in an issue of the flagship journal of the discipline.

There are a bunch of folks who think that anthro shouldn't be going off in all of these different directions away from *science*, away from anthropology. All people are doing is becoming more interdisciplinary and overlapping with interests in other disciplines, but that threatens folks who perceive themselves to be the models of the way it's supposed to be, who haven't changed, who are still using theories that they regard as truthful. [M]

This debate, she noted, was also being conducted via electronic mail. Over spring break, she received 150 mail messages on the issue. A member of a merged department that combined anthropology and sociology, she commented on the shared roots of these disciplines.

Historically we're the same discipline. . . . The early anthropologists were called sociologists, scholars of society. Turn of the century, late 1800s turn of the century, sociology and anthropology kind of fragmented and went different ways. So we share forefathers—not foremothers, forefathers— people who were looking at society and organizations in society. Sociologists, as I understand it, went more into society as a whole, theories to explain large groups of people, patterns in behavior, but society at large. Now that doesn't mean they don't have theories for the individual too but their relationship is more society and people, patterns, populations. Anthropology first of course was colonial and went into cross-cultural studies, the "other" and we have to get over that because that was nasty and ugly. But the early studies looked at *other* than us. I guess that was one of the traditional distinctions. Certainly, sociologists do cross-cultural studies now and anthropologists look at the United States. Now the differences are more the theoretical underpinnings. [M]

A jointly appointed professor of history and sociology also noted a turning point in history that allowed a sociologist, as she was by training, to use historiography.

> When I first started [doing interdisciplinary research], history was grabbing from sociology, which made my connections with it pretty easy. And when I first began, it was in a very social history phase, even to the extent of doing quantitative work and I actually did some of that. Increasingly, history has become enamored with, first, anthropology and then literary theory and so the kind of discursive turn in history, I think is still very alive and well. [D1]

Interdisciplinarity was easier to accomplish in history, she argued, because it is a discipline that "doesn't develop its own theory but kind of grabs from other disciplines." Sociology, on the other hand, seemed to find interdisciplinarity threatening:

> I think the discipline itself is very fractured. And I think that there are a lot of identity problems. I think what this is all about is what it means to be a sociologist. For some people being a sociologist means certain things; there is a very narrow definition and a fear that the discipline is kind of getting eaten away. [D1]

Although the state of the discipline dismayed her, she hoped that interdisciplinarity was gaining some ground in sociological circles. At her institution, at least, faculty were beginning to discuss the kinds of issues that raised questions about interdisciplinarity.

> I see my own colleagues here, some of them, trying to grapple with these issues and changing to some extent in what they read and a little bit in how they think. There is a little bit of movement, and within the discipline itself, there are signs of movement. There is an engagement with postmodernism, for example. It is sort of around the fringes, but there are

more people doing it now. It is not as though these trends of thought in
the humanities haven't had an impact, they have. But I think that is also
creating reaction on the part of the people who were trained in a particular mode of sociology—I don't want to make it age graded because it is
not. It's not age graded. [Others] are more interested in culture—cultural
sociology is the largest subdivision in sociology now. [D1]

Like the anthropologist who recounted the history of sociology and anthropology, she was intrigued by contrasting departmental arrangements for history
and sociology that she saw outside the United States. As a visiting professor in a
British university, she learned that these departments commingled much more
than they did in the United States:

Social history in many British universities . . . is located in sociology. . . .
I was in the sociology department doing history, so it was seamless.
And there was a sociologist who taught the historical methods course, he
did historical sociology. I felt very at home there actually. There
was also a regular history department there and I got to be quite close to
people in that department as well. . . . It seemed to me there weren't rup-
tures there either between the *proper* historians who do political history
and cultural history and intellectual history and the social historians who
are supposedly more sociological. The other thing that helped me was
that in the mid 70s, sociologists became more interested in history, generally, and historical sociology started to grow as a kind of a subfield within
sociology. [D1]

An associate professor of English who had recently been awarded tenure
was surprised when she learned that some faculty on her departmental tenure
committee still resisted the trend toward interdisciplinarity:

I think that the kind of move that I have made from a more sort of linguis-
tic-based approach to literature to a more context-historical interdisciplinary approach to the literature is a general trend within the field of literary studies, so it's not like I am any kind of pioneer and I think that my
trajectory is not an unusual one. However, it's still a problem. [B1]

In contrast an assistant professor of art history thought that he was at the forefront of a movement just beginning to form in his discipline.

> I think I hit quite a wave in a certain sense . . . art history has become so interdisciplinary—through its objects first of all: popular culture, material culture, fine art—and also through the question of methodology: How do we interpret these works? What does each methodology do? How does our methodology limit our vision? How do we open ourselves up to questions of race and gender? [E]

This expansion of art history was responsible for the creation of a new type of art historian—as well as for jobs for new breeds of art historians:

> So suddenly there is not only a debate about the objects of art study, but also a debate about how to study them. So the problem becomes how do we negotiate all these different complex theories? How do we do it? How do we negotiate all this complex information that's coming in from other disciplines? And that's why a person who just does critical theory in the department is becoming more and more important because I am supposed to interpret all this information coming in from other disciplines for the uses of art history right now. [E]

The faculty in his department, he claimed, predicted the need for a position such as his; to remain at the cutting edge of the discipline, they had to move in the direction of interdisciplinarity.

Other disciplines appeared to be changing much more slowly. In economics, for example, informants saw very few signs of change. Some were so subtle that they might be invisible to the uninformed observer. Even small victories, however, were cause for celebration. A tenured, female professor of economics enthusiastically recalled the interest stirred up by a new group of feminist economists at two recent annual meetings of the American Economics Association.

> What's really cool is [that] . . . we've had two sessions there each time and they were the best attended sessions at the whole conference. Because it's

new. It's kind of exciting. It's looking at what we do as economists from a different perspective. It's allowing people to, I think, to bring in other disciplines. It gives a more realistic picture of economic lives. It's not assuming the really strict assumptions that you have to do to get these models to work. So I think it's given people license to really kind of expand their thinking. I think that's why people find it exciting. [B]

Another professor of economics appeared less convinced that substantial change would occur in the discipline any time soon:

I think econ is the slowest of the social sciences because it, quite frankly, regards itself at the top of the social science hierarchy. It pretends to be physics. And it's very resistant to criticism from the outside either by economists who would be considered fringe types of people or *certainly* from other social scientists. People might think this is a bit harsh, but the majority of the economists don't think the majority of the sociologists have much interesting or useful to say. When you get to things like anthropology, forget it. . . . I think as a discipline we have tended to wall ourselves off to a greater extent than some. [G]

However, she, too, eagerly noted what she considered evidence of a movement toward interdisciplinarity:

I actually heard a paper at the national meetings in January that was based on survey data, they actually did questionnaires. I was flabbergasted to see that because that is not considered mainstream research methodology *at all* in economics. That's for sociologists to do and anthropologists, but in economics you need twenty-seven mathematical equations at the front end of your article before it will even be considered for publication in the mainstream journals. That is a bit extreme but not too far off the mark. [G]

She interpreted the appearance of new economics journals as a harbinger of things to come. Still, having experienced little success with her own feminist research in economics, she was cautious about hoping for too much.

I think discontent is starting to become a bit more widespread in economics itself. I think the reason you have a proliferation of new journals is because there are lots of people who have things to say that can't for a variety of reasons get into the mainstream journals. So you have what mainstream people would call fringe journals — "I have got important things to say and the *American Economic Review* won't publish me" and well, and if you have enough people like that and they all get together, well, gee, you have got a new journal. . . . I think that when you see that kind of thing happening that's a signal that there is dissension from the mainstream in a particular discipline. I think in the long run that is probably a good thing. Although there certainly will be a while when all of these new journals come out, when people get their stuff published in them, the ones who are still in a position to make decisions about promotion and tenure and all that other neat stuff will say, "Oh, yes, you have an article but it is in *these*." [G]

Another female economist, also involved in women's studies but at a different institution, also interpreted some signs of change.

I guess now the hottest topic in economics, and this might be where this move towards more interdisciplinary study has helped, is the endogeneity of tastes and preferences, how they really should be part of the [standard economic] model. So I think economists are starting to move to a broader definition of what economics is. They used to just truncate it right there. Now if you can assume that people's tastes and preferences are given . . . you literally do look at costs and you do look at benefits and that's it. But once you start looking at the interaction between those choices and what that could mean for future tastes and preferences, once people kind of evaluate the impact of that decision, then you've got all kinds of things that could happen. [B]

A colleague in the same department also questioned the standard model. His dissatisfaction with the ability of this model to explain change in underdeveloped countries led to his interdisciplinary excursions into other disciplines. Yet he understood the allure of a simple, parsimonious model of the world.

It is so much more comfortable to go with neoclassical theory. It is very elegant. It is very persuasive. It really can be used to explain an awful lot of things that we observe, but I am convinced that part of the reason that it can be used to explain those things is that most economists are white middle-class males. So what we are doing is explaining a world that we would love to have exist. If you are not a white middle-class male, the world looks very different to you and that theory doesn't do nearly as good of job of explaining the world. [W]

He noted that to accommodate his increasingly interdisciplinary viewpoint, he reconfigured himself as an institutional economist, that is, an economist who argued that the standard model was too restrictive. Leaving behind the "98 percent of economists in the U.S." who were trained in neoclassical economics, he was now aligned with "a very small minority" of economists.

Conversations about changes in scientific fields often focused on the influence of people and phenomena external to academia. Two psychologists at different institutions concurred that the "really interesting work" in psychology was happening in the interdisciplinary areas of cognitive science and neuroscience. A professor of psychology expressed a strong opinion about the state of the discipline.

I think psychology as a discipline is largely very ill and I think there are only two areas that are actually adding to knowledge: cognitive science and neuroscience. Both of those are really interdisciplinary things; they overlap with other disciplines. Cognitive science really overlaps with computer science, philosophy, to some extent with neuroscience but primarily computer science, possibly, cognitive psychology. Neuroscience is similar; it's overlapped with psychology with various other sciences. So those areas are inherently interdisciplinary. The rest of psychology is basically moribund these days, partly because it's committed to a set of very narrow methodologies. They're not thinking very hard about how to break loose from those perspectives. [J1]

External influences, he explained, were largely responsible for the stagnation in many areas of the field:

In large part it's very understandable because a lot of external pressure is being put on psychology to do only certain types of things. For example, clinical psychology is under enormous pressure to change everything to short-term criteria-oriented treatment. It is being forced into behavioral models by health care providers who are trying to drive costs down. So talky-talky psychotherapy increasingly is not being done because nobody will pay for it. Everything's short term, everything has to be fit into the framework of the Psychiatric Association's diagnostic manual, the DSM-IV, and psychologists are being dragged along. So that means the research paradigms in clinical psychology don't get beyond things that are definable in terms of that quasi-behavioralist paradigm. [J1]

A cognitive psychologist who was working in both neuroscience and cognitive science talked about the histories of these movements within psychology. Neither movement, he argued, was the result of a natural evolution in thinking within the discipline.

It's not completely natural evolution either in the cognitive science movement, which started in the late 70s, or the cognitive neuroscience movement, which started about ten years later. In both cases there was definitely some intrinsic, organic evolution—whatever you want to call it—natural things going on that really are critical and it couldn't happen without that. However, it was in both cases, there was a commitment of a foundation to move this thing, spearhead it, and dumping several million bucks into it. You know, several million isn't a lot in some circles, but in psychology it's still a lot—and it's more, it's probably more than several million. So that speeded things up both times and that's not, that's not evolutionary, that's revolutionary. [G1]

A biologist who worked on global change issues similarly argued that interdisciplinary science was in many cases driven by forces outside the university. In this case research sponsors were demanding that funded projects be relevant and responsible.

Disciplinary cultural barriers are somewhat breaking down in the past few years to decade because of concerns about global change type issues, overpopulation issues, environmental degradation issues and so more and more scientists are being forced by federal governments and funding agencies to justify their work and articulate their work in how it would solve society's problems. There still is a resistance to do that on the part of some number of scientists, although that number is getting smaller. [I1]

Observers of interdisciplinarity have often attributed a negative influence to institutional structures and academic disciplines. Yet institutions and disciplines are social groupings capable of growth and change and thus of welcoming new modes of inquiry and knowledge generation. In the sciences informants suggested that their disciplines responded to external influences as funding agencies created opportunities for interdisciplinary research; institutions and individuals were the recipients of their support. In the humanities and social sciences, informants talked about historical turns in their disciplines, moments when disciplinary doors were opened to new approaches to knowledge; particular departments responded by welcoming faculty committed to these innovative approaches. Some disciplines, however, appeared to resist interdisciplinarity more than others; economists, for example, were quick to comment on the insularity of their discipline. Still, it is important to recall Austin's (1990) observation that faculty, in addition to being influenced by disciplinary cultures, work within local contexts that can modify their disciplinary commitments. At institutions that value research and teaching equally, the pressure to maintain a traditional disciplinary stance appeared less intense. At these institutions even economics faculty crossed disciplinary borders and wandered across paradigms.

Tracing Interdisciplinarity:
Scholarly Outcomes

Faculty attributed a variety of professional and intellectual outcomes to interdisciplinary teaching and research. These included academic rewards such as promotions and tenure as well as tangible professional outcomes such as conference papers, articles, and books. Interdisciplinary projects also produced intellectual outcomes: changes in personal epistemologies such as new perspectives on disciplinary problems; greater understanding of particular problems or areas of study; and intellectual stimulation and growth stemming from new ways of thinking about a discipline or about the nature of scholarship.

Informants with the least experience in interdisciplinary scholarship generally focused on the tangible, professional outcomes of interdisciplinary teaching and research, reporting how they learned new concepts or principles from other disciplines or broadened their perspective on a vexing problem or phenomenon. Individuals who were more intensely and regularly engaged in interdisciplinary scholarship reported similar kinds of learning outcomes but also described how interdisciplinarity affected their disciplinary perspectives and ways of knowing. These individuals typically did more than add concepts or theories to their disciplinary repertoires; many carefully examined the epistemological and methodological traditions of their disciplines. In some cases, when their discipline yielded less than satisfactory answers, they struggled with the question of whether they could still count themselves as part of their disciplinary community. These kinds of radical epistemological changes were not common among my informants; rather most individuals sought to balance disciplinary and interdisciplinary ways of knowing. Most maintained disciplinary ties while developing coherent new ways of viewing and thinking about the world. Only occasionally, when attempts to combine disciplinary and interdisciplinary perspectives failed, did informants begin to doubt their disciplinary loyalties and identities.

Professional Rewards

Informants who pursued interdisciplinary work of all kinds—informed disciplinarity, synthetic, and conceptual interdisciplinarity—reported tangible professional outcomes as a result of their research and teaching. A number published articles and books and produced conference papers based on their interdisciplinary work. Many of their comments suggest that the widely held belief that resistance to interdisciplinary scholarship stymies publication efforts is exaggerated. A psychologist and a physician presented their collaborative research at their respective disciplinary conferences. The psychologist noted that the research generated some criticism, but the critique was based on the qualitative method used, not the interdisciplinary nature of the project. Similarly a collaborative project between a political scientist and a professor of art began with a team-taught course and culminated in a presentation at an interdisciplinary conference and articles in two journals.

An anthropologist with interests in cognitive psychology suggested that although psychologists favorably received his interdisciplinary work, the jury of anthropologists was still out: "I'll know in about two years [how my work is received by anthropologists] because I just turned a book in to a publisher that I am hoping will have some wider distribution than these psychological pieces. We'll see how they react" [S]. Despite his concerns he was successful in finding a publisher for his studies. An economist with an interest in critical thinking published in a number of different disciplinary journals; these were usually teaching-oriented journals in fields such as sociology and nursing. He did this writing in addition to his disciplinary writing for law journals.

Teaching responsibilities often produced research and publication opportunities. The interdisciplinary teaching activities of one informant resulted in an appointment to a national commission and eventually resulted in a book series on teaching about genocide and intolerance, sponsored by a national professional organization: "That's because of my holocaust work. The publications will all be interdisciplinary" [X]. This informant was also primarily responsible for the development and implementation of an interdisciplinary general education program at his institution, "a very radical approach to humanities education." This program, considered by the informant to be a major focus of his academic life, has been replicated by many American colleges and universities. "It has given us all," he reported, referring to the many faculty involved in the program over the years, "an excuse to do nondisciplinary education."

Another informant, an anthropologist, developed an edited volume as a result of team teaching an interdisciplinary course: "From that experience of team teaching, I got the idea of doing a book on multidisciplinary approaches to the study of gender that I edited with a fellow at [___] University" [M]. An associate professor of English and women's studies reported a similar outcome of interdisciplinary teaching.

> I am working on a book now that's very interdisciplinary in its method and its scope insofar as it involves thinking about the relationship between literary representations of things and broader cultural issues. So my research has really been shaped by being in women's studies. [C]

Earlier I argued that separating teaching and research activities, even temporarily for the purpose of clarity, could mask relationships between teaching and research. These statements from faculty informants attest to the connections between these responsibilities that are often seen as separate, even competing. At the liberal arts colleges, and also at the doctoral institution, faculty offered ample evidence of the interplay among teaching and research activities. For faculty in these kinds of institutions, linkages between teaching and research may be more frequent than for faculty at larger institutions. The greater teaching load at liberal arts and smaller universities makes combining research and teaching interests a viable strategy for accomplishing personal and institutional goals, and the size of the institution facilitates the kinds of interactions that can aid in bringing an interdisciplinary project to fruition.

Several informants contended that they were hired for current academic positions *because* of their interdisciplinary work. An assistant professor discussed the announcement for his position, noting that it required an interdisciplinary type. A tenured anthropologist reported that her university recruited her precisely because of her scholarship, which had always been interdisciplinary. A biologist believed that her interdisciplinary teaching and research experiences would probably land her a job as a director of environmental studies—should she decide to leave her current position:

> I actually think my best chance of leaving [this institution] is because of my interdisciplinary strengths. . . . I think that I could get a job as a director of an environmental studies program. I think that my [interdisciplinary] credentials are strong enough and my disciplinary credentials look good enough because of the posts that I've held within disciplinary societies—because of my activities nationally. But I have loved the opportunities for interdisciplinary interaction here, and I think in that way I came to the right place. [Other colleges] do not have a history of fostering interdisciplinary work. Their biologists are more truly biologists; they spend their time within the biology department for the most part. They are more well developed as biologists, I guess you could say, because their energies are going in that direction. But I think they miss out on the kinds of opportunities that I've had. [A1]

Informants also occasionally attributed promotions and tenure rewards to their interdisciplinary work. At the small liberal arts colleges where teaching was emphasized over research, all successful teaching experiences—disciplinary or interdisciplinary—were considered in reward decisions. Still, a few informants were concerned. Interdisciplinary teaching and team teaching, they claimed, was more difficult than traditional teaching and sometimes less successful—at least in terms of course evaluations. Junior faculty from these institutions tended to worry about poor teaching evaluations, but none suggested that interdisciplinary teaching was responsible for a negative promotion or tenure decision at their campus.

At the universities, interdisciplinary research could be a riskier venture, depending on the opinions of one's departmental colleagues. However, even a highly contentious tenure battle ended successfully for one informant. Given the fact that the entire corpus of this individual's research and teaching was interdisciplinary, her tenure must be viewed as a tangible, although contested, outcome of interdisciplinarity.

Rewards for interdisciplinary work also accrued to faculty in the form of institutional and outside grants for research projects. Although he noted that interdisciplinary projects might not always develop or progress smoothly, a biologist who directed interdisciplinary research teams focused on the positive, rather than negative, outcomes of interdisciplinary efforts.

> We have always said that as part of this project we will try to blend natural science and social science approaches and that blending has been difficult. I think it has something to do with cultural differences of the disciplines. It has to do with different languages, different perceptions of problems. But we have done a lot of talking in parallel. We certainly educated each other. At a minimum, we have done some good: we have promoted and funded, and sought funding for, a few good interdisciplinary projects and at a minimum, all proposals from both sides are now much better articulated in terms of the big picture because of those conversations. [I1]

This kind of outcome of interdisciplinary work blurs the line between tangible and intellectual rewards. The successful grant proposals that emanated from interdisciplinary forums on global change research are clearly tangible products that won research funds for their teams. The ability to better articulate the larger interdisciplinary picture, however, is an intellectual reward that stands alone and may precede the tangible reward. Although I separated the tangible and intangible rewards of interdisciplinary research and teaching for the purposes of discussion, the distinction is clearer in reporting than in reality.

Intellectual Outcomes

Informants who typically engaged in informed disciplinary scholarship were most likely to perceive new knowledge to be the primary outcome of interdisciplinary scholarship. Although these informants pursued interdisciplinarity with the hope of learning something new, they also prized the ability to engage in interdisciplinary conversations with colleagues. An economist found that teaching an interdisciplinary course led to informal exchanges with individuals in another discipline: "I learned a lot in that class and therefore I have greater awareness of certain things. So I will interact [with individuals in the political science department]—not in the formal case of exchanging papers, but talking about things they are working on, how they go about doing them, what might be involved and that kind of stuff" [H].

The ability to talk across disciplines and about other types of research is more than a social advantage. For at least one informant, it was a way to encourage interdisciplinary research projects across the university. He not only led his own interdisciplinary research teams but promoted interdisciplinary research within the university by sponsoring interdisciplinary forums for faculty interested in global change. He argued that he had become more of a generalist as a result: "Increasingly I find myself in positions where I need to acquire a certain amount of knowledge in a discipline so I can converse with people and convey what I am interested in to them and find out what they are interested in and then find out if there is a common ground" [I1].

An assistant professor of art history observed that his interdisciplinary interests facilitated interdisciplinary conversations.

> I have a good enough sense about the issues in a lot of different disciplines. This is something you see when you are interdisciplinary: The changes that are occurring in literature are also going on in visual arts and they're reflecting very important social issues, very important questions that the person on the street had, that the intellectual had. You see culture as something that doesn't simply run in these narrow disciplines, and therefore by trying to get a broader sense of the culture as a whole—albeit not doing as much work in the secondary literature of any one specific field—you find that you can talk to people. [E]

An associate professor of English who directed an interdisciplinary program also found the ability to understand different perspectives helpful in conducting meetings and getting work done in university committees:

> I think being interdisciplinary also makes one a better communicator. I have used my interdisciplinary inclination and interest as a tool in my administrating. When I sit on a university committee which is composed of people from all different disciplines, I feel as if I am able, more able, to slip into the perspective they are trying to argue. I was on the university

grant committee and I felt one of the problems there was people who could not transcend their own disciplines enough to be able to respect what someone was doing in another discipline. And so I think it's healthy in that way, too. [C]

Although interdisciplinary interaction can be personally satisfying and administratively useful, it may not lead to changes in knowledge or reassessment of disciplinary perspectives. More intense engagement in interdisciplinary topics seems to be required for this kind of intellectual change. An economist, for example, credited his collaboration with an anthropologist with helping him develop a more complex understanding of social change.

Probably the most important thing [my colleague] did was to contribute this sociological analysis of [social] class. I think it was always there, but now I have got some terms to use and I have got some theory. Economists have not ever dealt very effectively with the issue of class. I have always felt that it was important, but I didn't have the analysis other than the Marxist stuff to talk about it. [My colleague] helped me build a much broader sense of the importance of class and the role of class and the way classes get shaped and changed and so on, and that is now part of the repertoire. [W]

Comparing himself to a "sticky ball rolling down a hill," he described his interdisciplinary learning as a process of accumulation and internalization: "I roll through this field and I pick up stuff and then it becomes part of me."

Interdisciplinary work often had the effect of expanding an individual's intellectual universe. A political scientist attributed the ability to ask a new set of questions to her interdisciplinary learning, enumerating the topics she pursued after an interdisciplinary team-teaching experience.

I do enjoy interdisciplinary work. I have immersed myself in it. Part of the reason why it is fascinating to me is this connection, it opens me up to these other things that have been really interesting, for example, critical studies—critical race theory, feminist legal studies—and that caused me to have to read things other than the traditional kind of constitutional law books. Intellectually, it just expanded things for me. [I]

In this case interdisciplinary conversations sparked a research interest and another interdisciplinary course. Neither the research nor the course would likely exist if the conversation had not taken place.

> In the law, postmodernism is a relatively new concept. Yet if you go into literature or into art, postmodernism is — it's just everything. So it has been real important to have been exposed to those concepts and *then* I start to try and find places in law where it has started to happen and that has been the basis of my expanding what I do. So, for example, just recently I got a course approved that I am going to be teaching next year. We're going to be doing queer legal theory. I never would have even come across that literature if it hadn't been for this interdisciplinary connection that exposed me to postmodernism and then exposed me to critical race theory and feminist theory and now the cutting edge of stuff in legal theory, queer legal theory. So that's really key for me. I wouldn't have gotten that without a collegial, interdisciplinary discussion. [I]

Interest theories typically suggest that there are two types of interest: individual and situational (Krapp, Hidi, and Renninger 1992). Individual interest, as its name suggests, is specific to the individual, is relatively stable, and is associated with increased knowledge. Situational interest, in contrast, is generated by a stimulus in the environment, for example, texts, films, or the ideas of another individual, and tends to be shared among individuals. As a result it may only have a short-term value and a marginal influence on an individual's knowledge and reference systems. Research on the role of interest in learning, however, has consistently demonstrated that both situational and individual interests have important effects on learning (Krapp, Hidi, and Renninger 1992).

Faculty with a strong interest in an interdisciplinary topic may decide to pursue a prolonged interdisciplinary research or teaching process or to engage in a formal interdisciplinary collaboration. Those participating in faculty colloquia or conferences may exhibit a more situational interest that may be sustained for a shorter period of time and may require a less intensive effort. This kind of interest could be short-lived and have a limited influence on the individual's academic life. Of course, there is the possibility that a situational interest can become an individual interest — participation in an especially interesting conference may eventually lead to participation in an interdisciplinary collaboration. As demonstrated in this study, one interdisciplinary excursion can lead to others.

For many informants interdisciplinary teaching and research filled a void by offering intellectual stimulation previously unobtainable. For the political scientist quoted above, interdisciplinary conversations made life at her institution bearable. What she lacked in collegial interaction in her department, she found in interdisciplinary interactions: "Those things, for me, are everything. They make being here what it is. I would not be here and I would not be in this job if it weren't for *that*" [I]. At another institution an associate professor offered the same explanation for her interest in interdisciplinary topics and involvement in an ongoing interdisciplinary seminar.

> At the end of my first year here I was just sort of lonely and I didn't know very many people here and I felt a desire for a kind of intellectual community that I felt I'd had in graduate school and it just wasn't happening in my department. I had heard there was this faculty seminar and I didn't even really know what it was about, I just wanted to go. And it's been a really important part of my life since. . . . [B1]

Several informants confessed that they pursued interdisciplinary projects because they became bored with their disciplinary agendas. An economist enrolled in law school because he "was bored by a lot of conversations in my midst" and wanted some intellectual excitement. "I was not going to be a lawyer or anything like that and so, for me, it was just sort of a sidelight of my reading program." The law, he argued, was a refuge for individuals devoted to the liberal arts: "You can spend your whole career writing on the jurisprudential theories evoked in Kafka's work. That's quite an acceptable research program in law" [F]. A psychologist reflecting on his academic career noted a similar motivation and the reason he pursued several lines of research:

> I would say it's probably true of me that, for better or worse, I get bored doing the same thing for a very long period of time. I immerse myself and work very intensely and I think if I look back over my career, I at least change the problems I'm working on every five to seven years. [G1]

As if to deflect the common "dilettante" label, he quickly added, "certain themes have been there since graduate school." A physicist defended his attention to different research topics as reflection of a personality trait, and he suggested that he was merely one variety of faculty member:

> Many academics are very comfortable with becoming really expert in an area and mining it, really becoming a deep specialist in a certain field, and that is important. That's really important. There are other people who sort of take a broad view of things or whose personality is maybe very sequentially monogamous as far as academic disciplines go—I spend a few years on this subject then I move on and spend a couple of years on this subject. Those are people who more naturally gravitate to doing interdisciplinary work. For those kinds of people, I think the main reason for doing this kind of work is the intellectual challenge and excitement. It's not for everybody and I wouldn't say it has to be for everybody. [E1]

A professor of Romance languages and women's studies argued that the intellectual stimulation of interdisciplinarity was likely to engender other intellectual outcomes and that what was learned through interdisciplinarity would eventually help one be a better teacher and researcher.

> So that's also what interdisciplinarity means, it means that no matter how much you already know and are specialized in your own area, there's always something new you can learn that will eventually—you don't have to be capitalist about it, but there will be a payback. You will get something out of it. If nothing else, you will just get some excitement out of it, you know, stimulation, but probably, you'll also get something else. You will have some new insights that will help you teach whatever you are teaching better or write whatever you are writing better. If it's at all connected, it will help you think it out better. [N]

Maintaining Disciplinary Ties

In the literature on interdisciplinarity that appeared in the 1970s and 1980s, interdisciplinarity was usually considered a means to an end, a useful approach to answering social or technological questions that could not be addressed adequately by a single discipline. An interdisciplinary strategy, then, might be the best way to answer a particular question, but interdisciplinarity itself was not an epistemological imperative. In more recent discussions, particularly from feminist and postmodernist standpoints, interdisciplinarity is more than a useful approach, it is a requirement. Disciplinary approaches to research and teaching result in partial knowledge; interdisciplinarity is therefore the only possible route to understanding.

A substantial number of faculty who do interdisciplinary work share these sentiments, yet only a few informants in this study seemed to have moved to a place beyond discipline. And even these individuals were reluctant to leave their disciplines behind. Most maintained a disciplinary identity while critiquing their discipline. For most informants a combination of disciplinary and interdisciplinary approaches appeared to offer the best of both worlds.

Many informants adhered to the prevalent view that academic disciplines are important and useful. A jointly appointed sociologist-historian commented on her continuing interest in "traditional sociological concerns," remarking on

> class and hierarchical relations in society, relations of domination and subordination. These are things that are still very much at the center of my work and they are things that I am not about to let go of. And when I play around any kind of literary theory or cultural studies, I try very hard not to lose sight of the material world that constrains people's everyday lives and try to make links between how they understand those lives and how those lives are constrained. To me, that is what is interesting, what is important. [D1]

She later acknowledged the difficulty of maintaining a legitimate interest in classically sociological issues in light of the epistemological stances made popular by cultural studies, an emerging field that is often used as a model of scholarship by advocates of interdisciplinarity. An associate professor of English also noted the contrast between her version of interdisciplinarity and that of faculty in cultural studies.

> There is a way in which I still have a completely, 100 percent primary commitment to literature, which I think makes me different from some

other people who have sort of crossed over, who have thrown out disciplinary stuff altogether and have reimagined themselves as doing something like cultural studies. I still think of myself as primarily focused on literature and . . . looking closely at texts and really thinking about them and thinking about issues of language, issues of interpretation, with a whole bunch of historical perspectives. That's absolutely still part of my intellectual life. [B1]

She was personally satisfied as a result of using the academic strengths she developed while specializing in literature.

I do think that at this point in my life my strengths are still those that I got in graduate school, which is to be a close, textual reader with certain kinds of interpretative skills and I never want to give that up. That's what's personally most rewarding for me, so for me, it's always going to be a matter of going back and forth between a commitment to a primary thing and then other stuff. I don't see it—for me—I don't see a kind of completely breaking down barriers. [B1]

Realizing that she might be perceived as too comfortable with the status quo, she laughed and hurriedly added, "But I think the university should figure out a way to break down those barriers."

The informants quoted above expressed some mild concerns about their disciplinary commitments. The first worried about being "an old fogy"; the second about being left behind by "the groovy people" who wrote papers on cultural studies and presented them at well-attended panels at the annual Modern Language Association meetings. Neither, however, was willing to abandon her discipline or its questions. An anthropologist engaged in synthetic interdisciplinary research linking anthropology and psychology expressed a similar reluctance to leave his chosen discipline behind:

In some respects I wouldn't want to leave anthropology because tomorrow afternoon I might want to do an ethnography. I have long thought about the kind of ethnography that I would like to do. I don't see myself doing experimental studies ten years from now. This is a method and for a range of questions, and it's an interesting method, but it's not necessarily the only thing I want to do. In fact the next project that I have been thinking about is to look at the history of the field of child psychology and look at the cultural and political issues that shaped its emergence. That has no scientific side; it's an entirely interpretative project. [S]

Similarly the associate professor of English wanted to maintain her commitment to that field: "I went into this field because I really love literature and I still have a kind of fundamental primary commitment to literature. I love teaching my interdisciplinary courses, but I also would hate it if I could never teach a class on nineteenth-century poetry" [B1].

Nor did a psychologist whose work I classified as conceptual interdisciplinarity believe she was "beyond discipline." She talked about the "social theorizing" that she did before becoming an academic, before graduate school, and even before attending college. That framework, she argued, had not changed. However much she might question purely disciplinary approaches to her topic, she nonetheless maintained that they offered useful guidelines and information.

> I don't think I'm beyond discipline . . . this thing that I developed outside an academic setting is something that I think is really useful for understanding the kinds of things that I want to [understand] as an academic. And that I pick and choose from those things that really help me understand. If they don't help me understand what I *know* is out there, then I just don't use those things. Having [that] framework also helps me see when certain types of approaches or certain ways that people ask questions really are distorting. I tend to incorporate things that open up another piece that I hadn't thought about in that way. I've found in my life that there really are all these kinds of multiple layers of understanding and some of it you do, some of it is brought to you through other people, and as you mature and grow you can see other levels of that. Reading works that way. Your experiences with people work that way as well. And sometimes what I come in contact through different disciplines opens up a piece that I had that I really didn't fully see. [T]

Even informants whose work appeared to me to be primarily interdisciplinary rather than disciplinary appeared reluctant to cast themselves as purely interdisciplinary. Many, in fact, noted the lasting impact of their disciplinary training. Those who tended to pursue synthetic or conceptual interdisciplinary research and teaching were often surprised that despite long and involved engagements with interdisciplinary scholarship, they were continually cognizant of their disciplinary training and perspectives. Several commented on the difficulty of breaking through established ways of thinking. An economist with a twenty-year history of interdisciplinary collaboration admitted:

> Probably the more troubling part of it is . . . that when I try to think about ways in which social change might occur in society and what implications that has for economics, it still is extraordinarily difficult for me to think in terms that don't fall back into the neo-classical paradigm. I am interested in building a new theory, but all the tools and all the terms that I use as I talk about building a new theory are neo-classical ones. [W]

Although he had recast himself as an institutionalist, an economist who argued against the applicability of the neoclassical paradigm for particular societies, the impact of his disciplinary training endured. A psychologist working on cognitive science questions argued that virtually all faculty bore the imprint of their disciplinary training: "Everybody I've met in this business shows the tremendous impact of their own discipline. It's extremely rare to find somebody who's equally facile or views the world equally through two different disciplinary lenses" [G1]. Despite several excursions into interdisciplinary territory, he believed that he still approached problems from a psychological perspective.

> In the cognitive science work it was clear, I always maintained a psychologist's view and I still do, I still do. Part of it is I'm assessing how important is this particular problem or claim or whatever from a psychological point of view, that is, I'm thinking [about] how much in psychology, cognitive psychology, hinges on this? Who will care? Whereas clearly [my collaborators from other disciplines are] not thinking that way. Then you develop certain intuitions about what's important cognitively. I'm the kind of cognitive psychologist who relies heavily on intuition. Not everybody's like that. And maybe I even overdo it, but that's not something that's going to be natural for a medical physicist or systems biologist, to

> rely extensively on their own psychological intuitions. So you know we'll be running experiments—and I'm always a subject in my own experiments—and I get ideas about what's going on. . . . And that might reflect that psychology's the first discipline I knew, so that's what I'm really geared to. [G1]

Even when faculty moved away from "scientific" methods and toward more interpretative ones, the influence of scientific training still permeated their thinking. A sociologist who now concentrated on archival, historical work explained that her present way of thinking about problems was "sort of sociological."

> I still use some of that variable stuff in my head. I play little thought experiments to try to kind of make clear what it is I am trying to explain and why this explanation works better than that one. And I play thought experiments and that comes straight out of my methodological training in sociology. [D1]

Despite intentions, informants admitted that they were sometimes unable to break through traditional disciplinary perspectives. An economist who taught numerous thematic courses stressing critical thinking observed that faculty tend to fall back on what they know best, even in a carefully orchestrated interdisciplinary format.

> Those of us who were organizing [the class] were dead set on making sure that there was continuity in this course and that there was a sense of integration as we moved from one area to another. The amount of planning that went on was incredible. We had faculty working with one another. We had the overstructure in there. The students come in, and it disappears. Pffft. The faculty came in and did their thing. The geographer did his weather stuff and the biologist did his biology stuff. The philosopher did his philosophy stuff. . . . It went right out the window. I think most of us, even though we say that there are linkages, do what we are comfortable doing, that even though the faculty came to these meetings and prepared—and I think they were serious about wanting to do a good job—

when the actual teaching occurred they did what they were comfortable doing. They didn't really become interdisciplinarians. [O]

He argued that a special kind of individual was needed to teach interdisciplinary courses, an individual who was not afraid to step into unfamiliar territory with students.

Those of us who were involved in organizing it said, "Well, that was a nice attempt. There certainly was some gain. But we're not going to repeat this again. If we're going to do this, we're going to take two or three faculty who are really serious about willing to subject themselves to the challenge of a different way of thinking, be open with the students about not knowing everything." . . . I should have known better: when you bring a group of experts into a classroom, it's not going to work. I thought we could overcome that. We didn't. [O]

These informants may have encountered what Dewey (1916/1966) called habits. Habits, for Dewey, were attitudes, inclinations, predispositions, and preferences. They are the means by which individuals encounter and make sense of the world (Cuffaro 1995). Kestenbaum (1977) argued that "in Dewey's terms . . . to have a paradigm is to have a habit" (p. 4). For Margolis (1993) habits of mind are comfortable, entrenched ways of thinking that are so second nature to individuals that they are virtually subconscious. Although Margolis's habits of mind are not necessarily synonymous with disciplinary paradigms, disciplinary ways of viewing the world often take on the characteristics of habits of mind. Dewey and Margolis both explain, through their respective concepts, why commonly accepted disciplinary ideas might be confusing to individuals outside the discipline. Dewey (1916) noted that although habits can be active, they can also become fixed and passive and can "possess us instead of our possessing them" (p. 49). Focusing specifically on scholarly habits of mind, Margolis commented,

since habits of mind are intimately tied to communication, the people we communicate with freely—all the more so on some scientific or otherwise technical issue that exploits concepts and arguments far from ordinary discourse—are people who share specialized habits of mind with us, and hence, as we say, see things the way we do. "Talking past each other" yields the converse case. All this makes habits of mind even more likely to be socially shared than (say) styles in a physical activity, like skiing, and harder to escape. Incompatible habits of mind block communication, easily evoke resentment and distaste and frustration, all of which would tend to reinforce a natural propensity toward coordination of habits across individuals and make breaking with socially shared habits of mind harder than breaking with socially shared physical habits." (pp. 17–18)

Both Margolis and Dewey argued that habits are detrimental when they prevent individuals from seeing phenomena or problems from different perspectives. Dewey was concerned with habits when they "put an end to plasticity . . . to the power to vary and to change, to see and respond with freshness" (Cuffaro 1995, p. 20); Margolis found habits of mind problematic when they precluded perspectives that might advance thinking or result in a breakthrough.

Disciplinarity may be a habit of mind, an embedded way of seeing the world that can promote understanding at one time, preclude it at another. Interdisciplinary research and teaching require that faculty break habits of mind in order to gain a new perspective on an issue or phenomenon. For some faculty this may be both difficult and unconscionable. Others find it exhilarating—and necessary.

For some informants the need to maintain disciplinary associations or to return to disciplinary research and teaching after excursions into interdisciplinarity appeared to be a reaction to immersion in interdisciplinary scholarship. An associate professor of Romance languages and women's studies pondered the question of what to do next:

I have this set of projects that, if ever I had the time, I would do. And I don't know whether I will ever do them or not. But some of them, now that I think about it, would very much *not* be interdisciplinary in the sense that I am talking about. . . . So where is my future work going to go? I don't know. I think I will go back to the novel. [K]

An associate professor of English who was currently directing a women's stud-ies program made a similar prediction: "I will tell you that having been in this job for three years and doing these interdisciplinary projects, my next book is definitely going to be on a literary work! I miss it. I definitely miss it" [C].

Such comments about returning to disciplinary work could be interpreted as a desire for the "simplicity" of disciplinary work. The complicated nature of interdisciplinary work, the uncertainty involved with working outside one's dis-cipline, and the time and effort involved in interdisciplinary scholarship seemed to leave some informants yearning for more-bounded research and teaching projects. For some informants, however, scholarly interests dictated the research or teaching approach chosen. Some questions simply do not re-quire an interdisciplinary strategy.

Several informants combined interdisciplinary and disciplinary agendas. A political scientist pursued two research tracks—one that reflected the disci-plinary interests that she developed in graduate school, the other an interdisci-plinary interest stimulated by a recent teaching experience. For her the disci-plinary line of research was a safety net—rewarding from an institutional and professional standpoint, if not a personal one.

> My traditional area of research, which will continue throughout my ca-reer, is on the amending clause of the constitution which just plays a very minor role in my teaching. It also reflects kind of a former self. It's this thing I was very interested in when I was in graduate school and I ended up doing my dissertation on it. New issues regarding amending the consti-tution come up all the time, so it's an area where I can produce work and I intend to continue. I like it still. [I]

She preferred, however, her more recent work in the area of critical race theory, which grew out of an invitation to teach a class for the black studies program at her college. She discussed

> this other area that is more challenging, interesting. It's more expansive now in terms of personal growth. So that's what I am doing. . . . I am really retooling . . . so that I can begin to write in the area that I have become interested in. [I]

An economist also pursued both interdisciplinary and disciplinary interests but did not appear to prefer one more than the other. In fact he noted how these interests were, after a number of years, beginning to mesh and form a more cohesive research program.

> I have two or three tracks of research going on for a long while. One of the tracks is the things that I have been doing with [a colleague at the same college], and that goes back eighteen or nineteen years. We are working on another book now. We have been pretty consistent in that what we have been looking at is how we can use this language, this modified theory we get by putting liberation theology and economics together to explain how change occurs. . . . [Another colleague] and I are [now] working on environmental issues and we are trying to address the same question: how can we use the kind of marriage of theology and economics to understand more effectively questions of environment and social change associated with building sustainable environments. That happens to connect with another strain of research that I have been on for a quite a while which is environmental research. A colleague who is out on the West Coast and I have been working together for seven or eight years on issues of sustainability. . . . So, those two threads—my interdisciplinary thread over here and my clearly disciplinary thread over here—are now kind of connected. The things that I've been doing with [one colleague] are spilling over into the research that I am doing with [another colleague] and the things that I am doing with him are spilling over to the research I am doing with [yet another colleague]. [W]

The lengthy engagement of this informant in both interdisciplinary and disciplinary research and the linkages that he now sees between these tracks demonstrate that faculty do not have to abandon disciplinary teaching or research to do interdisciplinary scholarship. Nor may they wish to do so. Intellectual stimulation and satisfaction result from following those questions, whatever type of question they may be, that most interest the individual.

Challenging Disciplinary Beliefs

Informants who primarily pursued synthetic or conceptual interdisciplinary scholarship—rather than disciplinary, transdisciplinary, or informed disciplinary teaching and research—were most troubled by the question of their
relationship to their home discipline. In particular, individuals with ties to
women's studies focused on the challenges that interdisciplinarity posed to
their disciplinary knowledge and training and noted epistemological or ontological changes that they experienced as a result of embracing interdisciplinarity.

Two professors of economics reflected on their current thinking about
their disciplines; mathematical models seemed particularly troublesome:

> There is no question about the fact that it was getting involved in women's
> studies that led me to question the kinds of things that economists do. You
> get very indoctrinated in graduate school. The academic structure and
> the reward structure make it pay off to follow that same straight and nar-
> row path. I am not saying that I would still be the dutiful neoclassical
> economist with the mathematical models if it hadn't been for my involve-
> ment with women's studies, but that has certainly moved the process along
> a lot more rapidly than it would have otherwise. [G]

> I guess I'm defining economics more broadly. I may not have a math-
> ematical model to describe what I'm doing, but I'm still looking at the
> cost and the constraints, which to me are the basic parameters or the basic
> focus of economics. . . . What economists will say is economics [is] those
> things that you can see and measure on the marketplace. But there are
> other kinds of markets. Marriage markets, power markets, where some-
> thing is exchanged and people exchange those things in a way that they're
> maximizing some kind of utility or they're doing it for their own gain. [B]

Other informants also questioned established disciplinary perspectives. An
English professor who was also heavily involved in women's studies found new
ways of understanding and interpreting literature as a result of exposure to
interdisciplinary approaches such as cultural studies: "I do think my thinking
has changed in terms of what are the interesting, and I think important, ways

to read a literary work. There's definitely the context of the culture as a whole" [C]. She also admitted that she now looked more critically at her discipline as a result of her association with women's studies.

> I really never thought about different disciplines and how they might construct things differently, what our discipline included and what it deliberately excluded in order to be itself, but I do think much more deliberately in those terms now. Maybe because women's studies is not only composed of so many disciplines but is a kind of orphan, you know, a little orphan out here that is vulnerable and that people tend to try and attack in disciplinary terms. [C]

An associate professor of philosophy who also taught women's studies experienced some profound changes in her view of her discipline: "I have a hard time saying anymore what philosophy is because the old answers just don't seem to work" [J]. She criticized traditional modes of philosophical inquiry:

> I don't think there's anything such as the scientific method that we all learned in grade school. I think the philosophical method is similarly a mythic structure. If there's something in there operating that big machine, it's not what it was alleged to be. . . . When I think about keeping one's brain fully engaged—I mean, I'll settle for that—having the reflective critical posture, being able to look at the foundations of knowledge rather than comforting myself with postulates and axioms, and see what comes out of it. [J]

She asked if philosophy could no longer be defined by its method, what was it? Unwilling to offer a pat answer, she suggested that blurring the discipline's boundaries, not defining them, was the best alternative.

> To me the philosophers are the ones who are still thinking about these questions—who haven't accepted a disciplinary boundary, who refuse to take the settled things, whatever that may be in the timeframe, uncritically and unreflectively—and are trying to put together the various knowledges and the various methodologies in a way that supports human flourishing. You know, that's the only definition I can offer to my students. It's not

clear that that distinguishes us from a lot of other activities, but I think that's the good news rather than the bad news. [J]

Methodology and epistemology were also at the center of a psychologist's quarrel with psychology—for that matter with most social science disciplines.

The big picture, which I don't usually tell people, is that I think that I have a responsibility and an obligation to contribute to the telling of stories about black life and black history. So one aspect of that that I've chose to focus on is people's family lives—and I really do see research as just an extension of story telling—so I feel like I have this responsibility to add this sort of type of perspective or vision. And because I see it as partly storytelling, I want to tell a really comprehensive, integrated, and coherent story about people's experiences. This is not like a perspective that people who see themselves as social scientists have. [T]

It is sometimes difficult to say whether interdisciplinarity is the cause or the effect in these cases. Questioning disciplinary methods often leads to solutions based on interdisciplinarity, but exposure to interdisciplinarity can also challenge one's ideas about the "right" way to approach a problem or question. Some faculty, for example, the economist who attributed changes in her ways of thinking about economics to her involvement in women's studies, suggest a clear pattern of cause and effect; others may have difficulty deciding which came first in this chicken-and-egg issue. Whatever the case, it is clear that intense interdisciplinary activity is often associated with intense reflection on disciplinary tenets and, at times, results in changes in disciplinary perspectives. This association was indirectly but vividly demonstrated by the number of informants who sprinkled their interviews with comments about problems of objectivity, generalizability, universality, and truth—constructs that have been destabilized by epistemological challenges from proponents of critical theory, postmodernism, feminism, and alternative research methods.

A Question of Identity

During their interviews many informants reflected on the question of disciplinary identity. Some, typically those who pursued interdisciplinary activities that did not call into question fundamental tenets of their disciplines, were able to maintain a disciplinary identity without difficulty. These individuals did not make an epistemological or ontological shift to participate in interdisciplinary projects. Other informants, however, experienced varying degrees of discomfort as a result of incongruities they sensed between their interdisciplinary and disciplinary scholarship. For individuals who were bothered by their inability to reconcile traditional disciplinary tenets and perspectives with interdisciplinarity, epistemological and ontological shifts resulted in new ways of thinking about knowledge, about their professional identity, and about research and teaching commitments.

The desire to maintain a disciplinary identity was quite strong among informants. Even individuals who worked in modes that required the most interdisciplinary movement, such as conceptual interdisciplinarity and transdisciplinarity, considered themselves to be members in good standing in their disciplines. They were able to maintain this disciplinary identity because they believed that their interdisciplinary scholarship did not challenge the foundations or methods of their home disciplines—as they perceived them. And since it is possible to do interdisciplinary work that is consistent with a variety of paradigms, an anthropologist who worked in cognitive science was still able to consider himself an anthropologist "even though I have, by design, focused my empirical work outside of anthropology. . . . I still see myself as deeply rooted in anthropology as a member of the anthropology department" [S]. Contrasting his work to that of traditional psychological anthropologists, he revealed the consistency between his epistemological stance and positivistic approaches to anthropology and psychology in his search for universal cognitions.

I'm not a very typical psychological anthropologist. They often try to show how culture produces certain specific psychological effects and that it associates cultural variation with significant and real variation in the nature of the psyche. My concern is much more universalist. I don't deny that there are fundamental differences in our thought, depending on the cultural context in which we do that thinking. It's patently obvious that if we go to Java, they're thinking about the world differently than if we go to Cincinnati, but it doesn't follow from that their fundamental cognitions are different and I am more concerned with showing how those fundamental cognitions are similar than I am with showing how they might differ. [S]

Similarly a biologist was able to maintain her disciplinary identity because she found a way to define her current interdisciplinary methods as consistent with her scientific predilections. Speaking of a biography she was writing, she commented:

what I was doing initially was real science. I was developing hypotheses about what kinds of facts might exist and where I would find them. And then testing those hypotheses and then revising hypotheses and trying to imagine what kind of man he was and then looking for evidence. So I was conscious, I was very aware, when I first started working on it that "Hey, this is science." I'm just working with archives instead of plants and little plots in the field. [A1]

In a later conversation she iterated the connections she perceived between biography and botany: "Science is narrative. Science is telling a story. That's what makes sense. It's not the facts, but how you string them together to tell a story that makes the science." She attributed her deep interest in her subject matter to her decision to focus on topics, disciplinary or interdisciplinary, that were closely aligned with her field.

I think I identify myself as a biologist. There is something in the core of me that is that and that I want to develop. . . . I think what keeps me from becoming someone else, what keeps me in a biology department or at least brought me back from women's studies, maybe, into environmental studies . . . [is that] as a botanist being involved in women's studies, there's not a direct link, it's much more abstract. It's questions of how we know what we know and how knowledge is shaped and all that but it's not directly related to the subject matter whereas environmental studies is. As a plant ecologist I have something from within my discipline to directly offer. So I'm working much closer to home in terms of interdisciplinary work. And I think that's because I know that there is this essence of me that is a biologist that I want to satisfy. [A1]

Although this informant was undoubtedly sincere in her desire to nurture the biologist inside, her move from women's studies may be motivated by more than subject matter. When the first women's studies programs were founded in the 1970s and 1980s, this biologist was actively involved in first creating a program, then designing a major in women's studies for her institution. Since then feminist disciplinary critiques have developed into more searching epistemological inquiries that often indict scientific disciplines for their assumptions about objectivity and truth. Scientists with traditional teaching and research concerns may therefore find today's women's studies programs less hospitable and comfortable than in the past. This informant admitted that although she still found the idea of a "meta-look at disciplines" attractive, for her the feminist critique of knowledge was no longer compelling.

Some informants were able to reconfigure their thinking *and* remain within their discipline. The economist who discussed his rejection of neoclassical economic models was able to maintain his disciplinary identity by redefining himself as an institutionalist. At first he was concerned that his ideas might alienate him from the disciplinary community, from those he called colleagues. Eventually he found a refuge with a small minority of like-minded economists who also challenged the prevailing paradigm.

> I said to myself, "Gee, am I no longer an economist because I am interested in these questions?" I suspect that is one of the reasons that I wanted to keep teaching macroeconomic theories: [to] keep there at the center. . . . There was that fear of what will my colleagues think of this. . . . Basically, would I somehow become a pariah and no longer respected in the discipline? I learned after a while that there is a critical mass of people like me out there who are challenging the existing paradigm from a lot of different directions. . . . It took a while to get to the point where I realized that all those groups were out there, and there were some people who were well respected, and that I could continue to be well respected as an economist even if I was out on the fringes. [W]

For another informant timing was the key to maintaining a disciplinary identity. His interests were reflected in a growing disciplinary trend.

I've been fortunate in that the interdisciplinary directions I've gotten interested in, the fields moved in that direction. So if I started to look a little
bit less like a cognitive psychologist because of spending so much time
worrying about relationships of cognition to brain, fortunately for me, the
field's moving in that direction. So I don't look too deviant. [G1]

Another anthropologist who embraced interdisciplinarity in graduate
school was able to do conceptual interdisciplinary work, teach sociology in a
merged sociology/anthropology department, and still feel like an anthropologist.

When I first came here it was just a sociology department. The administration had taken one of the soc tenure tracks and said make it anthropology, so I came. . . . Now we have three anthropologists currently on the
staff. . . . I still think that it certainly has left its mark on me: I did interdisciplinary teaching within my own department because I had soc and
anthro students. . . . [But] *there is* a different perspective to the world in
sociology and no matter how much we as a department are trying to mask
that difference to make us work as colleagues, there is a different base of
theory, of literature. I'm learning more about the sociology. That's not a
problem, it's very interesting. I'm still an anthropologist. [M]

Having established earlier that her version of anthropology had always been
interdisciplinary, she was able to combine these activities in ways that she
deemed intellectually consistent.

Writing of interdisciplinarity and the annexation of disciplines, Fish (1994)
asked whether "the practice of importing into one's own practice the machin-
ery of other practices operates to relax the constraints of one's practice" (p.
239). He argued that it did not: "terms and distinctions could arrive intact in
the passage from one discipline to another only if they had some form independent of the disciplines in whose practices they first became visible" (p. 239).
However, since terms and distinctions are socially constructed, they will always "be relative to the socially constructed activity that . . . made them its
own" (p. 239). The moment something is imported into a practice, it is "already marked" by the discourse it supposedly opens; it is assimilated in terms

that the practice recognizes. Fish's observations seem to describe aptly the manner in which many informants pursued interdisciplinarity. No matter how frequent the invocation of other disciplinary methods or information, the existing disciplinary beliefs were unscathed because new methods, ideas, or directions were conceptualized as intellectually consistent. These informants pursued interdisciplinary scholarship in ways that allowed them to preserve their epistemologies or ontologies; their disciplinary identities were not compromised.

While Fish's notion of uncontaminated transfer is useful in considering how methods, concepts, or beliefs are borrowed among disciplines, this scenario is harder to abide when the "terms and distinctions" are feminist, poststructuralist, or postmodern critiques. The interdisciplinary nature of these forms of critique precludes importing anything into another discipline; rather the critique itself reconfigures the spaces in which feminists, poststructuralists, and postmodernists construct their research and teaching.

Some informants, confronted with the incommensurate nature of disciplinary and interdisciplinary perspectives, therefore revised their disciplinary, epistemological, and ontological commitments. When interdisciplinary research and teaching required ontological shifts, informants found it more difficult to identify with their discipline. A few created composite identities that included all the disciplines or fields in which they explored. The director of a black studies program who held divinity and sociology degrees expressed his preferences.

> I am uncomfortable, for instance, if I am introduced to a bunch of people as a sociologist, or introduced as a theologian, or even introduced as simply as a director of a black studies program. I would rather be known by the composite of those identities rather than one. [U]

A political scientist who taught in two interdisciplinary programs adopted a multiple identities as her teaching in women's studies and black studies became increasingly important to her. "I now identify myself around campus . . . as being in the political science department, the women's studies program, and the black studies program. So I feel that I have become increasingly more interdisciplinary in that regard" [I].

Other informants also dissatisfied with the usual labels implied that they were more than disciplinarians but did not see themselves as disciplinary composites. A professor of Romance languages suggested that colleagues tended to see her work as focused on literature: "I think there are plenty of people who if asked what I do, would say, "Well, she writes about women writers." And they would see me as a literature person, a person who is a literary critic" [N]. She did not, however, view herself that way: "I don't think of myself as a literature person who only does literature. I've *never* thought of myself that way" [N]. Rather, she argued, her work was much more akin to what today is called cultural studies, despite her dismay that the true roots of this field had been forgotten or ignored.

> I'm a little bit amused that today the new term is cultural studies and it seems to be emanating out of the English departments, when in my view, [it's been] people in the languages and literature departments who have been genuinely interested in the historical groundings of culture and the way that our history and our architecture and political events all interconnect with literary production. . . [N]

An anthropologist who described her own work as "increasingly archival, increasingly historical" wondered how colleagues defined her. They did not, she believed, consider her a typical anthropologist because her interests were so interdisciplinary.

> It's funny how I'm received—sometimes as an historian, sometimes as an anthropologist, sometimes as a social theorist. I was just invited to be a speaker for a gender studies conference. I gave the keynote lecture at a conference on imperialism. This is not to tell you how wonderful I am, I am trying to give you a sense of the interdisciplinarity. I have been double-billed to talk on nationalism with a political scientist who does anthropological work. I'm going to do a piece on sexual theory next month at another institution. The audiences are very, very different. Sometimes it's a gender audience, sometimes it's a colonial audience, sometimes it's a race audience, postmodern theory. . . [H1]

She did not think of herself solely as an anthropologist, but neither was she comfortable thinking of herself as a historian.

I don't identify myself completely as an anthropologist. But I know that when historians read my stuff, it looks really different to them. It's certain kinds of disciplinary conventions that I do not subscribe to. It's what I have to do in order to marshal certain kinds of evidence or the claims I am willing to make are broader than a lot of historians would make. I'm willing to do work that draws on different areas without it being comparative in a very localized sense, which is not the sort of history thing to do. I identified myself as an anthropologist when I was younger, but it was always, "I'm a Marxist anthropologist," "I'm a feminist anthropologist." And those words that would identify a critique in some ways of the discipline itself. [H1]

But, she argued, the critique of the disciplines was not the defining aspect of her work. A conceptual interdisciplinary thinker, she found excitement in speaking to different audiences and in making connections between disciplines in scholarship. "Forget the disciplinary crap," she exclaimed, "it's the questions they're asking" that are important.

A sociologist who successfully combined sociological and historical work described her love of historical work and the nagging sense that she was not really a sociologist.

As an undergraduate, I loved history. As a junior high school student, I loved history. As a high school student, I loved history. And somehow I ended up in sociology. And I sort of know how that happened, but—and it wasn't like I was carrying around this thing about history all this time. I really got into sociology and I really thought that was who I was and what I wanted to do, but I think I was never real comfortable with it. I was never really comfortable with a lot of the methods in sociology. A lot of the training and a lot of the theory is great, but I just really love being in the archives. [D1]

Her joint appointment in history and sociology spared her the decision of having to choose a single identity.

An economist learned too late that he had more in common with colleagues in other social science disciplines than most other economists. His interdisciplinary work emphasized that difference, but it also provided an op-portunity to pursue a broader range of interests.

> I [once] worked with a fellow in sociology who is a Marxist sociologist. We taught together a course on capitalism and socialism. One of the most powerful things that taught me is that I consider myself a social scientist. And the more we worked together, the more I realized the way he trained and the way I was trained were dramatically different. Economists' train-ing is very narrow and focused and much more quantitative. Whereas the sociologist, the historian—the breath of their reading is typically much, much greater than what we [economists] have. I just kind of, again it was maybe some of my naïveté; I think I should have known that. [O]

Informants whose interdisciplinary work distanced them from traditional disciplinary philosophies and methods questioned whether they could still call their departments and their disciplines their intellectual homes. Often they talked about not fitting in as well as they once did.

> To some extent I don't fit in the political science department. It's part of why I do interdisciplinary work, because I am really not interested in kind of pursuing the same theories or taking the central paradigm in the disci-pline and seeing how it fits in all these different situations. That's just not interesting to me at all. So my interest is kind of in learning the new stuff that I need to learn in order to make sense of the world that I am observ-ing and participating in. [L]

> There are some ways in which I see increasingly that I don't fit particu-larly well in economics and there are some levels on which that bothers me a great deal. [G]

Neither of these informants, however, considered their ability to teach stu-dents to be compromised by their critical stance toward their discipline. The ability to teach students, the political scientist suggested, allowed her to main-tain at least a marginal relationship with her home discipline.

It's easier to say where I fit in as a teacher rather than a researcher at this point because in the courses I teach we go through the standard theories of decision making, which I still think are important for people to understand. They're not important for my research because I understand them, but they're important for the students. [G]

The economist also believed that students needed exposure to fundamental theories, if only so that they might question them. Her job was to encourage a healthy skepticism.

[Feeling like I don't fit in] does not mean however that when I go into a classroom I say all this theory stuff is a bunch of crap because I don't believe that that's true. I think theory is useful and that tests of that theory are useful to the extent that they can help people solve problems because a lot of problems, most problems, have an economic dimension even if they are not primarily economic in nature. I think there are lots of interesting questions that can be answered with basic theory, basic theory, the kind of stuff that I would teach in a course like macroeconomics or even intro level. There are models of the economy that are useful as long as you don't regard them as *the* truth with a capital T. So to that extent I think that it is still important for me to teach the kinds of things that I teach in my standard courses. [G]

Commenting on the discomfort that her situation produced, this informant later commented, "I would like to think that I could fit better in a discipline that was transformed from what it is right now."

Other informants seemed to find safety, if not comfort, in numbers. A psychologist whose scholarly work was entirely interdisciplinary found a home in a large university department. Psychologists with different specialties were housed in different buildings and often did not know each other.

Because it's a very large department, it's been somewhat comfortable to be a person who doesn't really fit in psychology. . . . People are often trying to figure out why a psychologist is doing work on early-twentieth-century black families. My whole kind of graduate and academic life has been really a matter of not really fitting, period. [T]

An economist argued that the size of his discipline and the number of specialties and rarefied topics created a large number of specialty enclaves. Only a very few, highly visible economists were recognized by all.

> Given how segmented disciplines are now, there are some domains of economics that I belong to and write and contribute to and they know I exist but the discipline in the main is so big that very few people are recognized as existing. So everybody is marginal within a discipline that's that large and that specialized. Although some people are much more active politically and therefore much more noticeable. [F]

A professor with strong interdisciplinary leanings seemed to sum up the feelings of many of the informants whose interdisciplinary scholarship challenged disciplinary paradigms. They were neither disciplinary nor completely beyond discipline. The indeterminate place they occupied could be exciting at times but also lonely. They hoped to maintain disciplinary ties but often found those ties too confining. Her admission about her place in the academic world gave evidence of the contradictions often associated with interdisciplinarity: "So I am saying, yes, I think I fit in. And yes I still have that sensation periodically of not ever being quite content anywhere" [K].

Outcomes of Interdisciplinary Teaching and Research

For many the outcomes of interdisciplinary scholarship are the same as those of disciplinary scholarship. Interdisciplinary activities led to conference presentations and papers, journal articles, monographs, and books. Some were hired, promoted, and tenured on the basis of their interdisciplinary scholarly output. In addition informants learned as they pursued interdisciplinary topics, just as they did when they explored new disciplinary territory.

Many of the informants who pursued interdisciplinary topics did so occasionally, simultaneously, or alternately with disciplinary projects. Many talked about the enduring impact of their disciplinary training on their thinking, even when they were doing interdisciplinary research or teaching. The key to maintaining a disciplinary identity was to pursue interdisciplinary activities that were consistent with the preferred paradigms and epistemologies.

Only when interdisciplinary scholarship challenged disciplinary tenets and methods did it result in outcomes that one would not expect to result from disciplinary work. When interdisciplinary thinking was associated with larger epistemological questions of objectivity, truth, and empiricism, it often led informants to question their disciplinary ties. For this reason informants whose scholarship was influenced by postmodern, feminist, and critical theory were more likely than other informants who did interdisciplinary work to wonder where they belonged.

In *Academic Tribes and Territories* (1990), Tony Becher argued that the central source of faculty identity is the discipline. Consistent with views of the disciplines as cultures, this statement is rarely challenged. Although the discipline may be the source of professional, and perhaps even personal, identity for many or most faculty, faculty are increasingly critiquing disciplinary knowledge and consequently their right or their willingness to be considered disciplinarians. It may be that ontology and epistemology, not simply discipline, determine where we hang our intellectual hats.

Realizing
Interdisciplinarity

The early literature on interdisciplinarity would depress
even the most successful interdisciplinarian, with its relent-
less emphasis on the barriers to interdisciplinary scholarship: unfavorable reward structures, biased faculty, uninformed administrators. Julie Thompson Klein synthesized
this literature in her 1990 book, *Interdisciplinarity: History,
Theory, and Practice.* Struck by the boundary rhetoric, she
offered a litany of geopolitical metaphors—taken directly
from the literature on interdisciplinarity—that create the
impression that academic disciplines are foreign territories
and interdisciplinarians, hapless trespassers. Commenting
on "the inevitable paradox"—that even our vocabulary pre-
disposes us to talk about interdisciplinarity in terms of
disciplinarity, Klein specifically captured the problem; she
noted that most discussions of interdisciplinarity center on
disciplines or, more aptly, on the disciplinary boundaries
that define the content of the discipline and its methods
(pp. 77–78). More recent treatments of interdisciplinarity
have remedied some of the shortcomings of the early literature by including interdisciplinary teaching (for example,
Davis 1995) and interdisciplinary research in the social sciences and humanities (for example, Klein 1996, Salter and
Hearn 1995). Even the metaphors have changed. In a later
book Klein (1996) shifted her gaze, looking less intently at
how disciplinary boundaries divide and differentiate, to how

Chapter

they are crossed, blurred, and deconstructed.* Since the mid twentieth century, she argued, there has been a escalation of cross-disciplinary activities, even in hard disciplines such as physics (Klein 1993).

Softening Disciplinary Lines

The early literature on interdisciplinarity focused on the scientific disciplines, assuming these were exemplars for disciplines in general. Since disciplinary boundaries are more clearly drawn in the sciences, where content areas and methods are clearly defined, the image of fortified borders solidified. This imagery disguises the tentative nature of disciplinary boundaries that are, after all, products of human imagination. While there is clearly some degree of consensus among the members of disciplinary communities about what their fields include and exclude, there is also likely to be disagreement on particulars. Leo Apostel, a philosopher writing about interdisciplinarity, reminded his readers that

> *A discipline does not exist. A science does not exist. There are personas and groups practicing the same science or the same disciplines.* Our main problem is:
> a) that the inputs to all members, or groups of members of the same discipline are certainly not identical;
> b) that the work they do is not the same;
> c) that the conceptual models or instruments they produce are not identical;
> d) that their interlanguage is not the same for all interlocutors; and
> e) that the pedagogical procedures are not identical either. (emphasis in original; Apostel 1972, p. 147)

The informants in this study clearly demonstrated that even scientific disciplines are subject to individual interpretation. What one informant considered biology another did not. What was defined as disciplinary by some was

---

*Klein traced the idea of blurring disciplinary boundaries to the often quoted essay by Clifford Geertz, entitled "Blurred Genres," in which Geertz highlighted the ways in which analogies from the humanities were increasingly used in sociological and anthropological texts.

classified as interdisciplinary by others. The vagaries of personal constructions of disciplines and interdisciplinarity are compounded by changes within the disciplines themselves. As knowledge expands so do disciplines. Occasionally subfields become vestigial appendixes. Any discussion of interdisciplinarity therefore must begin with the acknowledgment that there is nothing permanent about the disciplines. They serve as epistemological corrals of concepts, theories, and methods linked by specialized languages, but they are, above all, social groupings that make and break their own rules of scholarship. As Klein wrote: "If there is an undisputed truth about disciplinarity, it is that disciplines change . . . " (1993, p. 186). Although he favors collectivist metaphors such as "tribes," "cultures," and "territories," Becher (1989) also acknowledges that disciplines are a troublesome unit of analysis.

> When one begins to look closely into their epistemological structures, it becomes apparent that most of them embrace a wide range of subspecialisms, some with one set of features and others with others. There is no single method of enquiry, no standard verification procedure, no definitive set of concepts which uniquely characterizes each particular discipline. (p. 43)

In describing their interdisciplinary research and teaching, the informants in this study implicitly defined interdisciplinary scholarship. These definitions varied considerably as is evident in the categories of the typology of interdisciplinary scholarship presented in chapter 4. As should be expected, informants' perceptions of interdisciplinarity were related to their perceptions of their discipline. For example, a few informants framed an argument in which scholarship must cross paradigms, as well as disciplines, in order to be interdisciplinary. Disciplinary habits of mind also colored impressions of interdisciplinarity, and informants' conscious or unconscious commitments to disciplinary conventions of rigor, depth, and specialization led them to approximate these in their interdisciplinary scholarship.

Rethinking Integration

Most definitions and categorizations of interdisciplinary work focus on the level of integration of the disciplines involved. The most commonly accepted distinctions—multidisciplinary, interdisciplinary, and transdisciplinary—maintain this emphasis (Newell 1998). These distinctions, perhaps because they are largely theoretical in nature, are difficult to apply to real projects. Researchers have difficulty determining a good method for measuring the integration of disciplinary perspectives or components. They disagree on whether processes or outcomes should be assessed to measure integration. It is unclear how much integration is enough integration to qualify as interdisciplinarity. Although scholars have circled around the question of integration for years, they have avoided asking the obvious question: is this conceptualization of interdisciplinary work accurate?

A definition of interdisciplinarity as integration is suitable for some scholarship conducted within a positivist paradigm. Integration results when two or more disciplines are combined in such a way that they become seamless, the individual contributions invisible. Differences are subsumed so that generalized statements can be made about phenomena. Epistemologies that value difference, however, may reject integration as the goal of interdisciplinarity if it requires ignoring difference, conflict, or contradictions because such actions belie the reality and complexity of phenomenon. In a positivistic model, unresolved conflict and contradiction suggest failure. In postpositivistic stances difference, conflict, and contradiction are required because of the plural nature of reality. Furthermore all work done within a positivist paradigm is not easily described as integrated. Some forms of interdisciplinarity, such as transdisciplinarity, for example, are often conducted in positivist paradigms but are more concerned with transcending disciplines than integrating them. My solution to the difficulty presented by the concept of integration was to look elsewhere for defining characteristics of interdisciplinarity.

Focusing on the questions that motivated interdisciplinary scholarship, I classified interdisciplinary research and teaching into four broad categories: informed disciplinarity; synthetic interdisciplinarity; transdisciplinarity; and conceptual interdisciplinarity. Informed disciplinary research and teaching call upon other disciplines to illuminate a disciplinary question. To achieve informed disciplinarity, some faculty infused their disciplinary courses with examples from a variety of disciplines; others were more selective and used fewer examples or contributions from other disciplines. Although many informants using this form of interdisciplinarity professed to the belief that interdisciplinary scholarship required integration of disciplinary perspectives, their descriptions of their scholarship suggest that they applied this requirement more rig-orously to research than to teaching. In the classroom the simple presence of another disciplinary perspective or the teaming of faculty from different disci-plines was often considered evidence of interdisciplinarity, regardless of whether disciplinary perspectives were integrated or presented as separate or conflicting. In contrast informants suggested that interdisciplinary research required a greater depth of understanding of other disciplines or a greater de-gree of integration than did interdisciplinary teaching.

Synthetic interdisciplinarity combines theories, concepts, and/or methods from different disciplines. It is often a simple matter to determine which com-ponents of the compound come from which discipline, whether one, both, or all of the disciplines involved have a strong paradigm that dictates content and methods. But the identifiable nature of the components is simply a marker of synthetic interdisciplinarity; the reason we are able to distinguish the disci-plines at work in synthetic interdisciplinarity is that clearly bounded content areas and distinctive methods define them. Furthermore the questions asked in synthetic interdisciplinarity tend to delimit the types of connections that are made between and among the involved disciplines because they specify a con-tent area and, often, the method of inquiry to be used.

Synthetic interdisciplinarity provides an opportunity to witness the nego-tiation between or among competing paradigms. Informants who pursued syn-thetic interdisciplinary questions usually combined scientific disciplines char-acterized by strong paradigms—for example, zoology and experimental psychology. A few, however, described research that crossed paradigms, that is, they combined a discipline with a scientific paradigm with a discipline with an interpretative paradigm. In at least one of these cases, the informant's disci-plinary commitments were tested as the scientific paradigm was reconfigured so that information from the interpretative paradigm discipline could be uti-lized.

In contrast to synthetic interdisciplinarity, which highlights the contribu-tions of disciplines, transdisciplinarity mutes the sources of theories and meth-ods, applying them across disciplines so that they are no longer associated with a single discipline or field. In a sense the discipline or field becomes a research setting and thus of secondary importance; the transdisciplinary question is the focus of attention. Although transdisciplinary scholarship was relatively infre-quent in this study, the individuals who pursued it seemed to do so frequently.

Transdisciplinary concepts, theories, and methods were tested in one discipline, then another. Both methods and theories are amenable to this kind of application.

Conceptual interdisciplinary questions have no compelling disciplinary basis; they can therefore include contributions from many disciplines. In this study conceptual interdisciplinarity involved questions about human societies; sociologists, anthropologists, and informants in languages and literature tended to pursue conceptual interdisciplinarity. In disciplines where content and method are not tightly regulated, disciplinary contributions were not limited by either the paradigm or the questions asked. Although interdisciplinary scholarship has often been lauded for its perceived ability to solve social and technological problems that cannot be answered by a single discipline, such commendations often imply that interdisciplinarity is merely a strategy for approaching complex questions. While some faculty undoubtedly agree, many faculty working in conceptual interdisciplinary modes, particularly post-structuralism, postmodernism, and feminism, argue that all questions require interdisciplinary answers. In this perspective interdisciplinarity is not simply *a* strategy; it is the *only* strategy. The category of conceptual interdisciplinarity therefore often implies a critique of the disciplines.

The differences among the categories of the typology of interdisciplinary scholarship are not merely differences of degree. Rather the questions that motivate the research or teaching are qualitatively different from one another. Conceptual interdisciplinary questions are not *more* interdisciplinary than synthetic interdisciplinary questions; they begin with a different kind of question altogether. And the kind of question asked is not independent of the disciplines involved. Synthetic interdisciplinarity and transdisciplinarity appear most often when scientific paradigms are involved; conceptual interdisciplinarity seems to characterize interdisciplinarity in interpretative paradigms. There are undoubtedly exceptions. But it is precisely because different epistemologies and ontologies underlie scholarly questions that a new scheme for understanding interdisciplinarity is needed.

Recognizing a Continuum of Experiences

While the types of interdisciplinarity that characterize a particular research or teaching project cannot be arranged on a continuum because of the different questions that motivate them, informants' experiences of interdisciplinary scholarship can be arrayed on several continua. One continuum describes the type of participation in interdisciplinary interactions: formal or informal. In this study informants' interactions ranged from informal activities such as conversations with colleagues from different fields, to more formal participation in interdisciplinary seminars or conferences, to formalized interdisciplinary teaching and research collaborations. Some informants had experienced a range of interactions while others had experienced, or had chosen to experience, fewer. Another continuum therefore is the frequency or intensity with which informants engaged in interdisciplinary activities. Some individuals engaged in interdisciplinarity infrequently, perhaps only a single interdisciplinary teaching collaboration. Other informants, often those with ties to interdisciplinary undergraduate or graduate programs, engaged in interdisciplinary teaching more often. Informants also varied in the number of interdisciplinary research projects they conducted.

Frequency of interdisciplinarity is related to the extent to which an individual's body of scholarly work is interdisciplinary. At one end is the single excursion into interdisciplinary teaching or research; at the other is an exclusive commitment to interdisciplinary approaches to scholarship. At this far end of the spectrum, faculty may completely renounce disciplinary work. Changes in disciplinary perspectives, however, do not necessarily result from more frequent interdisciplinary activity. If interdisciplinary work does not challenge disciplinary assumptions, change may not be necessary. Similarly it is possible that a single interdisciplinary conversation may have more influence on an individual's thinking or research than a yearlong involvement in interdisciplinary research collaboration.

A final continuum is the degree of disciplinary outreach a given teaching or research project entails. Some questions require a contribution from only one discipline, as when a borrowed method allows a particular analysis. Other questions require contributions from several, even many, disciplines; together these disciplines offer a more complete picture than could otherwise be devised. The terms *broad*, or *wide*, *interdisciplinarity* and *narrow interdisciplinarity* have been coined to indicate differences in the degree of interaction among disciplines (van Dusseldorp and Wigboldus 1994) and the epistemological distance among disciplines (Kelly 1996). Broad interdisciplinarity requires the interaction of many disciplines with different paradigms and methods, ignoring the fact that a scholar today can travel quite comfortably in the epistemological vehicle of choice across a number of disciplines. Different disciplines do not necessarily imply different paradigms. In this study outreach to one other discipline was the norm among informants from the sciences as the questions they asked suggested a specific combination of disciplines. In the humanities and social sciences, informants often reached out to a greater number of disciplines because of shared content areas among the disciplines.

Pursuing Interdisciplinarity

The processes by which informants do interdisciplinary work greatly resemble the processes by which they do disciplinary work. Differences often amount to variations on a theme rather than distinctive ways of accomplishing academic work. For example, when undertaking a teaching or research project, whether it is disciplinary or interdisciplinary, faculty typically begin by reading about a topic. Informants in this study reported that they read extensively to prepare for interdisciplinary projects—more extensively than they would for a disciplinary project and of course in disciplines other than their own. Some read in only one or two disciplines; others ranged more widely, depending on the type of interdisciplinary scholarship undertaken. Faculty teaching a collaborative course generally read the disciplinary works suggested by their partner and perhaps by others. Attempting to approximate the disciplinary norm of specialization, informants often chose a narrow topic as a basis for an interdisciplinary project, strategically defining topics that would allow them to develop expertise. Their comments about the depth of their reading and the specialized nature of their research revealed both their strategies for accomplishing interdisciplinary work and their anxieties about it.

Specialization often requires or inspires faculty to develop a network of colleagues with like interests. Interdisciplinary work also encouraged individuals to expand their network of colleagues. The nature of interdisciplinary work motivated some informants to attend interdisciplinary conferences, institutes, and workshops. These interdisciplinary meetings, typically smaller and more specific than disciplinary conferences, were well suited to obtaining helpful information from colleagues and developing a network of individuals working on the same topic. On campus many informants also participated in interdisciplinary forums, colloquia, and seminars that offered opportunities to learn what others were thinking about the same topics, to crystallize thinking, and to share ideas with individuals who might offer a valuable critique.

In the disciplines collaboration often follows a pattern. In some fields it is the norm; the nature of the problems under study requires teams of researchers who work on pieces of the puzzle. In others it is less common; research topics are not easily divided into component parts, and individual scholars tend to toil alone. About half of the informants in this study collaborated with a colleague or colleagues from another discipline in a research or teaching project. In some cases collaboration occurred in fields where it is *not* the norm, for example, in English literature and theology. In addition collaboration was as serendipitous as it was purposeful. Several informants described accidental meetings that resulted in research and teaching collaborations. These same individuals, as well as others in the study, also solicited the help of collaborators. Both planned and unplanned activities occurred across the disciplines represented.

Teaching interdisciplinary courses, whether individually or in teams, inspired informants to reflect on pedagogical styles and educational purposes. Learning another discipline reminded them what it is like to be students, and informants who taught interdisciplinary courses often empathized with their students, acknowledging that interdisciplinary approaches could be unfamiliar and confusing. This heightened awareness of student needs often resulted in informants taking extra care and time to explain goals and assignments to students and to reassure them about the quality and direction of their work in interdisciplinary classes. Both cognitive and affective challenges arose in interdisciplinary classrooms, and interdisciplinary courses inspired reflection on the purposes of education. Although they conceded that interdisciplinary approaches often sacrificed content coverage, most informants valued the perceived superiority of interdisciplinary approaches for developing students' thinking skills, particularly the ability to critique thoughtfully what they had learned.

As interdisciplinary teaching heightened pedagogical awareness, interdisciplinary research often inspired epistemological reflection. Whereas informants might use competing disciplinary perspectives to advantage in the classroom, many found them unacceptable in research. Disciplinary conflicts among the members of interdisciplinary research teams might be resolved early in a project's history, but for the most part potential conflicts were avoided by carefully selecting collaborators who shared basic beliefs about content and methods.

Contextual Influences on Interdisciplinarity

Portraying disciplines, departments, and institutions as barriers to interdisciplinarity whitewashes the variety of contexts in which interdisciplinarity is conducted. Departments, institutions, and disciplinary associations are variously responsive to interdisciplinarity, and faculty respond to these academic contexts in numerous ways. Overstating the influence of context can led to a deterministic view of faculty life, but inattention to context conceals faculty agency in negotiating institutional, departmental, and disciplinary realities. In many institutions familiar barriers to interdisciplinarity such disciplinary norms, departmental structures, and institutional reward systems exist, but they do not prevent all faculty from pursuing interdisciplinary work. Some adjust to their contexts, even if critical of them, and continue with their work. Both senior and junior faculty in this study substantiated this ability to adjust to, or ignore, negative influences in their environments. Despite concerns about colleagues' opinions, senior faculty pursued their interdisciplinary interests — while warning junior members of their departments to avoid them until after tenure. Junior faculty in this study acknowledged the potential for departmental conflicts, ignored the warnings, and persisted in their interdisciplinary scholarship. The height of a barrier, of course, is in the eye of the beholder. Faculty who are determined to pursue interdisciplinary research and teaching projects may see possibilities where others see pitfalls. But perhaps departmental, institutional, and disciplinary contexts are not now—or may never have been—as hostile to interdisciplinarity as reported. Certainly informants described a variety of departmental, institutional, and disciplinary responses to interdisciplinary scholarship and their perceptions of these environments varied widely. Some described departmental colleagues as open to and supportive of interdisciplinarity while others felt alienated or even ignored by faculty and administrators. Several forged ties with colleagues in other disciplines as much out of necessity as by choice. Since the climate of an institution or department is highly dependent on the mix of individuals that comprise it, changes in personnel can make the difference between acceptance and rejection of interdisciplinary work.

Concerns about collegial disapproval in the liberal arts colleges revolved around the fear that interdisciplinary teaching was a drain on departmental resources. A particular concern was that departmental colleagues would have to teach courses that the person teaching in an interdisciplinary program would have taught. Resources were also a continuing question for directors of interdisciplinary programs. When not guaranteed sufficient faculty through contractual arrangements, directors found recruiting teaching faculty from departments a difficult task. Even at institutions where contracts eased the staffing situation, directors worried that changes in administration and in the attitudes or needs of contributing departments could create problems.

Informants tended to assess administrative support for interdisciplinary work in terms of structural or financial support. For example, at one institution informants suggested that the large number of joint appointments signaled an institutional openness to interdisciplinarity. At the universities funding for interdisciplinary programs at the graduate and undergraduate level, as well as for special projects, was an important barometer of the climate for interdisciplinarity. At the liberal arts institutions, where teaching was weighted more heavily than research in hiring, promotion, and tenure decisions, financial support for interdisciplinary course development was interpreted as a sign of administrative sanction.

Observers of interdisciplinarity typically have framed the disciplines as negative influences on interdisciplinary scholarship, but some informants contested this image, describing their disciplines as increasingly open to interdisciplinarity. For example, historians and anthropologists talked about the inroads each made into the other's fields. Scientists argued that external influences, such as funding agencies and sponsors and funding incentives, pushed the interdisciplinary research agenda. In the humanities interdisciplinarity was thought to be an increasingly normal aspect of academic life, except in economics, where informants were typically pessimistic about disciplinary response. While the views of these few informants may not be representative, they do reveal the importance of individual perceptions of disciplinary attitudes and remind us that disciplines are changing and growing social entities.

Interdisciplinary Outcomes

Interdisciplinary scholarship can yield both professional and personal rewards. Informants attributed a variety of tangible professional outcomes—conference papers, articles, and books—to their interdisciplinary activities. A few revealed that they had been hired by their institutions precisely because of their interdisciplinary work, not in spite of it. Others contended that interdisciplinary work helped them attain promotions and tenure. Informants were equally excited about the intellectual outcomes that resulted from interdisciplinary engagement. Faculty with varying levels of interdisciplinary experience talked about what they learned about their own and other disciplines. Their learning was a source of personal satisfaction and, for a few, relieved their boredom with disciplinary topics. Learning a new discipline also had the distinct benefit of expanding an individual's range of teaching options and research questions.

Interdisciplinarity could open new intellectual vistas, but it did not require informants to abandon their disciplines. Most pursued their interdisciplinary interests from the comfort of their home discipline. Often informants noted the enduring impact of their disciplinary training; disciplinary concepts, theories, and ways of looking at the world were ever present. Few informants were inclined to supplant their disciplinary teaching and research with an interdisciplinary agenda; the majority interspersed interdisciplinary and disciplinary projects. A few longed to return to purely disciplinary work after a hiatus. As long as interdisciplinary work was consistent with disciplinary tenets and methods, informants maintained their disciplinary identity. On occasion, however, interdisciplinarity left epistemological scars. When interdisciplinarity caused informants to question previously held disciplinary beliefs, professional discomfort resulted. Informants then broached the question of disciplinary identities and how much they could question and critique their discipline and still remain a member of their community. When epistemological conflicts became too severe, informants searched for alternate identities.

Feeding Interdisciplinary Interests and Talents

Informants spoke candidly about institutional and departmental environments that both encouraged and discouraged interdisciplinary research and teaching. Administrators, department chairs, and disciplinary faculty can learn much from these accounts about developing higher education environments that facilitate and support interdisciplinarity.

Once faculty members establish an interest in a particular interdisciplinary topic, they often find it useful to attend workshops, institutes, and conferences where they can deepen their knowledge of the area and connect with potential colleagues. The annual meetings of most disciplinary associations do not address interdisciplinary topics and faculty must find interdisciplinary interaction elsewhere. The dilemma for faculty at institutions where travel funds are limited is the need to choose between disciplinary and interdisciplinary meetings. Lack of travel funds can create the impression that disciplinarity and interdisciplinarity are in competition. In such a circumstance, junior faculty may feel obliged to choose disciplinary meetings so that their commitment to their discipline is not questioned. Although doubling travel funds is not a feasible answer for most institutions, faculty in need of additional funding may be served through a program that allocates special travel funds on a competitive basis to faculty pursuing interdisciplinary research or teaching projects.

Off-campus opportunities should not be the only institutional response to the needs of faculty doing interdisciplinary work. Colleges and universities can sponsor workshops, institutes, and conferences that make use of local experts, encourage interinstitutional collegiality and collaboration, and enhance institutional visibility and prestige. Grants officers may be helpful in locating potential external funding for particular topics.

The institutions that I visited varied in their willingness and ability to support interdisciplinary activities. Informants portrayed two of the institutions as largely indifferent to interdisciplinarity and occasionally as hostile to it; the other institutions were perceived as more accommodating and welcoming. At one of these supportive institutions, one individual in particular personified the proactive faculty/administrator. He described the activities of what he called "a facilitating organization."

We are always sniffing around looking for projects that need to be done or looking for resources that we can compete for. When we find projects and or resources, we then look around for an interdisciplinary mix of people, often people who have never known each other exist, bring them together and show them how to behave, actually help them write the proposals. Often we are a key part of the proposal process. [We] bring a group of people together. Educate them about the opportunity. Educate them about how the opportunity can be played out. Educate them about the fact that the university really is supporting this effort. Provide them with airplane tickets to go to wherever they have to go to get the information needed to make the proposal a success. Then we have our own staff, who know how to work with people who haven't been interdisciplinary and prepare interdisciplinary workshops. [I1]

These workshops encouraged people from several different disciplines to share their perspectives on a common theme. In addition the organization often co-sponsored seminars and provided the extra funding "to bring in the first team." "If it is possible to get someone who is doing an unusual project, or has been very successful with interdisciplinary work," he explained, "we will make sure that person gets here."

Institutions that hope to encourage interdisciplinarity must consider the needs of interdisciplinary teachers as well. Colleges and universities that offer interdisciplinary programs must address important issues such as staffing and budgeting that directly affect faculty and students. In addition they need to consider the needs of faculty who, in pursuing interdisciplinary teaching projects outside of interdisciplinary programs, often find themselves without mentoring, peer, or monetary support. A number of informants in this study served or were serving as directors of interdisciplinary programs and felt a particular responsibility to maintain the health and vitality of interdisciplinary programs on their campuses. These directors were often the only full-time faculty in a program; they typically borrowed faculty from other departments to provide a program of studies. At the mercy of these other departments, directors worried every year about who would be available to teach program courses. At small colleges this was particularly troubling since the pool of potential faculty was very limited.

Institutions have a responsibility to ensure that students enrolled in interdisciplinary programs and courses have access to a faculty who can support their learning needs. Joint appointments between departments and programs can ease the shortage of faculty considerably, and contractual commitments can help interdisciplinary programs maintain their academic standards. Institutions that require program directors periodically to hunt for faculty reveal their values and priorities. College and university administrations can encourage departments to share their faculty and recognize departments and faculty who serve interdisciplinary programs. Program directors can be encouraged to recruit widely and administrators can aid in the identification of potential instructors. Institutions can also create incentives for departments to loan or jointly to appoint faculty. Incentive funding can come in the form of discretionary departmental funds that can be used for activities such as colloquia, guest speakers, equipment purchases, or seed money for course or research project development, or funds for replacement faculty.

When enrollments warrant, full-time faculty, perhaps with joint appointments in departments, should be hired to staff interdisciplinary programs. At some colleges interdisciplinary programs with burgeoning enrollments are poorly staffed while departments that graduate one or two majors per year maintain a full faculty. Faculty with strong interdisciplinary interests might be encouraged to move from underenrolled departments to interdisciplinary programs. Faculty should not be expected, however, to teach and advise students in interdisciplinary programs without proper training and support. Retooling for an interdisciplinary assignment takes time and energy, and this commitment should be recognized. Immigrants to new programs or departments should be provided with faculty development opportunities such as course development funds, conference travel, and financial support for interdisciplinary projects, as well as discretionary funds for publications, equipment, or other supplies. Directors should assess the service role their programs provide to traditional majors, as well as examine their program enrollments to bolster the case for additional faculty.

Excessive teaching responsibilities can detract from faculty research productivity, but, for some faculty, teaching interdisciplinary courses can contribute to productivity; several informants in this study generated research projects from their interdisciplinary teaching. Informants who collaborated on interdisciplinary teaching and research often produced scholarly work; furthermore, by presenting at different disciplinary and interdisciplinary conferences and tailoring articles for different audiences, these individuals effectively doubled the output from a single project. Although informants managed to develop and teach interdisciplinary courses without administrative assistance, they appreciated policies and practices that eased the pressure. Developing interdisciplinary and team-taught courses required more preparation time than a disciplinary course and informants benefited from provisions of summer salary, course releases, and funds for teaching or research assistants to compile and organize course materials. Informants' experiences suggest these incentives are good investments in faculty productivity.

Focused, interdisciplinary dialogues can be powerful mechanisms for promoting interdisciplinary scholarship. Colloquia, seminars, and other forums offer faculty regular and continuing opportunities to engage in interdisciplinary conversation about topics of interest. Informants contemplating or engaged in interdisciplinary scholarship acknowledged these opportunities for dialogue as important no matter what their career stage; both new faculty seeking colleagues and senior faculty trying out new ideas found in colloquia a congenial place to meet and become intellectually acquainted with colleagues from across departments. As one informant put it,

> the institution has a challenge and a responsibility to be imaginative and innovative, to get people to come together and think about issues of common concern — because there are lots of issues of common concern and common inquiry, but we don't always do a very good job identifying what they are and creating a forum, an arena for their exploration. [T]

Departmental chairs can solicit ideas for interdisciplinary forums from faculty members and graduate students. With the assistance of an academic dean and chairs from different departments, cosponsored seminars can be developed. Institutions or divisions can provide funding for guest lecturers to supplement existing faculty talent and create visibility and interest across campus. Since fiscal constraints can force departments to choose between disciplinary and interdisciplinary activities, institutional funding can be used to supplement departmental funds or incentive funding used to reward departments that produce cosponsored programs.

At smaller institutions faculty often know one another and share information about teaching and research interests. Informants at these institutions noted that serendipity and proximity fostered interdisciplinary collaborations. Still, interdisciplinary seminars were valued opportunities for sustained conversation with colleagues across campus. Serendipitous meetings also occurred among faculty at large institutions, but the size of an institution can stymie interdepartmental interaction. Carefully planned programs can attract faculty from different schools, disciplines, and programs and may result in collaborative interdisciplinary projects. Sponsors of interdisciplinary forums should evaluate these programs to assess their usefulness and their contributions to professional development and outcomes. Evaluation should be timely but not hasty, since such interdisciplinary dialogues will undoubtedly take time to bear fruit.

A pervasive fear among faculty who do interdisciplinary work is that colleagues will neither appreciate nor reward it (for example, Hurst 1992). Faculty may be troubled by departmental colleagues who are skeptical of interdisciplinary scholarship and withhold collegial support. The lack of a collegial home base can undermine confidence and morale. Engagement in interdisciplinarity can be especially intimidating for junior faculty, who depend on the support of departmental colleagues for their promotion and tenure. Junior faculty who perceive unfavorable opinions about interdisciplinary scholarship among departmental colleagues may avoid projects they otherwise would have pursued. Stifling intellectual exploration rarely serves the interests of faculty or higher education in general.

Faculty must also recognize that disciplinary biases may be cloaked in seemingly neutral terms. Phrases such as *research trajectories* and *focused agendas* are often euphemisms for disciplinary conventions. While it is incumbent upon junior faculty, as informants suggested, to package their work carefully for disciplinary colleagues, it is equally important that faculty carefully review interdisciplinary work. Innovative work should be assessed with a flexible, but intellectually justifiable, set of scholarly criteria. Colleagues should also consider the time commitment required by interdisciplinary scholarship when assessing scholarly productivity. Departments may also need to rely on external reviewers when they do not possess the expertise to judge the quality of interdisciplinary scholarship. External review, however, is not a substitute for collegial review; sincere and concerted attempts to understand interdisciplinary research and teaching can create amicable environments for faculty with interdisciplinary interests.

Institutions that expect interdisciplinarity to thrive on their campuses must do more than support interdisciplinary scholarship through funding of existing programs or individual projects. They must create flexible interdisciplinary spaces where faculty can find temporary or second homes. The notion of such spaces is not new; the University of Chicago's divisional committees and the research institutes and organized research units that are increasingly found on university campuses are examples. Neither of these structures, however, is sufficient to serve all faculty with interdisciplinary interests. Faculty must be invited, for example, to join one of Chicago's committees; temporary attachments are uncommon (Dzubach 1991). Organized research units are typically dedicated to specific research projects, usually scientific or technical in nature. The interdisciplinary space of the future would provide interdisciplinary faculty, or faculty with interdisciplinary research and teaching interests, with a place to grow.

Faculty who are new to interdisciplinary research must be welcomed into interdisciplinary spaces where exploration and conversation are as valued as collaboration. These spaces may house ongoing interdisciplinary projects, but they should also be available to faculty who are still exploring interdisciplinary options. In addition faculty must be able to move in and out of these spaces according to their own schedules. The usual scenario of fixed appointments tied to grants does not allow for interdisciplinary incubation periods. Nor does it provide a home in disciplines where external funding is rare.

Interdisciplinary spaces need not be large facilities although a centralized location with office and conference room space is necessary to facilitate interaction. These modest accommodations can serve as places to hold colloquia and seminars, as meeting rooms for teaching and research teams pursuing interdisciplinary projects, or simply as places where individuals can go to learn about interdisciplinary opportunities and make connections with faculty with similar interests in interdisciplinary teaching and research. Such spaces should be considered faculty development centers that revitalize faculty and/or stimulate their intellectual juices. A strong advocate of interdisciplinarity, who was also a member of the administration at her institution, felt that it was her role and her responsibility to bring people together to foster innovation and knowledge generation:

> What I am interested in for myself and for other people—as an administrator and also as a faculty member—is making sure that as much as possible we are supportive of and encouraging of people who are interested in connecting with other knowledge seekers and that we help each other

as much as possible to learn more. That seems to me what interdisciplinarity is. And to the extent that we keep people from connecting, that we keep students from making connections, that we keep university structures from allowing groups of people to connect, then I think we are probably not fostering knowledge in the fullest way that we can. [N]

Investigating Interdisciplinarity

Interdisciplinarity has been hard to define because it takes on so many guises and because it is a moving target that responds to expansions and contractions in the disciplines themselves. Grounded definitions of interdisciplinary scholarship enhance our understanding of interdisciplinary scholarship because they capture interdisciplinarity in practice. And, since practices evolve, our understandings of interdisciplinarity must also evolve over time. The picture of interdisciplinarity offered by this study is of course incomplete, in part because it is limited in scope, but also because of the sheer variety of scholarship in colleges and universities today. The task for researchers in higher education and other fields is to update the picture of interdisciplinarity continually—as well as that of scholarship in general. Researchers should attend to questions of how scholarly work is conducted, how it is perceived and rewarded within and across disciplines, how interdisciplinary and multidisciplinary fields are created, and how they develop. Scholars should also carefully observe continuing and future shifts in disciplinary ontologies and paradigms that may signal far-reaching changes in the ways we think and learn.

In this study a few informants wholly committed to interdisciplinarity suffered professional identity crises. As committed interdisciplinarians, they were reluctant, even unable, to identify with a single discipline. What are the long-term effects of such disciplinary identity crises on faculty trained and located in academic departments? Will such individuals resolve their identity conflicts over time and if so, how? Researchers may wish to follow the careers of interdisciplinary faculty to see how changes and/or reconciliations occur over time and how institutions and colleagues respond to them. Higher education researchers could also examine the scholarly productivity of faculty in interdisciplinary programs, faculty with joint appointments, and faculty doing interdisciplinary work from disciplinary locations. Do the same measures of productivity suffice for disciplinary and interdisciplinary faculty? Are scholarship patterns similar or dissimilar? What accounts for the patterns observed? How might institutional contexts influence the productivity of interdisciplinary faculty?

Further study of individual faculty members' constructions of their disciplines is also needed to help us better understand how these constructions influence their scholarship and their perceptions of disciplinarity and interdisciplinarity. Researchers should pursue questions that help us understand how individuals develop these constructions, how they change over time, and how they perceive alternative constructions. These studies should begin with precollege and college students who are just beginning to recognize that there are such conventions as disciplines. Researchers should also explore the development of disciplinary constructions over time among graduate students and faculty. Why do individuals construct the same discipline in different ways? What are the ramifications of these personal constructions on individuals, careers, departments, and institutions?

A Concluding Allegory

One informant told me a disturbing story about an important figure in the field of ecology. In the 1930s this man wrote a classic study of the dustbowl, "a wonderful interdisciplinary treatise . . . that won all kinds of awards." A professor of botany at the University of Oklahoma, he explained what was happening in the dustbowl, why it was happening, and how the phenomenon was related to agricultural practices and government policies. As a result of the success of this book, Oberlin College hired the botanist. Later, in 1950, he was invited to Yale to found the first graduate program in conservation.

> He spent his last decade at Yale very happy, but he always felt that he had failed in his life because he hadn't been more of a scientist, that these interdisciplinary activities had caused him to spend less time with science and so he really hadn't developed in his true calling. [A1]

Other people felt the same way about him, my informant explained. Scientists were a little bit suspicious of him. In her interviews with individuals who knew the man, she detected assumptions that interdisciplinary work was by its nature less difficult, less rigorous, less prestigious.

So that while he was admired for what he did do, even at its best, it wasn't good enough. So I'm very much, these days, thinking about the costs to people of getting involved in interdisciplinary work, because this guy knew that we need to think in interdisciplinary ways to save the planet. He was absolutely convinced of that. And he spent a lot of time developing under-graduate and graduate curricula that were truly interdisciplinary—and yet he could say that and also devalue himself. It's tremendously sad. [A1]

Although this informant clearly loved interdisciplinary teaching and research and had been instrumental in forming two interdisciplinary programs on her campus, she also harbored fears that these activities made her less of a scientist. The parallels between her own story and that of the ecologist were stark.

Interdisciplinary scholarship has inspired many to call for, or even attempt, a reconceptualization of scholarship so that it acknowledges the contributions made by scholars working from different perspectives and in different modalities to the advancement of knowledge. In 1990 Ernest Boyer, then president of the Carnegie Foundation for the Advancement of Teaching, published an influential book calling for such a redefinition of academic scholarship. Concerned that academia had adopted a restrictive view of scholarship that privileged basic research and diminished other forms of scholarly work, Boyer called for an enlarged perspective in which faculty work was defined more broadly, to allow for the "full range of academic and civic mandates" (1990, p.16). This new typology of scholarship included the traditional scholarship of discovery, that is, basic research, but it also included the scholarship of integration, of application, and of teaching. For Boyer integration included making connections across disciplines, analyzing and interpreting data in revealing ways, and educating nonspecialists. The scholarship of integration, Boyer argued, is closely related to the scholarship of discovery because it involves research that is conducted at the boundaries "where fields converge" (1990, p. 19). The scholarship of integration is broader than interdisciplinary research alone, since it also includes interpretive and integrative scholarship, which Boyer defined as work that asks, "What do the findings mean? Is it possible to interpret what's been discovered in ways that provide a larger, more comprehensive understanding?" (1990, p.19).

We might ask why Boyer chose to distinguish interdisciplinary from disciplinary scholarship. He suggested that the two are closely related, but not the same. Yet there is little in the definition of the scholarship of discovery to exclude interdisciplinary scholarship, except allusions to "disciplined inquiry" and Boyer's telling list of disciplinary scholars who have contributed to the advancement of knowledge. Without diminishing the importance of Boyer's call for the inclusion of interdisciplinary work in the research canon and the credibility it lent to interdisciplinary scholarship, I nonetheless regret his decision to create a new category of scholarship to accommodate interdisciplinarity rather than to argue that there is more to the scholarship of discovery than "disciplined" investigation. In response to the work of Boyer and others (for example, Rice 1992, 1993), Michael Paulsen and Ken Feldman (1995) argued that the scholarship of integration is not a separate scholarly function but rather should be distributed among the functions of teaching, research, and service. I find this notion of interdisciplinarity preferable to one that separates teaching from research and disciplinary research from interdisciplinary research. The informants in this study demonstrated the veracity of Paulsen and Feldman's claim: interdisciplinary work occurs in these three domains, although interdisciplinarity in teaching and research were more common than interdisciplinarity in service activities.

Calls for the reconceptualization of scholarship are not academic exercises. The interdisciplinary research and teaching conducted by informants in this study differs in only one respect from disciplinary teaching, that is, in its attention to multiple disciplines. In all other respects it is barely distinguishable: it relies upon the same processes, occurs in the same contexts, and earns the same kinds of rewards. Reconceptualizing scholarship so that it treats disciplinarity and interdisciplinarity equally is the first step toward recognizing the current and growing diversity of our academic communities and enlarging our ideas about the pursuit of knowledge. There is no intrinsic worth in being a scientist, a literary theorist, a good teacher, a good disciplinary citizen, or an interdisciplinary scholar. As a community we create our value systems. We can also alter them.

A more inclusive definition of scholarship would accommodate faculty who not only choose an exclusive focus on interdisciplinarity, but those who move back and forth between disciplinary and interdisciplinary thinking. In this study alone, informants included an economist who collaborated with a theologian, a political scientist who earned the respect of biologists, individuals in anthropology, history, and sociology who shared common interests, an anthropologist who adopted psychologists' methods, and a psychologist who explored the worlds of linguists, philosophers, and neuroscientists. A more inclusive reconceptualization will ease the pressure on faculty who, because of epistemological and ontological imperatives, choose to take an exclusively interdisciplinary approach to teaching and research. Feminists, multiculturalists, postmodernists, poststructuralists, and cultural critics combine border-crossing conversations and collaborations with individual excursions into interdisciplinary research and teaching projects; for many, excursions into disciplinary scholarly work are rare. After a generation on college and university campuses, some of these approaches are still viewed with suspicion despite outward signs of success—journal articles, books, conference papers, and grants. Institutional reward systems and faculty attitudes often ignore these indices. Even in the most supportive institutions, interdisciplinary work has dedicated opponents. Many summarily judge interdisciplinary scholarship on principle rather than give it the same benefit of the doubt that is accorded disciplinary work.

Even informants with long histories of interdisciplinary work harbored disciplinary biases. While some of the study informants recognized the impediments to interdisciplinarity that are created by disciplinary training and immersion, others seemed unaware of the depth of their own disciplinary habits of mind. A biologist, for example, refused to call her work interdisciplinary, arguing that the concept of *interdisciplinarity* was contrived. Her stance, although extreme, was not much different from that of other informants who argued that interdisciplinarity required a solid disciplinary foundation. In contrast, informants from more relational disciplines, such as those in the humanities, frequently argued against the need for a disciplinary grounding in interdisciplinary work. The epistemological influences of the disciplines, even when unconscious, resulted in strong opinions about what counts as knowledge.

Definitions of scholarly work built on a single model of research unnecessarily divide the sciences from the humanities, teaching from research, and the disciplinary from the interdisciplinary. As faculty increasingly question their choices of inquiry methods and their underlying assumptions, the relationship of knowledge to society, and the lines drawn between disciplines, restrictive definitions impede rather than impel knowledge. A more inclusive understanding of scholarship can accommodate current movements such as interdisciplinarity and ably respond to future developments not yet conceived. Our challenge is to recognize disciplinary biases when they appear. To consider duly interdisciplinary scholarship in promotion and hiring decisions, we must amend the traditional question of whether scholarship advances the discipline. We must judge scholarship on the basis of its contribution to the advancement of knowledge. Any other evaluation privileges the discipline over the enterprise and diminishes both the scholarship and the community that produces it.

APPENDIX
Study Design and Conduct

Preparation for the Study

Early in the conceptualization of this research, I conducted a focus group of faculty familiar with interdisciplinary teaching at a summer workshop offered by the Association of Integrated Studies, an organization that encourages and supports interdisciplinarity and interdisciplinary teaching.* The purpose of the focus group was to determine whether faculty who taught interdisciplinary courses could articulate how they incorporated disciplinary components such as subject matter, language, and methods in their work. The literature suggested these disciplinary components would either facilitate or hinder interdisciplinarity and thus would be an important focus for a study of interdisciplinary research and teaching.

The format for the group was simple; I asked faculty to describe in detail the ways in which their discipline and disciplinary perspectives influenced their interdisciplinary scholarship. I suggested a variety of disciplinary components — including domains of inquiry, or subject matter; conceptual structures, or cognitive frameworks; symbolic or specialized languages; modes of inquiry, or discovery processes; epistemological values and normative factors; and relationships with other fields — to begin this discussion.

Ten faculty from a variety of disciplines and representing several institutional types — community colleges, liberal arts colleges, and comprehensive universities — engaged in this conversation. They easily recalled instances in which disciplinary considerations came into play. Since most had more experience and/or interest in teaching interdisciplinary courses than in conducting interdisciplinary research, they focused primarily on the issues of subject matter and language. Although they raised fewer issues about modes of inquiry, some did contribute these kinds of comments. In addition the participants discussed choosing pedagogical strategies consistent with in-

---

*Additional information on the study design, data collection procedures, and analysis is offered in Lattuca 1996.

terdisciplinary approaches to knowledge, team teaching, and participating in nonacademic experiences that encouraged an interdisciplinary view of the world. Overall the focus group suggested that faculty who were from a variety of institutions and disciplines and who varied in their emphases on research or teaching could readily hold forth on how discipline influenced their interdisciplinary thinking and activities.

Based on the focus group discussion, I developed a semistructured interview protocol that included questions related to disciplinary components and about motivations to do interdisciplinary research and teaching. The protocol consisted of fifteen open-ended questions keyed to the three guiding research questions focusing on processes, contexts, and outcomes. I also developed follow-up probes for particular questions. I tested this protocol in exploratory interviews with faculty members who had done interdisciplinary research and teaching.

Based on this pilot, I expanded the time frame for the interview. The informants often had more than one kind of interdisciplinary experience, and their accounts were detailed. The extended nature of their responses suggested that the semistructured protocol was still too restrictive; following it seemed to interrupt the flow of the interviewees' thoughts. In their descriptions of interdisciplinary activities, individuals covered many of the questions in the interview protocol without prompts. Probing at these intersections appeared to work as well as direct questioning and allowed the faculty members to describe and discuss the salient aspects of interdisciplinary activity.

From these exploratory interviews I also learned that some of my assumptions about the importance of disciplinary perspectives in interdisciplinary work were misguided. Before conducting the exploratory interviews, I tended to think of interdisciplinarity as an approach to research and teaching that grew out of disciplinarity. The literature on interdisciplinarity also suggested that once an interdisciplinary stance was internalized, disciplinarity was left behind. However, four of the five individuals I interviewed—each trained in a single liberal arts or science discipline—told me that they had always been interdisciplinary. None, however, disclaimed their disciplinary training or affiliations. In fact they eschewed the disciplinary/interdisciplinary dichotomy, speaking instead of disciplinarity and interdisciplinarity as mutually informing approaches to creating knowledge, to be contingently selected and/or combined according to the task at hand. I began to wonder whether this kind of simultaneity and interaction was common among faculty doing interdisciplinary work. Would it be different for faculty who did not claim to be "born" interdisciplinary?

These conversations also forced me to reconsider some common conceptions of interdisciplinarity that permeate the literature on interdisciplinary research and teaching. The faculty whom I interviewed eagerly discussed their interdisciplinary scholarship, but none advocated wholesale rejection of disciplinary perspectives. No one in this pilot group believed that interdisciplinary approaches were inherently superior to disciplinary ones; they simply used them to accomplish different things. Nor did they see their disciplinary perspectives as insurmountable obstacles to interdisciplinarity.

None described their interdisciplinarity an institutional liability, and none had been denied tenure as a result of their interdisciplinary leanings. At least two interviewees claimed that their interdisciplinarity was a prized commodity when they were hired as junior faculty. While two had moved from their original discipline-based departments to interdisciplinary programs, only one mentioned experiencing discomfort in the discipline-based department. Finally, few had actually collaborated with a colleague or colleagues from another discipline on a teaching or research project—casting doubt upon the claims that interdisciplinarity only occurs when individuals with different disciplinary perspectives successfully collaborate.

On the basis of these five conversations and the questions they raised in my mind, I revised my research design. I decided to conduct unstructured interviews guided by broad questions and flexible probes. The unstructured format required that I rely heavily on the participants' constructions of their work, but it permitted faculty to raise important issues that I could not anticipate. These interviews also convinced me that a missing element in the rhetoric and research on interdisciplinary is nuance. The opinions and experiences that faculty described were more complex than I had anticipated, and if I were to portray them accurately and thereby learn from them, I would have to let the faculty express their thoughts rather than respond to a list of assumption-laden questions. While I might not find other faculty who worked and believed as the five faculty members I had met during the exploratory interviews, I would at least be open to their accounts of their work, careers, and lives.

The Study

I selected thirty-eight faculty for interviews on the basis of their participation in interdisciplinary teaching or research activities and personal characteristics. The goal of the selection process was to provide an inclusive group of informants who had experienced a variety of the interdisciplinary interactions from a variety of perspectives. A maximum variation selection procedure ensured that these perspectives included those of junior and senior faculty, tenured and untenured faculty, men and women, faculty of color, and faculty from disciplines in the sciences, social sciences, and humanities. Institutional affiliation was limited to faculty in research/doctoral universities and selective liberal arts colleges where faculty are generally assumed to be actively involved in research as well as teaching. Two universities and two liberal arts colleges were selected as research sites.

The literature on interdisciplinarity offers little guidance as to the influence of institutional type on interdisciplinarity since virtually all the research conducted in this area investigated the experiences and attitudes of research university faculty. While the capacity of this study to illuminate the influence of institutional type on interdisciplinarity is severely constrained, it was nonetheless important to select faculty from more than one type of institution. I did not hope to not to make comparisons among institutions—given the size of the informant group these would be highly inconclusive—but to increase the probability that any common themes identified would be central to faculty regardless of institutional affiliation. Accordingly, four institutions—a research university, a doctoral university, and two selective liberal arts colleges—were identified.

Selecting Informants

I used a broad definition of interdisciplinarity that focused on interaction rather than integration, to guide the selection of informants.* This definition, developed by the Centre for Educational Research and Innovation (CERI) in Paris, was particularly useful because it specifies a range of elements that might be involved in an interdisciplinary interaction. The definition also suggests that these interactions exist on a continuum from informal to formal and the locus of any one interaction on this continuum may not necessarily predict its total impact on the faculty member. I also used it to develop the definitions of formal and informal interdisciplinary activities. In the initial stages of this research, I hoped to interview an approximately equal number of faculty in the formal vs. informal interaction categories. I learned during the exploratory interviews, and again during the data-gathering interviews, that these activities were not mutually exclusive. Setting quotas therefore was unrealistic and unnecessary.

The first step in the selection process was to develop a pool of faculty informants who had participated in interdisciplinary research and teaching activities in the selected institutions. This process varied slightly depending on the type of institution. Knowledgeable administrators on each campus assisted me by compiling lists of potential interviewees. These individuals included deans, administrators from offices of research and sponsored programs, and directors of interdisciplinary faculty seminars.

After generating the pool of faculty for each institution, I examined the personal characteristics of potential informants and selected a group of individuals that varied across rank, tenure status, gender, disciplinary affiliation, and type of interdisciplinary activity. Since faculty were often involved in a number of activities, formal and informal, adherence to a strict selection criterion was impossible. Similarly, important characteristics—disciplinary affiliation, tenure status, and gender—also overlapped. For example, an untenured woman faculty member in biology might satisfy three selection criteria; any attempt to achieve equal numbers of informants in all selection categories was therefore foiled. While this selection process did not include all individuals with interdisciplinary interests or experiences on the campuses selected, it did provide a pool of potential informants that varied along the several dimensions that emerged as important from the literature on interdisciplinarity.

---

*See chapter 1 for a detailed discussion of this definition.

Gaining the Cooperation of Informants

Initially I planned to interview thirty faculty members, ten each on the campus of the larger university campuses and five each at two selective liberal arts colleges. This number was subjected to upward or downward adjustment based on the characteristics of the informant pool and the information gathered during the interview process. Because I assumed that some faculty would be unable or unwilling to participate or would not actually meet the selection criteria, I selected approximately fifteen faculty each from the universities and ten each from the liberal arts colleges. I then mailed letters to each explaining the study and requesting participation. I followed up with telephone calls to determine whether the individual had actually engaged in the types of activities required and, if so, to ascertain if and when he or she would be available for an interview.

Thirty-three faculty members contacted in this first round agreed to be interviewed; twenty of these were university faculty, and thirteen were from the selective liberal arts colleges.* Initially, each of the four campuses was represented by from five to ten participants. Through snowballing, five additional faculty members were identified, contacted, and interviewed: one each from three campuses, two from the fourth campus.

Interviewing Informants

After scheduling an interview, each faculty informant was mailed a brief form requesting demographic, educational, and some professional data, as well as a consent form. Interviews were conducted in person at a site selected by the informant, typically the informant's office. All interviews were tape-recorded, with the permission of the informant, and fully transcribed for analysis. I requested permission to phone the informant after the interview to clarify responses. I offered informants the option of requesting transcripts of the interviews that could be checked for accuracy.

In the interviews I asked a few broad questions and probed, sometimes extensively, for additional information or clarifications. Although the form of each interview varied, I typically began by asking the individual to describe his or her research and teaching. This allowed the faculty member to begin the interview with a subject of immediate relevance and familiarity and gave me the opportunity to understand the scope of the research and teaching the individual had undertaken and where interdisciplinary work fit in this scheme. It also placed the emphasis on faculty experiences rather than my assumptions about what individuals considered interdisciplinary and

---

*All but two of these participants received their doctoral degrees from universities classified as Research I institutions. Two individuals received degrees from Doctoral I institutions. Presumably this set of informants experienced similar, if not equivalent, disciplinary immersion during graduate education.

what they considered important. This discussion often provided an easy segue into a conversation about how interdisciplinary work was accomplished. I was careful to follow up both disciplinary and interdisciplinary work as well as teaching and research activities. During these conversations I probed with questions about collaborative efforts, interdisciplinary conversations, and reading in other disciplines. Typically informants raised the issue of institutional and departmental contexts without prompting. They discussed promotion and tenure policies and practices, the role of departmental colleagues, and the overall institutional stance toward interdisciplinarity.

I also explored informants' perceptions of their departments and disciplines and how they believed disciplinary colleagues viewed interdisciplinary research or teaching. Eventually the interview would turn to issues related to the outcomes of interdisciplinarity. I asked faculty about the products of their interdisciplinary work, for example, conference papers, articles, or books, but also about how interdisciplinarity had influenced their teaching and research. I followed up with questions about future work and commitment to an interdisciplinary approach to teaching and research. Typically my last question concerned the informant's perceptions of the relationship between disciplinarity and interdisciplinarity. Before ending each interview, however, I asked informants if there was anything else we should talk about. In several instances this elicited further conversation.

Analyzing Informants' Accounts

I analyzed the interview data using an iterative process of analytic induction. I categorized excerpts from informants' accounts according to a framework consisting of three basis components: processes, contexts, and outcomes. I categorized statements that described or explained how faculty pursued interdisciplinary scholarship as process statements, that indicated how institutional, departmental, or larger disciplinary environments influenced informants' work as context statements; and that discussed the tangible and intangible results of informants' work as outcomes statements. These broad categories were not mutually exclusive. For example informants' statements often intertwined discussion of how faculty accomplished their work, or process; about how colleagues perceived it, or context; and about whether the institution did or did not reward it, or outcome.

The next step in the analysis process was to identify themes and subcategories within these larger categories of process, context, and outcomes. Although the literature suggested some a priori categories, I did not use these to search for the themes and patterns; instead I allowed categories to emerge from the data. During the many iterations of the analysis, I continuously compared informants' statements, descriptions, and observations to one another to refine the coding categories and analytic framework. Eventually these emergent themes and subcategories became the focus of my analysis.

I also mined the informants' accounts to determine how they explicitly or implicitly defined interdisciplinary scholarship and for detailed descriptions of interdisciplinary research and teaching projects. Examining these excerpts led me to a critical discovery, although I did not immediately recognize it as such. Comparison of the definitions and descriptions was the first step toward understanding important differences among faculty members' perspectives on, and approaches to, interdisciplinary research and teaching.

As I read and considered the words of informants, I could not avoid comparing these varied descriptions of interdisciplinary work. I was puzzled by differences among informants' approaches to research and teaching. My first attempts to understand these differences were driven by the literature, which suggests various, sometimes competing, schemes for classifying interdisciplinary work. One commonly suggested rubric is the multidisciplinary/interdisciplinary dichotomy; another resembles a typology of forms of borrowing—for example, whether one borrows methods or content from other disciplines. These and other rubrics are discussed in detail in chapter 4. After failing to adequately match my informants' constructions of interdisciplinarity with conceptualizations of interdisciplinarity from the literature, I concluded that a different way of thinking about interdisciplinary scholarship was needed and began again to look for emergent categories.

In this step of my analysis I eventually focused on the catalysts that prompted informants' interdisciplinary research and teaching. We often talk about the match between the question and the method in research design; my informants seemed to apply a similar principle: the question or issue they wanted to pursue determined the method they used to pursue it. The impetus for a research project was typically expressed as a question; the impetus for a course was more often framed as an issue. Regardless of this semantic distinction, the framing of the question or of the issue influenced the kinds of projects that informants developed.

My thinking about the differences between these questions and issues eventually led to the development of a typology of forms of interdisciplinary teaching and research that is based on the kinds of questions and issues that faculty pursue. As I compared faculty informants' descriptions of the processes used in interdisciplinary research and teaching, their perceptions of departmental, institutional, and disciplinary contexts, and outcomes of interdisciplinary scholarship they reported, the typology gave greater meaning to the patterns of scholarship that I observed. To refine the typology, I selectively contacted informants by telephone for reactions to the categories. I was especially interested in comments from informants who had pursued more than one type of interdisciplinarity; these informants, it seemed, would be able to discuss the categories as lived experiences rather than as abstract ideas. These conversations, which were also recorded and transcribed, constituted another iteration of the analysis. The typology became an alternative to existing categorizations of interdisciplinary scholarship and was critical in helping me understand the perceptions and experiences of the informants.

Limitations of the Study

I delineated a method that was in keeping with the exploratory nature of this study and the goal of developing a complex picture of interdisciplinary scholarship. That method had some limitations. First, the process of selecting informants relied largely upon nominations by knowledgeable administrators and faculty. These individuals may have overlooked or even purposely excluded some individuals from consideration. I attempted to resolve any omissions by interviewing additional faculty suggested by informants during the course of the study. Still, an exhaustive selection process could not be guaranteed, even on smaller campuses.

My decision to interview only faculty with doctoral degrees in liberal arts fields constrains the picture of interdisciplinary work presented here. I made this decision because I assumed that these individuals would have stronger disciplinary views than faculty from fields such as business and education, which amalgamate a variety of disciplines. As I interviewed faculty about their graduate training and educational backgrounds, it became increasingly obvious that some of my assumptions about their graduate education were mistaken. The amount of work that individuals did outside their discipline during their doctoral programs varied. Furthermore a few individuals read widely outside their disciplines of their own volition. I found that I could not assume that liberal arts doctorates were necessarily less interdisciplinary than doctorates in applied fields such as education, engineering, or business. Including informants from these and other applied fields may or may not have altered this picture of interdisciplinary work. Further study of the relationship between graduate experiences and interdisciplinarity is needed. Researchers should consider conducting comparative studies of both traditional disciplinary programs as well as professional and multi-/interdisciplinary programs to illuminate the influences of these kinds of programs on students' understandings of and attitudes toward disciplines and interdisciplinarity.

I also limited research sites to faculty in selective liberal arts colleges and universities. I did not include faculty from interdisciplinary schools or divisions or from institutions that are committed, through their mission statements and structure, to interdisciplinary study. These institutions and divisions may offer more supportive contexts for interdisciplinary teaching and research that influence the frequency and quality of interdisciplinary experiences. I omitted informants from these settings because I assumed that there would be less variation in experiences, epistemologies, and ontologies among faculty who had already demonstrated a commitment to interdisciplinarity by their choice of institution or division. Instead I sought a diverse pool of informants whose range of experiences and beliefs would suggest the scope of interdisciplinary activities in a typical college or university. A comparative study of faculty in traditional and interdisciplinary colleges would demonstrate differences and similarities in their experiences and beliefs.

Finally, I relied on self-reports of interdisciplinary research and teaching. While it might have been possible for me to examine syllabi, research articles, and books in search of evidence of interdisciplinarity, my limited understanding of many of the disciplines of the faculty would render such judgments suspect, but the alternative choice, that of restricting the study to faculty in one or two disciplines, would have defeated the goal of generating a more nuanced picture of interdisciplinary work. I chose instead to use the interviews with faculty as opportunities to extensively question them about their work, in essence, asking them to teach me about their teaching and research.

BIBLIOGRAPHY

Allaire, Y., & Firsiruto, M. E. (1984). Is 'organizational culture' culture bound? *Human Resource Management* 25, 72–90.

Apostel, L. (1972). Conceptual tools for interdisciplinarity: An operational approach. In Organisation for Economic Cooperation and Development, *Interdisciplinarity: Problems of teaching and research in universities*, 141–80. Paris: OECD.

Austin, A. E. (1990). Faculty cultures, faculty values. In W. G. Tierney, ed., *Assessing academic climates and cultures. New Directions for Institutional Research*, No. 68, 61–74. San Francisco: Jossey-Bass.

Bakhtin, M. (1981). *The dialogic imagination*. Austin: University of Texas Press.

Baldwin, D. R., & Faubian, B. J. (1975, Spring). Interdisciplinary research in the academic setting. *SRA, Journal of the Society of Research Administrators* 6, 3–8.

Baldwin, R., & Austin, A. E. (1995). Toward greater understanding of faculty research collaboration. *Review of Higher Education* 19(1), 45–70.

Barnett, R. (1990). *The idea of higher education*. Bristol, PA: The Society for Research into Higher Education and Open University Press.

Bauer, H. H. (1990). Barriers against interdisciplinarity: Implications for studies of science, technology, and society (STS). *Science, Technology, & Human Values* 15(1), 105–19.

Becher, T. (1987a). The disciplinary shaping of the profession. In B. R. Clark, ed., *The academic profession: National, disciplinary, and institutional settings*, 271–303. Berkeley: University of California Press.

———. (1987b). Disciplinary discourse. *Studies in Higher Education* 12(3), 261–74.

———. (1989). *Academic tribes and territories: Intellectual enquiry and the cultures of disciplines*. Bristol, PA: The Society for Research into Higher Education and Open University Press.

Biglan, A. (1973a). The characteristics of subject matter in different academic areas. *Journal of Applied Psychology* 57(3), 195–203.

———. (1973b). Relationships between subject matter characteristics and the structure and output of university departments. *Journal of Applied Psychology* 57(3), 204–13.

Birnbaum, P. H. (1977). Assessment of alternative management forms in interdisciplinary projects. *Management Science* 24(3), 272–84.

———. (1979). A theory of academic interdisciplinary research performance: A contingency and path analysis approach. *Management Science* 25(3), 231–42.

———. (1981a). Academic interdisciplinary research: Characteristics of successful projects. *SRA, Journal of the Society of Research Administrators* 13(1), 5–16.

———. (1981b). Integration and specialization in academic research. *Academy of Management Journal* 24(3), 487–503.

———. (1982). The organization and management of interdisciplinary research, a progress report. *SRA, Journal of the Society of Research Administrators* 13(4), 11–23.

———. (1983). Predictors of long-term research performance. In S. R. Epton, R. L. Payne, & A. W. Pearson, eds., *Managing interdisciplinary research*, 47–59. New York: John Wiley & Sons.

Birnbaum, P. H., Newell, W. T., & Saxberg, B. O. (1979). Managing academic interdisciplinary research projects. *Decision Sciences* 10(4), 645–65.

Blackburn, R. T., & Lawrence, J. H. (1995). *Faculty at work: Motivation, expectation, satisfaction*. Baltimore: Johns Hopkins University Press.

Blau, P. M. (1973) *The organization of academic work*. New York: John Wiley & Sons.

Bloland, H. G. (1995). Postmodernism and higher education. *Journal of Higher Education* 66(5), 521–59.

Boyer, E. L. (1990). *Scholarship reconsidered: Priorities of the professoriate*. Princeton: The Carnegie Foundation for the Advancement of Teaching.

Braxton, J. M. (1983). Department colleagues and individual faculty publication productivity. *Review of Higher Education* 6(2), 115–28.

Cameron, D. (1985). *Feminism and linguistic theory*. London: MacMillan.

Cameron, S. W., & Blackburn, R. T. (1981). Sponsorship and academic career success. *Journal of Higher Education* 52(4), 369–77.

Cameron, K. S., & Ettington, D. R. (1988). The conceptual framework of organizational culture. In J. Smart, ed., *Higher Education: Handbook of Theory and Research*, Vol. 6, 356–96. New York: Agathon Press.

Carter, M. (1988). Problem solving reconsidered: A pluralistic theory of problems. *College English* 50(5), 551–65.

Clark, B. R. (1983). *The higher education system: Academic organization in cross-national perspective*. Berkeley: University of California Press.

Code, L. (1991). *What can she know? Feminist theory and the construction of knowledge*. Ithaca: Cornell University Press.

Collins, P. H. (1986). Learning from the outsider within: The sociological significance of black feminist thought. *Social Problems* 33(6), 514–32.

Cotterell, R. (1979). Interdisciplinarity: The expansion of knowledge. *Higher Education Review* 11(3), 47–56.

Crane, D. (1969). Social structure in a group of scientists. *American Sociological Review* 34(3), 335–52.

———. (1972). *Invisible colleges*. Chicago: University of Chicago Press.

Cravens, D., & Heathington, K. (1976). Organizing for interdisciplinary research in a university setting. *Journal of the Society of Research Administrators* 8(1), 3–10.

Cuffaro, H. K. (1995). *Experimenting with the world: John Dewey and the early childhood classroom*. New York: Teachers College Press.

Davis, J. R. (1995). *Interdisciplinary courses and team teaching: New arrangements for learning*. Phoenix: American Council on Education and Oryx Press.

Dewey, J. (1966). *Democracy and education*. New York: Free Press. (Original work published 1916.)

Doll, W. E., Jr. (1993). Curriculum possibilities in a 'post'-future. *Journal of Curriculum and Supervision* 8(4), 277–92.

Donald, J. G. (1983). Knowledge structures: Methods for exploring course content. *Journal of Higher Education* 54(1), 31–41.

———. (1990). University professors' views of knowledge and validation processes. *Journal of Educational Psychology* 82(2), 242–49.

Dressel. P., & Marcus, D. (1982). *Teaching and learning in college*. San Francisco: Jossey-Bass.

Dzubach, M. A. (1991). *Robert M. Hutchins: Portrait of an educator*. Chicago: University of Chicago Press.

Epton, S. R., Payne, R. L., & Pearson, A. W., eds., (1983). *Managing interdisciplinary research*. New York: John Wiley & Sons.

Fairweather, J. (1993). Faculty reward structures: Toward institutional professional homogenization. *Research in Higher Education* 34(5), 603–23.

Feldman, M. S. (1995). *Strategies for interpreting qualitative data*. Thousand Oaks, CA: Sage Publications, Inc.

Fenker, R. M. (1975). The organization of conceptual materials: A methodology for measuring ideal and actual cognitive structures. *Instructional Science* 4(1), 33–57.

Finklestein, M. (1984). *The American academic profession: A synthesis of social scientific inquiry since World War II*. Columbus: Ohio State University Press.

Fish, S. (1989). *Doing what comes naturally*. Durham: Duke University Press.

———. (1994). *There's no such thing as free speech and it's a good thing*. New York: Oxford University Press.

Foucault, M. (1979) *Discipline and punish: The birth of the prison*. (A. Sheridan, Trans.). New York: Random House.

———. (1980). *Power/knowledge: Selected interviews and other writings, 1972–1977*. C. Gordon, ed., (C. Gordon, L. Marshall, & K. Soper, Trans.). New York: Pantheon Books.

Fox, M. F., & Faver, C. A. (1984). Independence and collaboration in research: The motivations and costs of collaboration. *Journal of Higher Education* 55(3), 347–59.

Fox Keller, E. (1993). Fractured images of science, language, and power: A postmodern optic or just bad eyesight? In E. Messer-Davidow, D. R. Shumway, & D. J. Sylvan, eds., *Knowledges: Historical and critical studies in disciplinarity*, 54–69. Charlottesville: University Press of Virginia.

Frank, R. (1988). 'Interdisciplinarity': The first half century. In E. G. Stanley & T. F. Hoad, *WORDS: For Robert Burchfield's sixty-fifth birthday*, 91–101. Cambridge: D. S. Brewer.

Geertz, C. (1980). Blurred genres. *The American Scholar* 49(2), 165–79.

Geeslin, W. E. & Shavelson, R. J. (1975). An exploratory analysis of the representation of a mathematical structure in students' cognitive structures. *American Educational Research Journal* 12, 21–39.

Gergen, K. J. (1994). *Realities and relationships: Soundings in social construction*. Cambridge: Harvard University Press.

Gibbons, M., Limoges, C., Nowotny, H., Schwartzman, S., Scott, P., & Trow, M. (1994). *The new production of knowledge: The dynamics of science and research in contemporary societies*. Thousand Oaks, CA: Sage Publications, Inc.

Gillespie, D., & Birnbaum, P. (1980). Status concordance, coordination, and success in interdisciplinary research teams. *Human Relations* 33(1), 41–56.

Gold, H. J. (1977). *Mathematical modeling of biological systems: An introductory guidebook*. New York: John Wiley & Sons.

Gold, S. E., & Gold, H. J. (1983). Some elements of a model to improve productivity of interdisciplinary groups. In S. R. Epton, R. L. Payne & A. W. Pearson, eds., *Managing interdisciplinary research*, 86–101. New York: John Wiley & Sons.

Gorodetsky, M. & Hoz, R. (1985). Changes in group cognitive structure of some chemical equilibrium concepts following a university course in general chemistry. *Science Education* 69(2), 185–99.

Graff, G. (1992). *Beyond the culture wars: How teaching the conflicts can revitalize American education*. New York: W. W. Norton and Company.

Gumport, P. J. (1991). Feminist scholarship as a vocation. In G. P. Kelly & S. Slaughter, eds., *Women's higher education in comparative perspective*, 283–96. Netherlands: Kluwer Academic Publishers.

Hagstrom, W. O. (1971). Inputs, outputs, and the prestige of university science departments. *Sociology of Education* 44(4), 375–97.

Hanisch, T. E., and Vollman, W., eds., (1983). Interdisciplinarity in higher education. United Nations Educational, Scientific, and Cultural Organization, Bucharest (Romania). European Centre for Higher Education. (ERIC Document Reproduction Service No. ED 249 864)

Hattery, L. H. (1986). Interdisciplinary research management. In D. E. Chubin, A. L. Porter, F. A. Rossini & T. Connolly, eds., *Interdisciplinary analysis and research:*

Theory and practice of problem-focused research and development, 13–28. Mt. Airy, MD: Lomond.

Hausman, C. R. (1979). Introduction: Disciplinarity or interdisciplinarity? In J. Kockelmans, ed., *Interdisciplinarity and higher education*, 1–10. University Park,: The Pennsylvania State University Press.

Heath, S. B. (1999). Discipline and disciplines in education research: Elusive goals? In E. C. Lagemann & L. S. Shulman, *Issues in education research: Problems and possibilities*, 203–223. San Francisco: Jossey-Bass.

Heathington, K. W., Cunningham, J. O., & Mundy, R. A. (1978). Management of interdisciplinary research in universities: The state of the art. *Educational Researcher* 7(1), 11–14.

Heckhausen, H. (1972). Discipline and interdisciplinarity. In Organisation for Economic Co-operation and Development, *Interdisciplinarity: Problems of teaching and research in universities*, 83–89. Paris: Center for Educational Research and Innovation.

Hermerén, G. (1985). Interdisciplinarity revisited — promises and problems. In L. Levin & I. Lind, eds., *Interdisciplinarity Revisited: Re-assessing the concept in light of institutional experience*, 15–25. Stockholm: Organisation for Economic Cooperation and Development, Swedish Board of Universities and Colleges.

Hewson, P. W. & Hewson, M. G. (1984). The role of conceptual conflict in conceptual change and the design of science instruction. *Instructional Science* 13(1), 1–13.

Hill, C. E. (1990). *Writing from the margin: Power and pedagogy for teachers of composition*. New York: Oxford University Press.

Hollinger, R. (1994). *Postmodernism and the social sciences: A thematic approach*. Thousand Oaks, CA: Sage Publications, Inc.

Holstein, J. A., & Gubrium, J. F. (1998). Phenomenology, ethnomethodology, and interpretive practice. In N. K. Denzin & Y. S. Lincoln, eds., *Strategies of qualitative inquiry* 137–57. Thousand Oaks, CA: Sage Publications, Inc.

Hood, J. C. (1985). The lone scholar myth. In M. F. Fox, ed., *Scholarly writing and publishing: Issues, problems, and solutions*, 111–25. Boulder: Westview Press.

Hurst, P. J. (1992). The research university as an organizational context for collaboration: Cross-departmental research collaboration in environmental studies. Unpublished doctoral dissertation, University of Michigan.

Ikenberry, S. O., & Friedman, R. C. (1972). *Beyond academic departments*. San Francisco: Jossey-Bass.

Jacobson, B. (1981). Collection type and integration type curricula in systems of higher education. *Acta Sociologica* 24(1–2), 25–41.

James, L. R., James, L. A., & Ashe, D. K. (1990). The meaning of organizations: The role of cognition and values. In B. Schneider, ed., *Organizational climate and culture*, 40–84. San Francisco: Jossey-Bass.

Jantsch, E. (1972). Inter- and transdisciplinary university: A systems approach to education and innovation. *Higher Education* 1(1), 7–37.

Jurkovich, R., & Paelinck, J. H. P., eds., (1984). *Problems in interdisciplinary studies*. Brookfield, VT: Gower Publishing Company.

Kast, F. E., Rosenzweig, J. E., & Stockman, J. W. (1970). Interdisciplinary programs in a university setting. *Academy of Management Journal* 13, 311–324.

Kelly, J. (1996). Wide and narrow interdisciplinarity. *Journal of General Education* 45(2), 95–113.

Kestenbaum, V. (1977). *The phenomenological sense of John Dewey*. Atlantic Highlands, NJ: Humanities Press.

King, A. R., & Brownell, J. A. (1976). *The curriculum and the disciplines of knowledge: A theory of communication practice*. Huntingdon, NY: Robert E. Krieger Publishing Company.

Klein, J. T. (1985). The interdisciplinary concept: Past, present and future. In L. Levin & I. Lind, eds., *Interdisciplinarity revisited: Re-assessing the concept in the light of institutional experience*, 104–22. Stockholm: Organisation for Economic Cooperation and Development, Swedish Board of Universities and Colleges.

———. (1990). *Interdisciplinarity: History, theory, and practice*. Detroit: Wayne State University Press.

———. (1996). *Crossing boundaries: Knowledge, disciplinarities, and interdisciplinarities*. Charlottesville: University Press of Virginia.

Kleinman, S. (1983). Collective matters as individual concerns: Peer culture among graduate students. *Urban Life* 12(2), 203–25.

Kocklemans, J. (1979). Why interdisciplinarity? In J. Kocklemans, ed., *Interdisciplinarity and higher education*, 123–60. University Park: The Pennsylvania State University Press.

Knorr-Cetina, K. D. (1981). *The manufacture of knowledge: An essay on the constructivist and contextual nature of science*. Oxford: Pergamon Press.

Krapp, A., Hidi, S., & Renninger, K. A. (1992). Interest, learning, and development. In K. A. Renninger, S. Hidi, & A. Krapp, eds., *The role of interest in learning and development*, 3–25. Hillsdale, NJ: Lawrence Erlbaum Associates.

Kuhn, T. S. (1970). *The structure of scientific revolutions* (2nd edition, enlarged). Chicago: University of Chicago Press.

———. (1977). *The essential tension*. Chicago: University of Chicago Press.

Lagemann, E. C. (1999). An auspicious moment for education research? In E. C. Lagemann & L. S. Shulman, eds., *Issues in education research: Problems and possibilities*, 3–16. San Francisco: Jossey-Bass.

Latour, B. (1986). Visualization and cognition: Thinking with eyes and hands. *Knowledge and Society: Studies in the Sociology of Culture* 6, 1–40.

Lindas, N. (1979). Conclusions from the American society of public administration assessment of four interdisciplinary research projects. In R. Barth & R. Steck, eds.,

Interdisciplinary research groups: Their management and organization, 278–94. Seattle: Interstudy.

Lodahl, J. B., & Gordon, G. (1972). The structure of scientific fields and the functioning of university graduate departments. *American Sociological Review* 37(2), 57–72.

Luszki, M. B. (1958). *Interdisciplinary team research: Methods and problems.* New York: New York University Press.

Lynton, E. A. (1985). Interdisciplinarity: Rationales and criteria of assessment. In L. Levin & I. Lind, eds., *InterDisciplinarity revisited: Re-assessing the concept in the light of institutional experience*, 137–52. Stockholm: Organisation for Economic Cooperation and Development, Swedish Board of Universities and Colleges.

Lyotard, J. F. (1984). *The postmodern condition: A report on knowledge.* (G. Bennington & B. Massume, Trans.). Minneapolis: University of Minnesota Press.

Margolis, H. (1993). *Paradigms and barriers: How habits of mind govern scientific beliefs.* Chicago: University of Chicago Press.

Mayville, W. V. (1978). *Interdisciplinarity: The mutable paradigm. AAHE-ERIC/Higher Education Research Report No. 9.* Washington, DC: American Association for Higher Education.

Miller, M., & McCartan, A. (1990). Making the case for new interdisciplinary programs. *Change* 22(3), 28–35.

Miller, R. C. (1982). Varieties of interdisciplinary approaches in the social sciences. *Issues in Integrative Studies* 1, 1–37.

Mourad, R. P. (1995). *Implications of five postmodern philosophical critiques for the pursuit of knowledge in higher education.* Unpublished doctoral dissertation, University of Michigan.

Mulkay, M., Potter, J., & Yearly, S. (1983). Why an analysis of scientific discourse is needed. In K. D. Knorr-Cetina & M. Mulkay, eds., *Science observed: Perspectives on the social study of science*, 171–203. London: Sage Publications, Inc..

Naveh-Benjamin, M., McKeachie, W. J., Lin, Y., & Tucker, D. (1986). Inferring students' cognitive structure and their development using the 'ordered-tree' technique. *Journal of Educational Psychology* 78(2), 130–40.

Newell, W. T. (1975). *Management of interdisciplinary research in universities faces problems.* Paper presented at the meeting of the American Society for Engineering Education, Fort Collins, CO. (ERIC Reproduction Service Document No. ED 118 395)

———. (1994). Designing interdisciplinary courses. In J. T. Klein & W. Doty, eds., *Interdisciplinary studies today. New Directions for Teaching and Learning, No 58*, 35–51. San Francisco: Jossey-Bass.

———. (1998). Professionalizing interdisciplinarity: Literature review and research agenda. In W. H. Newell, ed., *Interdisciplinarity: Essays from the literature*, 529–63). New York: College Entrance Examination Board.

Newell, W. T., Saxberg, B. O., & Birnbaum, P. H. (1975). Measures of effectiveness and efficiency for university interdisciplinary research organizations. (Working Paper No. 3) Research Management Improvement Program, University of Washington.

Nielsen, J. M. (1990). Introduction. In J. M. Nielsen, ed., *Feminist research methods: Exemplary readings in the social sciences*, 1–37. Boulder: Westview Press.

Nilles, J. M. (1975). Interdisciplinary research management in the university environment. *SRA, Journal of the Society of Research Administrators* 6(9), 9–16.

———. (1976). Interdisciplinary research and the American university. *Interdisciplinary Science Reviews* 1(2), 160–66.

Organisation for Economic Cooperation and Development. (1972). *Interdisciplinarity: problems of teaching and research in universities.* Paris: OECD.

Over, R. (1982). Does research productivity decline with age? *Higher Education* 11(5), 511–20.

Parsons, T., & Platt, G. M. (1968). *The academic profession: A pilot study.* Washington, DC: National Science Foundation.

Paulsen, M. B. & Feldman, K. A. (1995). Toward a reconceptualization of scholarship: A human action system with functional imperatives. *Journal of Higher Education*, 66 (6), 615–40.

Pearson, A., Payne, R., & Gunz, H. (1979). Communication, coordination and leadership in interdisciplinary research. In R. Barth & R. Steck, eds., *Interdisciplinary research groups: Their management and organization.* Seattle: Interstudy.

Pelz, D. C. & Andrews, F. M. (1976). *Scientists in organizations: Productive climates for research and development, Revised edition.* Ann Arbor: Institute for Social Research, University of Michigan.

Perrault, G. (1984). Contemporary feminist perspectives on women and higher education. In C. C. Gould, ed., *Beyond domination: New perspectives on women and philosophy*, 283–309. Totawa, NJ: Rowman and Allanheld.

Peterson, M. W., & Spencer, M. G. (1990). Assessing academic culture and climate. In W.G. Tierney, ed., *Assessing academic climates and cultures. New Directions for Institutional Research*, No. 68, 3–18. San Francisco: Jossey-Bass.

Peterson, M. W., & White, T. H. (1992). Faculty and administrator perceptions of their environments: Different views of different models of organization? *Research in Higher Education* 33(2), 177–204.

Petrie, H. G. (1986). Do you see what I see? The epistemology of interdisciplinary inquiry. In D. E. Chubin, A. L. Porter, F. A. Rossini & T. Connolly, eds., *Interdisciplinary analysis and research: Theory and practice of problem-focused research and development*, 115–30. Mt. Airy, MD: Lomond.

———. (1992). Interdisciplinary education: Are we faced with insurmountable opportunities? In G. Grant, ed., *Review of research in education, Vol. 18*, 299–333. Washington, DC: American Educational Research Association.

Phenix, P. (1986). *Realms of meaning: A philosophy of the curriculum for general education, Second Edition*. Ventura, CA: Ventura County Superintendent of Schools Office. (Original work published 1964)

Piaget, J. (1972). The epistemology of interdisciplinary relationships. In Organisation for Economic Cooperation and Development, *Interdisciplinarity: Problems of teaching and research in universities*, 127–39. Paris: OECD.

Pineau, C., & Levy-Leboyer, C. (1983). Managerial and organizational determinants of efficiency in biomedical research teams. In S. R. Epton, R. L. Payne, & A. W. Pearson, eds., *Managing interdisciplinary research*, 164–76. New York: John Wiley & Sons.

Pintrich, P. R., Marx, R. W., & Boyle, R. A. (1993). Beyond cold conceptual change: The role of motivational beliefs and classroom contextual factors in the process of conceptual change. *Review of Educational Research* 63(2), 167–99.

Porter, A. L. (1983). Interdisciplinary research: Current experience in policy and performance. *Interdisciplinary Science Reviews* 8(2), 158–67.

Porter, A. L., & Rossini, F. A. (1985). Forty interdisciplinary research projects: Multiple skills and peer review. In B. W. Mar, W. T. Newell, & B. O. Saxberg, eds., *Managing high technology: An interdisciplinary perspective*, 103–112. New York: North-Holland.

Price, D. (1970). Citation measures of hard science, soft science, technology, and non-science. In C. Nelson & D. Pollock, eds., *Communication among scientists and engineers*, 3–22. Lexington, MA: D. C. Heath and Company.

Pye, L. (1975). The confrontation between discipline and area studies. In L. Pye, ed., *Political science and area studies: Rivals or partners?* 5–22. Bloomington: Indiana University Press.

Reichers, A. E., & Schneider, B. (1990). Climate and culture: An evolution of constructs. In B. Schneider, ed., *Organizational climate and culture*, 5–39. San Francisco: Jossey-Bass.

Reif, F., & Strauss, A. (1965). The impact of rapid discovery on the scientist's career. *Social Problems* 12(3), 297–311.

Reskin, B. F. (1978). Scientific productivity, sex, and location in the institution of science. *American Journal of Sociology* 83(5), 1235–43.

Resnick, L. B. (1991). Shared cognition: Thinking as social practice. In L. B. Resnick, J. M. Levine, & Stephanie D. Teasley, eds., *Perspectives on socially shared cognition*, 1–20. Washington, DC: American Psychological Association.

Reuben, J. A. (1996). *The making of the modern university: Intellectual transformation and the marginalization of morality*. Chicago: University of Chicago Press.

Robertson, I. T. (1981). Some factors associated with successful interdisciplinary research. *SRA, Journal of the Society of Research Managers* 13(2), 44–50.

———. (1983). The interdisciplinary researcher: Some psychological aspects. In S. R. Epton, R. L. Payne, & A. W. Pearson, eds., *Managing Interdisciplinary Research* 164–76. New York: John Wiley & Sons.

Rorty, R. (1979). *Philosophy and the mirror of nature*. Princeton: Princeton University Press.

———. (1991). *Objectivity, relativism, and truth: Philosophical papers, Vol. 1.* Cambridge: Cambridge University Press.

Roschelle, J. (1992). Learning by collaborating: Convergent conceptual change. *Journal of the Learning Sciences* 2(3), 235–76.

Rosenau, P. M. (1992). *Post-modernism and the social sciences: Insights, inroads, and intrusions*. Princeton: Princeton University Press.

Rosser, S. (1997). Feminist critique of science as usual. In S. Rosser, *Re-engineering female friendly science*, 81–101. New York: Teachers College Press.

Rossini, F. A., & Porter, A. L. (1981). Interdisciplinary research: Performance and policy Issues. *SRA, Journal of the Society of Research Administrators* 13, 8–24.

———. (1984). Interdisciplinary research: Performance and policy Issues. In R. Jurkovich & J. H. P. Paelinck, eds., *Problems in interdisciplinary studies*, 26–45. Brookfield, VT: Gower Publishing Company.

Rossini, F. A., Porter, A. L., Kelly, P., & Chubin, D. E. (1979). Frameworks and factors affecting integration within technology assessments. In R. Barth & R. Steck, eds., *Interdisciplinary research groups: Their management and organization*, 136–58. Seattle: Interstudy.

Roy, R. (1979). Interdisciplinary science on campus: The elusive dream. In J. Kocklemans (Ed.), *Interdisciplinarity and higher education*, 161–96. University Park: The Pennsylvania State University Press.

Rudolph, F. (1977). *Curriculum: A history of the American undergraduate course of study since 1636*. San Francisco: Jossey-Bass.

Ruscio, K. P. (1987). Many sectors, many professions. In B. R. Clark, ed., *The academic profession: National, disciplinary, and institutional settings*, 331–68. Berkeley: University of California Press.

Russell, M. G. (1983). Peer review in interdisciplinary research: Flexibility and responsiveness. In S. R. Epton, R. L. Payne, & A. W. Pearson, eds., *Managing interdisciplinary research*, 184–202. New York: John Wiley & Sons.

———. (1990). The impact of interdisciplinary activities on departmental disciplines. In P. H. Birnbaum-More, F. A. Rossini, & D. R. Baldwin, eds., *International research management: Studies in interdisciplinary methods from business, government, and academia*, 81–96. New York: Oxford University Press.

Russell, M. G., & Sauer, R. J. (1983). Creating administrative environments for interdisciplinary research. *SRA, Journal of the Society of Research Administrators* 14(4), 21–31.

Saljo, R. (1985). On the identification of competence in interdisciplinarity in a monodisciplinary world: The Tema experience. In L. Levin & I. Lind, eds., *Interdisciplinarity revisited: Re-assessing the concept in the light of institutional experience*, 93–102. Stockholm: Organisation for Economic Cooperation and Development, Swedish Board of Universities and Colleges.

Salter, L., & Hearn, A. (1996). *Outside the lines: Issues in interdisciplinary research.* Buffalo: McGill-Queen's University Press.

Sax, L. J., Astin, A. W., Korn, W. S., & Gilmartin, S. K. (1999). The American college teacher: National norms for the 1998–99 HERI faculty surveys. Los Angeles: Higher Education Research Institute.

Saxberg, B. O., & Newell, W. T. (1983). Interdisciplinary research in the university: Need for managerial leadership. In S. R. Epton, R. L. Payne & A. W. Pearson, eds., *Managing interdisciplinary research*, 202–10. New York: John Wiley & Sons.

Saxberg, B. O., Newell, W. T., & Mar, B. W. (1981). Interdisciplinary research — a dilemma for university central administration. *SRA, Journal of the Society of Research Administrators* 13(2), 25–43.

Schein, E. H. (1986). *Organizational culture and leadership: A dynamic view.* San Francisco: Jossey-Bass.

Schneider, B. & Rentsch, J. (1988). Managing climates and cultures: A futures perspective. In J. Hage, ed., *Futures of organizations*, 181–200. Lexington, MA: Lexington Books.

Shavelson, R. J. (1972). Some aspects of the correspondence between content structure and cognitive structure in physics instruction. *Journal of Educational Psychology* 63(3), 225–34.

Sherif, C. W. (1987). Bias in psychology. In S. Harding, ed., *Feminism and methodology: Social science issues*, 37–56. Indianapolis: Indiana University Press.

Shinn, T. (1982). Scientific disciplines and organizational specificity. In N. Elias, H. Martins, & R. Whitley, eds., *Scientific establishments and hierarchies*, 239–64. Dordrecht: Reidel.

Smart, B. (1993). *Postmodernity.* New York: Routledge.

Stasz, C., Shavelson, R. J., Cox, D. C., & Moore, C. A. (1976). Field independence and the structure of knowledge in a social studies minicourse. *Journal of Educational Psychology* 68(5), 550–58.

Stewart, C. J. (1980). Faculty identification and interdisciplinary teaching and research in a multidisciplinary setting, The School of Public Health. Unpublished doctoral dissertation, University of Michigan.

Strike, K. A., & Posner, G. J. (1985). A conceptual change view of learning and understanding. In L. West & A. Pines, eds., *Cognitive structure and conceptual change* 211–31. Orlando: Academic Press.

———. (1992). A revisionist theory of conceptual change. In R. Duschl & R. Hamilton, eds., *Philosophy of science, cognitive psychology, and educational theory and practice* 147–176. Albany: SUNY.

Taylor, J. (1986). Building and interdisciplinary team. In D. Chubin, A. Porter, F. Rossini, & T. Connolly, eds., *Interdisciplinary analysis and research: Theory and practice of problem-focused research and development*, 141–54. Mt. Airy, MD: Lomond.

Teich, A. H. (1986). Research centers and non-faculty researchers: Implications of a growing role in American universities. In D. E. Chubin, A. L. Porter, F. A. Rossini, & T. Connolly, eds., *Interdisciplinary analysis and research: Theory and practice of problem-focused research and development*, 215–27. Mt. Airy, MD: Lomond.

Thorburn, S. M. (1985). *Faculty development opportunities in interdisciplinary general education programs*. Unpublished doctoral dissertation, University of Maryland.

Thro, M. P. (1978). Relationships between associative and test structure of physics concepts. *Journal of Educational Psychology* 70(6), 971–78.

Toulmin, S. (1972). *Human understanding, Vol. 1*. Oxford: Clarendon Press.

Trimbur, J. (1989). Consensus and difference in collaborative learning. *College English* 51(6), 602–16.

van Dusseldorp, D. & Wigboldus, S. (1994). Interdisciplinary research for integrated rural development in the developing countries: The role of social sciences. *Issues in Integrative Studies*, 12, 93–138.

Van Mannen. J., & Barley, S. R. (1984). Occupational communities: Culture and control in organizations. *Research in Organizational Behavior* 6, 287–365.

Van Mannen, J., & Schein, E. H. (1979). Toward a theory of organizational socialization. In B.M. Staw, ed., *Research in organizational behavior, Vol. 1*, 209–64. Greenwich, CT: JAI Press.

Vosskamp, W. (1986). From scientific specialization to the dialogue between the disciplines. *Issues in Integrative Studies* 4, 17–36.

Whitley, R. (1976). Umbrella and polytheistic scientific discipline and their elites. *Social Studies of Science* 6(3–4), 471–97.

Wilson, R. (1998, November 27). Ph.D. programs in women's studies proliferate on campuses. *Chronicle of Higher Education* 45(14), A10–A12.

Wong, H. Y., & Sanders, J. M. (1983). Gender differences in the attainment of doctorates. *Sociological Perspectives* 26(1), 29–50.

INDEX

academic departments. *See* departments
Academic Tribes and Territories, 242
accommodation, as type of learning, 166
administrators. *See also* institutional
    influence on interdisciplinarity, 45–46,
    181–82, 189–91, 196
American Economics Association, 204
Andrews, F.M., 47
anthropology
    as interdisciplinary, 200–202, 221–22, 237–
    38, 253
    epistemology in, 107
    examples from, 91–92, 135, 145–46, 149,
    232–33, 235
Apostel, Leo, 244
applied disciplines, 32–33
area studies, 8, 113
Aristotle, 5
art history, as interdisciplinary, 204
assimilation, as type of learning, 166
Austin, A. E., 209
auxiliary interdisciplinarity, 11

Bakhtin, M., on language, 166
Barley, S. R., 35
barriers. *See* interdisciplinarity, barriers to
Bauer, H. H., 30, 34
Becher, Tony
    on academic specialization, 40–41, 61
    on collegiality, 175
    on disciplines, 29, 32–34, 36, 39, 242, 245
    on values of the university, 34–35
Biglan, Anthony, 32, 34
biochemistry, 73–74

biology
    as interdisciplinary, 208
    examples from, 74–75, 84–85, 146–47,
    233–34
biophysical chemistry, 75
Birmingham Centre for Contemporary
    Cultural Studies, 100
Birnbaum, P. H., 12, 13, 39–40, 49
black studies
    as interdisciplinary, 56, 57, 97
    faculty of, 14, 59
Blackburn, R. T., 49, 169
Blau, P. M., 47
boundaries. *See* disciplines
Boyer, Ernest, L., 60, 263–64
Boyle, R. A., 51
Bridgman, P. W., 26
Brownell, J. R., 27, 28

Cameron, D., 30
Carnegie Foundation for the Advancement of
    Teaching, 9, 44, 263
Centre for Educational Research and
    Innovation, and interdisciplinarity
    (CERI), 9, 17–18, 19, 55, 270
Chomsky, N., 15
Chubin, D. E., 31
climate. *See* institutional
Code, Lorraine, 104–5
cognitive style in disciplines, 32–33
colearning vs. expertise, 133
constraints on interdisciplinarity. *See*
    interdisciplinarity, barriers to

University of Sussex (Britain), 9
University of Tromso (Norway), 9
University of Tsukuba (Japan), 9
University of Virginia, 5
University of Wisconsin, and experimental
    education, 7–8, 9
urban studies, 56, 57, 88–89

Van Mannen, J., 35
Vosskamp, W., 31

ways of knowing, in disciplines, 2
Whitley, R., 27, 28
women. *See* faculty

women's studies
    and epistemology, 15
    as critique, 234
    as interdisciplinary, 3–4, 15, 56, 59
    conceptual interdisciplinarity in, 97
    examples from, 133, 135, 149, 183–84, 206,
        229–30
    faculty of, 14, 59
workshops. *See* conferences
World War II, and interdisciplinary research,
    8
writing across the curriculum, 57

Yale University, 5, 6